Chicken Poop for the Soul

Chicken Poop for the Soul

In Search of Food Sovereignty

Kristeva Dowling

CAITLIN PRESS

Caitlin Press Inc.
8100 Alderwood Road,
Halfmoon Bay, BC V0N 1Y1
www.caitlin-press.com

Edited by Betty Keller and Vici Johnstone.
Text and cover designed by Vici Johnstone.
Printed in Canada

Caitlin Press Inc. acknowledges financial support from the Government of Canada through the Canada Book Fund and the Canada Council for the Arts, and from the Province of British Columbia through the British Columbia Arts Council and the Book Publisher's Tax Credit.

Library and Archives Canada Cataloguing in Publication

Dowling, Kristeva
    Chicken poop for the soul : in search of food sovereignty / Kristeva Dowling.

    Includes bibliographical references.
    ISBN 978-1-894759-60-1

      1. Dowling, Kristeva. 2. Farms, Small—British Columbia—Bella Coola River Valley. 3. Subsistence farming—British Columbia—Bella Coola River Valley. 4. Self-reliant living—British Columbia—Bella Coola River Valley. 5. Farms, Small—Government policy—British Columbia. I. Title.

HD1476.C32B75 2011   630.9711'1   C2011-901966-3

To the ethical farmers who work with their hearts and souls to keep their animals happy, their land fertile, and their families' histories and dreams alive. And to all the animals whose plight goes ignored yet who suffer at the hands of the intensive livestock farming industry so the masses can be nourished.

Contents

Introduction   13

The Seeds of Sustainability   19

    My property wish list   22

    Creating a garden   22

    The advantages of planning   27

    The clan grows (not according to plan)   29

    How ethical can you get?   35

    Cabbage anyone?   36

    The value of heritage   38

    The genetically modified threat   42

    Why buy heritage?   44

    Heirloom seeds   45

Year Two at the Howling Duck Ranch   47

    The beet affair   47

    Building the permanent garden   49

    Mr. Mallard meets his maker   51

    Gordon gets into the grain   53

    Egg profits: Keeping it local   61

The Food Sovereignty Project   70

    Do I go or do I stay?   70

    Planning to provide   71

    Counting chickens before they're hatched   73

    Are you my mother?   74

    The dedicated poultry barn   75

    Teach a woman to fish   80

Planning the Garden for Self-Sufficiency   83

    The asparagus incident   84

    Spring harvesting   85

    Cougar capers   88

    The pie plants of penchants   90

    To brassica or not to brassica   92

    "Indeed the tears live in an onion ..."   92

The new tomato patch 94

People who want glass houses 96

Beans, beans, the musical fruit 100

The King of Wheat's wheat comes to Bella Coola 109

Eating with the seasons 112

Milk 115

Ruminants with a view 115

The raw and the cooked 117

Got milk? 119

Before the fall: Raw milk pasteurizing 125

Hard cheese 130

Summer Harvesting 132

The best laid plans 132

Mrs. Mallard meets a mate 136

The twenty-mile community feast 139

A Feast of the Fields sample menu 143

The running of the chicks 145

A potato party for one 146

Hi-ho, hi-ho, it's off to work experience I go 150

Preserving the Harvest and Generally Persevering 154

The pantry 154

Pantry contents (Winter 2008–9) 154

Haute cuisine–style fast food 163

Calling for reinforcements 166

The staff of life 169

Yeast wrangling 101 172

The tough realities of food sovereignty 176

City Girl Gets a Gun 182

The only thing to fear … 191

A time to kill 193

Woman running fairly close to the wolves 196

Butchering 101   202

    Clarence-style kosher butchering   202

    Turkey plucking   208

    To breed or not to breed   215

    Food insecurity and unpalatable realities   217

Bears I Have Known   223

    They were here first   223

The Project in Full Swing   236

    The Rod and Gun Club dinner and dance   236

    Crouching farmer, soaring feed costs   237

    Sweetness and light   239

    The Jenny Craig Cornish Crosses   246

    Taking stock   249

    Searching for that one percent   250

Your Money and Your Mouth   255

Epilogue   265

    Farming: The social nexus   265

Additional Recipes   268

Notes and Sources   271

    Seed resources   271

    References   271

Acknowledgements   272

Introduction

ONE DAY IN JANUARY 1997 I found myself standing in a grocery store in Prince George, BC, looking with dismay at the bare produce section. The grocery store truck drivers had just gone on strike, and as I stood there I could hear snippets of conversation as people filtered past me: "How bloody long is this going to last?" "When are they going to get some decent stuff on these shelves?" "How dare those strikers do this to us?" "They shouldn't have the right to strike!" "I need a pineapple for this recipe, but I'm not going to buy any of these. Look at them! They're disgusting."

While the shoppers vented their outrage, I turned to look outside at the falling snow. There had to be three or four feet of it already on the ground and it was forty below zero. It was going to be a long while before we would see green grass again. I began to wonder, *What will I do if the strike continues for a long time? It will be June before I can even plant a garden, and July or August before I can harvest anything from it. I don't really have a stocked pantry. Boy, I could starve to death before the strike is over!* And there it was: I realized then just how dependent I was (we all are) on North America's food production and distribution system.

I was also shocked that day by my fellow shoppers' lack of awareness and surprised by their attitudes. In reality there was still a lot of food on the shelves if you could be flexible about that pineapple and find a recipe that calls for apples or bananas instead. It was this revelation that made me begin to question the necessity for Canadians to have pineapples in January. While the people around me were revealing their impatience and total dependency, I started making mental notes about my "wants"—that is, what I've grown accustomed to having—versus my "needs." I began a plan to reduce my family's dependency on others for our basic necessities, specifically food.

I soon realized that before I could even begin this project I had to ask myself some probing questions, which to my astonishment were difficult to answer: How much food do we eat each year? In what quantities? How will we produce, acquire or preserve this food? What if the hay we have on hand doesn't last for the goats? What if our supplier stops making hay each year? When I thought seriously about how I would feed myself, my family and my animals, I realized just how dependent I was on the system. I was humbled and somewhat unnerved.

In truth, I have always been concerned with food. From a very young age, my mother included me in the kitchen. I can remember baking cakes and cupcakes with her when I was as young as four years old. I especially remember one Valentine's Day, when in spite of her better judgment, she let me make a heart-shaped cake for my dad. It was blue! When at fifteen years old I announced in a capricious passion for animal rights that I wanted to become vegetarian, my mum was less supportive, but at least she let me stop eating the meat on my plate. Then I found myself out with friends for pizza and unthinkingly eating with gusto my favourite: capicolla and green pepper. It was not until the slice was well and truly down the hatch that it occurred to me that the capicolla had once been an animal.

Much later I did make a more informed leap to vegetarianism, and when I discovered the horrors of the dairy industry, I promptly converted to veganism. Several years and some wonderful culinary discoveries later, I was diagnosed with dangerously low B12 levels. My doctor gave me the ultimatum: either I take weekly injections of B12 or I start eating meat again. I declined the offer of the injections and bought fish on the way home. At first I struggled to get it past my lips, but within half an hour of eating that first mouthful of flesh, I knew my body needed it. In fact, it practically sang out for it. Within days I felt better than I had in years. Gradually I moved from fish and canned tuna (the only things I could eat and not throw up) to chicken and beef, and finally, because by then I was living in New Zealand, I found an organic source for lamb.

I had gone from eating meat to vegetarianism to veganism and back again, but it wasn't just a struggle for my stomach: I had been sweating over the ethics of eating meat since my teen years. So I began to do some research. I read literature on the politics of food and animal rights—Carson, Robbins, Singer—took a tour through various Buddhist philosophies, and ended my journey with basic homesteaders and farming revolutionists like Logsdon, Mollison, Fukuoka and so on. I had also been formally studying social anthropology during these years, first at the University of Northern BC in Prince George, then at Waikato University in New Zealand, learning how human societies and customs have evolved throughout history, always intrinsically linked to, and dependent upon, animals for their food, clothing, shelter and customs. I concluded that eating meat and depending on animal products is what we have always done and what we should always do.

By this time I had learned that there is no clear line on one side of which lies digestive virtue. After all, even vegans must consider the loss of rain forest and wildlife habitat to soybean fields, the environmental cost of transporting those soybeans to their plates, and the inordinate amount of energy used to convert soybeans into tofurkey, wrap it in attractive packaging and get it to the "store nearest you" in time for Thanksgiving. Or how about the millions of animals that are killed by the combines used to harvest wheat, beans and lentils? I decided that the least hypocritical position was to make my ecological footprint as small as possible, which meant extracting myself as much as possible from the corporate agricultural system. In other words, get out of the supermarket and into the local farmers' markets, and whenever possible grow some food myself.

In July 2003 I returned to BC and to the beautiful Bella Coola Valley to do the fieldwork for my master's degree in social anthropology; my husband, David, who is a New Zealander by birth, followed me that December. In the spring of 2005 we bought a four-acre farm and I plunged into the grand experiment of growing as much of our own food as possible.

It was two years later that Vancouverites Alisa Smith and James B. MacKinnon published their book *The 100-Mile Diet,* in which they share the challenges of eating locally for an entire year. The book and their journey of discovery were inspired by a meal they had with friends and family at their cabin in northern British Columbia. When suddenly faced with feeding company from their much neglected larder, they rummaged on the forest floors, skillfully plucked fish from a nearby stream, gathered apples from an old orchard and cleaved food from their nearly abandoned vegetable plot.

Satiated by their hard-earned meal and alarmed by new-found knowledge of just how far most Canadian meals travel from farm to plate, their conversation wove itself around to the ultimate challenge: could they eat locally for a whole year? *The 100-Mile Diet* was an international sensation and drew worldwide media attention to the idea of eating locally, but after I finished reading it, I realized that the next obvious challenge would be to actually *produce* a whole year's food. Being philosophically opposed to corporate agriculture's inhumane treatment of animals and wishing to limit my footprint on the earth, I decided to simplify my life, limit my retail consumption, provision for myself and my family as much as possible, supplement the foods I could not grow myself through the efforts of my neighbours whenever possible, and become as close to a modern-day hunter-gatherer as I could be.

I didn't plan to go back to living in a cave or sitting around a campfire, but I wanted to construct a life where, like a hunter-gatherer of old, I was in direct control of my food sources. But as I had not been raised in a clan of hunter-gatherers, I would need to learn to hunt and fish and grow and kill my own food. It's what I call "personal food sovereignty."

The idea of "food sovereignty" is not a new one. The concept was developed by the global farmers' movement known as La Via Campesina and was launched to the general public at the World Food Summit held in Rome in November 1996 under the auspices of the United Nations Food and Agriculture Organization. While there is no universal definition for food sovereignty, the most common one used by the international community is: "the right of peoples, communities, and countries to define their own agricultural, labour, fishing, food and land policies, which are ecologically, socially, economically and culturally appropriate to their unique circumstances. It includes the true right to food and to produce food, which means that all people have the right to safe, nutritious and culturally appropriate food and to food producing resources and the ability to sustain themselves and their societies" (Glipo and Pascaul Jr, www.nyeleni.org/IMG/pdf/FoodSovereigntyFramework.pdf).

With the help of neighbours, many of them farmers, sport fishers and hunters, my husband and I gradually learned to detach ourselves from the system, regained independence, formed new, healthier attachments and rediscovered the concept of community. Over the next four years our farm became a living testament to what I believe in. My life and my food choices had become a conscious political statement.

The decision to leave that farm five years later did not come easily. I loved the land I was living on, my animals, the homestead we had created and the community I was part of. The picture was, in fact, nearly perfect. But in the end I had to take stock of the harsh realities of the Valley—the predator pressure was too great and the population too small. Consequently, I knew that if I wanted to take food sovereignty and the idea of farming seriously, I would have to move on. I had to let that dream go, at least for the short term.

However, I can't let go of my commitment to personal food sovereignty, and fortunately I don't need to own a farm or even a piece of land to do that. I have already found alternative ways to control and earn my food. I make friends with farmers and work out trade agreements for my labour. I visit farmers' markets and thereby support farmers in the region. I helped friends to process 340 kilograms of "garbage apples" into wine and reaped some of the results as my reward. I hunt and gather in the area for meat and wild foods in season. This spring I will tap some birch trees in the nearby woods to make syrup and dig up the lawn of the house I'm renting to grow veggies. I will buy surplus fruits and vegetables in season and preserve this bounty through freezing, dehydrating and canning. And finally I can forgive myself for needing chocolate and coffee and buy fair-trade organic roasted and/or made-in-BC products. Being committed to food sovereignty or sustainability does not depend on owning a farm—I can do it wherever I live.

When I started off on this journey I thought that I would simply be growing my own food, learning to process and preserve it and quietly eating it. I thought I would eat well and share nice dinners with friends. I didn't think the act of drinking milk would become a political debate. I didn't count on becoming hot and bothered about farmers' right to farm and consumers' right to choose. I had no idea I would have educated thoughts about the politics of predators. But I have. I am now passionate about these issues and I can't go back. My life, and the simple act of eating, has taken on a richer meaning. I now live and eat much more consciously.

I thought I would be lost and lonely without my farm, but now I am not only forced to meet other farmers—which quells the loneliness—but I also have enough time to help out on their farms, which satisfies the farmer in me. I find myself sharing some of what I have learned with others, and through this ironic twist of fate I am doing something I did not dream I'd ever be doing—inspiring others.

The Seeds of Sustainability

I DO NOT HAVE A BACKGROUND IN FARMING or agriculture. I was raised in the city of Vancouver, but when I was a child, my grandfather kept a large garden, and even though I didn't spend much time with him, I knew that gardening was in my blood. Until I reached my thirties I had only been to a farm once. I was five years old when my dad took me to a farm in Langley owned by a colleague at work. We had been invited for a barbecue, and while I do not recall the dinner or anything about the people on the farm, I do remember seeing the cows, a cow-pie (I didn't know what it was!), and the big red barn stacked with hay, and climbing into the loft to look out over the pasture. I loved it all—the space, the smells, the sounds. After that I hounded my dad every now and then: "Please can we live on a farm, Daddy? Pleeeeeease." Alas, my pleas went unnoticed and I grew up in the city though I never really felt at peace there.

My passion for growing food crystallized a number of years later when I was living in New Zealand where my husband, David, was born. I was in heaven because it is possible to grow food there nearly all year long without much effort. I never did own a producing farm in New Zealand, but I didn't have to as there were plenty of opportunities to farm vicariously, and so I did, volunteering on a few farms and soaking up as much knowledge as I could. In fact, my first vegetable garden grew almost in spite of me. This was a great place for a floundering beginner to start her farming venture—a country where nearly everyone is doing it or knows how to do it and is willing to teach you; where parsley plants obligingly relocate their offspring into the cracks of the sidewalk to appear the following spring completely unannounced and fight you to the death if you try to pull them out; and where you might be lucky enough to live next door to a consummate gardener, exemplary sybarite and welcoming host called Tony the Greek.

My husband and I built a house on three acres outside Palmerston North in the Pohangina Valley. It was here that I got my first chickens and ducks. Tony the Greek donated a "chicken starter kit"—three hens and a rooster—and the chickens did the rest of the work, happily replicating themselves on a fairly regular basis. Each spring a hen would go "broody" and sit on a clutch of eggs, and three weeks later she would emerge from some corner of the garden with her babies in tow.

The following year Tony the Greek gave us a Muscovy duck starter kit, which was less successful than the chicken kit, and I soon learned what the term "like a sitting duck" meant. We were excited when the duck went broody and was sitting on a nice batch of eggs. I don't remember how far into the incubation process she was, but one morning when I went out to check on her, all that was left were her feet. We never did successfully hatch baby ducks in New Zealand.

After six years of living outside of Canada, I started to formulate a plan to return home to live and farm in a rural location. For about fifteen years I had been dreaming of living in the Bella Coola Valley because I thought it had potential for good agricultural development. So when I went there to do the fieldwork for my master's degree and a job opportunity arose as well, I asked my husband what he thought of the idea of selling our home in New Zealand and moving to this remote, economically depressed village on the west coast of British Columbia. Can I sell an idea or what? When David agreed to relocate, we sold the property. The buyers, charmed by the poultry-capades, wrote the chickens and ducks into the agreement to purchase! I stayed on in Canada to begin work, and David joined me six months later.

Hidden away at the end of North Bentinck Arm, a long fjord on BC's wild central coast, the town of Bella Coola was founded on the traditional lands of the Nuxalk people. It lies 458 kilometres from the nearest traffic light or Tim Hortons and is closer to a cruising blue whale than to a Walmart. Until 1953 the Valley was not accessible by car. Highway 20, also known as the Alexander Mackenzie Highway, began in Williams Lake but went only as far as Anahim Lake; the government refused to extend it to Bella Coola because they considered the terrain too difficult. Local volunteers, fed up with the government's obfuscations, completed the road themselves, setting out from both Anahim Lake and Bella Coola with bulldozers and determination. This "Freedom Road" remains a difficult route; in fact, the forty-three-kilometre stretch known as "The Hill" still terrifies many a driver with its 18 percent grades and hairpin turns.

It is, however, possible to arrive in Bella Coola by air as there is a small airport, although "airport" is perhaps an overstatement since there is usually only one flight from Vancouver per day, and a few extra flights in the summer to cater to increasing tourism. Even these are sometimes cancelled because of the mattress of cloud and fog that often smothers the mountain peaks while at the same time making the climate of Bella Coola one of the most temperate in Canada. The Valley is in the zone six climate belt, which means it has humid but mild winters although it also condemns it to summer temperatures that are sometimes not high enough for full crop maturation. A hundred years ago the Valley, with its rich river flats, was a major producer of potatoes, but forestry, fishing and the development of Freedom Road disrupted that way of life.

When we first moved to the Valley, we rented a house. I was working full-time and it was hard to find time for my garden, so I would get up two hours early and spend the early morning with my hands in the dirt, weeding. It was like therapy for me to be outside with my fingers in the earth and the birds singing to me, and I would work my way around the veggie patch as the sun made its way over the mountain to greet me. I would finish this morning escape by sipping coffee on my garden seat and basking in the fresh air. It was exquisite. You can't buy that kind of tranquility. However, I knew I wanted to live on my own land with my own patch of dirt and my own flock of chickens, so after a few months we started looking for property.

My property wish list

Good Soil: In New Zealand, after buying and trying to develop a farm in a wonderful location but on poor soil, I learned that you must buy the best soil you can for the money you have.

Good Water: Having relied on rainwater for six years in New Zealand, I simply couldn't go back to drinking chlorinated water.

Good Climate: I'm a wimp. I couldn't see myself surviving a real northern Canadian winter, so my farm had to be on the coast where temperatures are relatively mild. Also, when growing food, you need a decent amount of rain. Irrigation actually ruins soil, so I wanted a place where the rain could provide the majority of my farm's watering needs.

Established Fruit Trees: Fruit trees take many years to produce. Therefore, it was important to find a property with some established trees.

Affordable: Last but not least, the property had to be affordable. This is increasingly difficult to find in Canada, BC in particular.

Eventually we found a four-acre piece of ground that met all my criteria, and in the spring of 2005 we moved to our new haven, the Howling Duck Ranch. The property had lots of great advantages—good soil, good irrigation, great location—and the house was in good shape, but to become a working farm we needed to clear more land and add outbuildings, specifically a "little red barn," which is an essential fixture on any self-respecting farm. Unfortunately, two of our four acres were in lawn, which took more than three hours to mow on a ride-on lawn mower; it was, as a friend said, a "two beer lawn." I wanted to replace it with a food garden and eventually establish a market garden. We had some work to do.

Creating a garden

When we bought our property it had the makings of an English estate with approximately two acres of lawn drawing the eye south to a pond, a white latticed pergola and bridge, a small garage, an enveloping circle of trees, and to the south a Matterhorn-like peak forming the background. There was only one small chicken coop without fencing, no barns for animals, no garden and only a half-dozen or so well-established, albeit overgrown, fruit trees. Although we had over four acres of land, only two were cleared, and once you subtracted the areas we would be designating for goats, ducks, turkeys and chickens, we really only had the equivalent of a large city lot to work with. I wanted to keep it that way, partly for manageability but also because I wanted to see just how much food I could grow in that small a space. It is one thing to be able to spread out and grow rows and rows of fruit and veggies, but not everyone has that kind of space. I wanted to begin with a garden that anyone with a decent-sized backyard could achieve. This plan was also in keeping with one of the first principles of permaculture: work from your home out. Keep things close to the house and manageable.

Although the permaculture system of agriculture was developed by Australians Bill Mollison and David Holmgren, I had come across it while living in New Zealand, and I was especially interested in the "permanent" part of it. Permacultural design creates a "food forest," the idea being to use food species to mimic the architecture and beneficial relationships between plants and animals that are found in a natural forest or other natural ecosystem. Food forests are not naturally occurring but are designed and managed ecosystems—typically complex perennial polycultural plantings—that are very rich in biodiversity and productivity.

An aerial view of the Howling Duck Ranch outlined in yellow. Photo Michael Wigle.

Mustard lettuce is a spicy salad green that readily reseeds itself.

Spring came early to the Valley that first year, and I realized that if I wanted to have a garden by summer, I had to start converting grass to soil—and fast. Over the years I've read all that I could get my hands on in terms of intensive veggie gardening, most notably *Four Season Harvest* by Elliot Coleman, and I adapted many of his suggestions for my own garden. Being an organic, ethical farmer intent on living lightly on the earth, Coleman says that developing no-till, permanent beds is fundamental to sustainability. However, when you are just beginning a garden, especially one that is replacing a lawn, I decided that you can't *not* till. (I revised that opinion within a few years.)

Being a purist, I began by trying to hand-dig a garden out of the lawn. I didn't want to use fossil fuel–powered machines unless I absolutely had to. However, after several days of back-breaking labour I caved and gave in to my husband's flawlessly reasonable insistence: "Why don't we use the rototiller that came with the place so you can put your energy into actually growing something for us?"

The garden space that I paced out for him to rototill incorporated three blueberry bushes and two highbush cranberries growing on the lawn close to the house. Together these bushes would mark the northwest corner of my garden. Two thirty-five-year-old cherry trees with an intertwined root system formed a natural boundary to the south. Then, after leaving a nice wide space that could accommodate my truck and other vehicles dropping things off at the farm, I marched east from the house as far as I could and put a stake into the ground. In very short order David had turned this six-by-nine-metre rectangle of lawn into a garden. This was to be the extent of my vegetable patch for the first season. In order to build the soil nutrients, I divided the garden into three sections so that the chickens (soon to arrive) could turn over one area, leaving their nutrient-rich deposits, while I planted another.

In the meantime I was so eager to start my vegetable garden that I bought seedling plants from the local nursery and snuck them into spaces between the plants in the existing flower beds. That year I grew the best broccoli, cauliflower and cabbages of my life. At the time I couldn't decide whether it was beginner's luck, the particular weather pattern that year, or the fact those plants liked being placed next to ornamentals that did it, but each following year my attempts paled in comparison to the bounty I reaped that season. It has since been suggested that the previous owners had probably thoroughly fertilized their flower beds, and I was seeing the benefit.

Having taken note of the number of marauding deer, we enclosed the veggie patch in a two-metre-high fence and covered the fence with old fishing net. I then placed wire fences around all the new plantings and mulched heavily in order to battle the weeds without chemical additions. Because I planned to give my animals free range, the fruit trees and shrubs needed heavy protection, especially from the goats who, theoretically, were only ever supposed to have monitored free range time, so in addition to the wire, we put rails around the trees like little personal fences so the goats that eventually joined our farm project couldn't lean on the wire and access the branches. I'd seen this done on farms in New Zealand to keep the sheep and cows from grazing too close to new plantings. In the years ahead our animals didn't always cooperate in this regard, but overall I won the battle and in time had a nicely established and productive food forest orchard and I was able to take the fencing off some of the more established trees.

I modeled my garden layout on Elliot Coleman's measurements: each bed should be no wider than your legs can comfortably spread for ease of hand planting and weeding. Not being a giant of the western world, my beds were about a metre wide (maybe slightly more).

That first year I bought seedlings and planted everything I could get my hands on: tomatoes, sweet peppers, hot peppers, Japanese eggplants, broccoli, cauliflower, squash and an assortment of salad greens. I had the ridiculous notion that if I planted it, it would grow. I was sadly mistaken. Bella Coola summers are not long enough or hot enough for the heat-loving veggies like peppers, tomatoes, eggplants or squashes to be very successful. However, I did manage to harvest salad greens right into October.

My first permanent beds were asparagus, strawberries and garlic. We harvested our first strawberries that year and every year afterwards. As ideally garlic should be planted in the fall and over-wintered, I left it in the ground until the second year. Okay, I did cheat and try one bulb the first season just to see how it would taste! However, I harvested the garlic scapes each year for use in salads and for making garlic scape pesto, which I put on my own home-made angel hair pasta. Oh. My. God.

We were well on our way to becoming farmers.

The advantages of planning

In a permacultural system everything gardens, and animals and insects are in the leadership position. All of the animals, both the domestic ones and the wild ones that range on your land, are critical components of any sustainable system because without their participation and contribution an ecological balance cannot be achieved. From the birds and bees who fertilize your crops to the manure-making mammals such as horses, chickens, goats, sheep and cows, their contribution to the development of a sustainable system is paramount. In addition, one of the key principles in this system is to have each component, be it machine, flora or fauna, do triple duty. So, for example, a horse can provide you with power, manure and lawn-mowing duties. However, in terms of the small farm or homestead, chickens are the true workhorses. I knew from my Antipodean experience that they were easy to raise; therefore, the first addition to my farm venture would be chickens. From day one my chickens provided eggs, meat, manure, weeding services and soil development through their scratching and compost turning. Later they did spring and fall garden cleanup, foraged on fallen fruit, chased bugs and cabbage moths, and did all this with enthusiasm. They also provided entertainment, a factor that is not defined in the permaculture principles but should be!

In a perfect world, one's homestead would grow according to a plan, just like the books say. The reality is that when you are working with the seasons, animals, and people's whims, plans are modified by the unexpected, accidental, and totally unpredictable. So it was that after months of planning, my husband and I had found an uneasy compromise between his preference for no animals and my own vision of self-sufficiency, which included numerous farmyard animals and a red barn for a horse. The attraction of the property for him was that it was essentially a no-maintenance deal: a vinyl-sided house with central heating and a ride-on lawnmower in the garage. Thankfully, in his experience, chickens were practically "no-maintenance," too. As luck would have it, there was a chicken house already on the property, so with a minimal amount of prompting he eventually agreed we could plan for a few chickens.

The living conditions of commercially raised hens, even in so-called free range operations, had always been enough to spur me on to getting my own chickens, but the real impetus had come one quiet morning a few months before we moved onto our own property. I was in the kitchen making an omelette for breakfast and cracked some store-bought eggs into a bowl. Having gotten used to the deep orangey-yellow of pasture-raised chicken eggs from my own flock in New Zealand, I was unimpressed with the pallid complexion of the yolks of these store-bought eggs. I had tried on a few occasions to feed them raw to my dog, Tatra, but she always threw them up. Not once had I experienced this with my own eggs, which she had happily scarfed down like the breath of life itself. For several years I had wondered—not really wanting to know the answer—what awful ingredient is in store-bought eggs that my dog couldn't tolerate? What were we feeding ourselves that a dog couldn't eat? When I told this story to some of my friends, they all claimed a similar intolerance for regular store-bought eggs. Many complained of sore stomachs after eating them, and most had quit eggs altogether.

On that morning as I began to whisk the eggs together, I smelled an unpleasant waft of old fish, like a tuna can left a few days too long in the garbage under the sink. In fact, I began doubting my housekeeping, stopped stirring and looked in the trash to see. Perhaps there were fish bones in there, off-gassing. Finding the garbage pail empty, I checked the usual places for an offending aroma: the fridge, the sink, behind the stove. Nothing. Wracking my brain and doubting my sanity, I picked up one of the egg shells and sniffed. There it was: a foul, fetid, fishy smell! Enough is enough! At that point I decided to stop eating eggs until we could raise our own chickens. I made a call to my friend Darrell, who had an incubator, and he offered to start some eggs for us.

The clan grows (not according to plan)

On the first of the twenty-one days until chick-hatching day, I arrived home from work with a puppy—Tui—that a colleague had found being thrown against a brick wall by some children. This colleague was living in one of the hospital apartments in town so he couldn't keep her, and I couldn't bear the thought of leaving the pup to fend for herself, so I agreed to take her.

We weren't really equipped to deal with a new pup nor was another dog part of the official plan, but I hoped that my older dog, Tatra, would help with the puppy training. However, while Tatra could be relied on to stay home when asked to, I knew that a new pup would need fencing, so we constructed a small fence around the chicken coop where we would house both dogs—temporarily, of course. Not long after the fencing was complete, we came home to find both dogs on the front porch. I discovered a freshly dug hole under the fence—definitely the handiwork of Tatra—so we dug a trench and buried the chicken wire fencing. Two days later the puppy was sitting on the front porch when we came home and Tatra was still in the yard. We'd solved one problem but created another: why was Tatra still confined but not the pup? We looked around the perimeter of the fence for ways the pup could have gotten out. Perhaps a hole too small for Tatra? But this was not likely because Tatra was not all that much bigger than the pup. There were no signs of holes through or under the fence. We were stymied.

Two nights later a friend solved the problem. We were having a dinner party, and our friend was just making a toast to the chef when suddenly he began laughing and pointing at the chicken coop. Turning our heads to follow his finger, we watched as the little puppy scaled the four-foot fence like a clumsy Spiderman, teetered on the top, then tumbled head over heels toward freedom and the front porch. Tatra was left behind, unimpressed with the unfairness of it all. Turning to my husband I said, "Well, that is clearly not working. We'll have to build a permanent doghouse." He lowered his fork with a sigh, knowing that by "we" I meant him.

The following weekend David built the classic *Peanuts*-style doghouse, complete with insulated walls, a raised floor and a tiled roof. The puppy spent one night in it. The next day Darrell phoned. "Put the coffee on," he said, "I'm coming over. I have something for your pond." Fifteen minutes later he came through our gate carrying a cardboard box under his arm. "These will have to stay warm for another two weeks," he said as he walked into the garage without disclosing what "they" were. I lifted the lid to see six adorable week-old Muscovy ducklings: soft, brown and yellow, torpedo-shaped balls of joy. While my husband listed the economic and logistic reasons not to keep them, they stole my heart, and I looked over a yellow ball of fluff at him.

"How can you refuse?" I blinked at him.

Ignoring my pleading eyes, he ended with what he thought was a triumphant flourish of irrefutable logic. "We don't have any housing for them!"

"We can drag the doghouse you just built over to the pond. They'll love it over there!" I announced victoriously. On a roll, I continued by itemizing all the small alterations the doghouse would need in order to be converted to duck housing, including a front door, hinged and lockable at night to save the ducks from predators.

"And it will need a ramp up to the front door because ducks don't like to walk on steps," Darrell chimed in helpfully.

Without a word, my husband walked to the back of the garage and got out his circular saw. Within a few days, the alterations to accommodate the ducklings had been made—without complaint. The following weekend my husband built another doghouse and painted the puppy's name on it in big bold letters: T-U-I. He really outdid himself on this one. The puppy spent precisely one night in its newly constructed, complete-with-name-tag doghouse.

During its construction, I thought that David was looking a bit overwhelmed with the task, so I offered to help. He sent me up to the farm supply store for some nails. I returned from the store with a roll of page wire, some posts—and a pygmy goat! At first my husband was charmed by this miniature novelty. "You are now a truly liberated woman with a ruminant of your own and all," he announced. But soon the panic set in: "What do we do with a goat? The chickens are going to hatch soon!"

"Isn't he adorable?" I said, watching intently as the little goat took in his surroundings.

David looked at the goat, put down his hammer and sighed. "Yes, he is cute. But what will we do with him?"

"So-o-o cute. And look, he's got one white foot."

"But where is he going to sleep?"

"Well, I think we should go Canadian and call him Gordon."

He looked at the goat's foot then back at me, blank.

"Geesh, how can you not get the reference? Gordon Whitefoot, of course."

He pressed on with practicalities. "Where are we going to put him?"

"Well, we can do another shuffle. The goat can have the new doghouse."

"But it has a big window in it," he said, knowing it would make no difference to the predicament but nonetheless unable to hold it back.

"Well then," I replied, "we will have a ruminant with a view!"

I think my husband calculated that if he stopped building doghouses, no new animals would arrive. So the following weekend, with seven days to go until the only actual planned additions to the farm's livestock were to hatch, he enlisted the help of a contractor and built a larger fence around

The "ruminant with a view" dog-cum-goat house built by my husband, David. We housed the Muscovy ducks in this "doghouse" until the grizzly bear took away their feed one afternoon.

the chicken shed, and we released Gordon into it—temporarily, of course. The vision before me morphed into a photo from some Greek Island cookbook. I had never seen anything so excruciatingly adorable in my life—a beautiful miniature goat standing beneath a dwarf weeping birch tree as if he'd been there since the dawn of time.

A few days later while we were admiring Gordon in his new home, Nils—the farm store owner who had sold Gordon to me—arrived with a laden truck. "I know you said you didn't want any more animals, but I've just had an offer on my business. I'm moving back to New Brunswick and really need to unload my animals. Would you be able to take Gordon's sister?" A plaintive ba-a-a-a came from the truck, and the response from Gordon filled the air with irresistible charm—well, at least to me. She was completely black except for a small white spot on her head that looked like a doily.

"We should call her Sundown," I said, and registered the puzzlement on my husband's face. "You know, in keeping with the Canadiana theme we have going on." Still facing that puzzled look, I began to sing, "Sundown, you'd better take care if I find you've been creeping round my back stairs ..."

Nils recognized it right away and, smiling, turned to leave. "I feel much better knowing they are going to people like you."

As our numbers and species of animals grew, we assured ourselves that we had planned for no more.

"Is there a grand plan here?" my husband ventured, exhausted by the flurry of building activity.

"Grand? Yes," I replied confidently, but I was interrupted by the ringing of the phone. It was Darrell, who had been incubating the chicken eggs for us.

"You're going to have to come right now and get your eggs," he barked uncharacteristically.

"But I'm in the middle of something, Darrell ..."

"Well, it's ... uh ... hmm ... kinda urgent ... sort of," he said, his voice trailing off and softening a little.

"I thought you were going to—" I started to say.

"You have to come right now!" he interrupted. "I've been making a plexiglass hatch door for your chicken shed, you know, so they can see out? And … uh well, I kinda cut my thumb off … a bit."

"Jesus, Darrell, are you okay?"

"You have to come get these eggs!"

"Okay, but you should get to the hospital. I'll meet you there first and get the eggs later," I said, hoping reason would prevail.

"No! Get the eggs first!" When he paused, I could almost see him looking down at his thumb and considering his condition. "I'll be okay."

Clearly I wasn't going to win this. "Well, how bad is it? Do you still have a thumb?"

"Yeah, sort of," he answered vaguely.

"God, Darrell, what does that mean?"

"Well … I can see bone. I kinda peeled it like a banana," and his voice trailed off.

A wave of nausea washed over me and set my alarm bells ringing. *Oh my God, he's going into shock. Lord, he should get to the hospital.* "I'll be there in a moment," I said quickly and hung up before he could object. Then quickly I dialed a friend at our little local hospital and painted a slightly brighter version of the situation. She agreed to walk the two blocks to get him while I drove down. By the time I arrived, he was already in hospital and a nurse was attending to what was left of his thumb. Although the injury would require an air-vac trip to Vancouver, Darrell was still more worried about the chicks than his thumb, and before getting into the air ambulance, he told me everything I would need to know about becoming a mother to baby chicks.

It is very stressful being a chicken mother-to-be. I drove home with the incubator cradled on the seat beside me and spent the next two days and nights listening to the stifled yet insistent "peep-peeps" coming from inside the box. Unbeknownst to me at the time, chicks can begin to peep two to three days before they hatch, which can be quite unnerving for the uninitiated. I found myself not sleeping as I listened to their chatter, worrying that the chicks would suffocate in their shells. What was taking them so long? Why weren't they coming out? What was all the peeping about? Happily, within a few days twenty-two chickens managed to hatch without any help from us, and we set up a temporary pen for them in the garage.

As the chickens grew bigger, it became clear the goats would soon have to move out of the chicken house, and for the second time my husband went outside to discuss the merits of *al fresco* living with the pup. And because more chicks had hatched than we had anticipated, we needed a bigger fenced area for them, so I offered to drive to town to get more posts. David, however, being aware that Nils was still in the process of liquidating his stock and having seen the size of Nils' dogs and knowing he had a horse on offer as well, politely declined my offer to go to the store for more posts and wire. Instead, he went himself, and then with naive enthusiasm and a (false) sense that he'd established some boundaries, he began enlarging the chicken run. Eventually the fencing for the chickens was finished and a new enclosure was built for the goats, complete with doghouse number two. David valiantly built two more structures: a house

We enjoyed watching our first batch of chicks grow into a healthy and happy flock of roosters and hens.

for Sundown, which was installed next to Gordon's house in the new goat pen, and a final doghouse, which the dogs never really adopted because, it seems, David's chat about the advantages of living in the fresh air had been too convincing.

The new baby chicks were finally old enough to be moved. Having spent their first six weeks in the garage, they found the outdoors exciting. It was thrilling to see them run around their yard, scratching for tasty morsels and running awkwardly after the occasional winged bug that dared enter their pen. It was even more thrilling when Darrell arrived a few days later to visit the chicks for the first time, with his thumb firmly reattached and with the doctor's promise that it would soon be in good working order.

How ethical can you get?

Most chickens and eggs no longer come from real farms but huge indoor factories where millions of hens are kept in the most inhumane, disease-ridden conditions imaginable—even when they have fancy names such as free-run, free-range, organic and so on. Just because the egg carton says "free-range," meaning the chickens technically have access to grass, doesn't necessarily mean they've had a chance to feel the earth beneath their feet. Most of these factory-farmed hens (including the organic and so-called free-range varieties) never see the light of day, let alone get the chance to become a mother. Thanks to genetic modification, we are breeding broodiness out of hens because what industry wants is a hen that lays an egg every day like clockwork. They generally die of exhaustion at the ripe old age of two or younger.

My version of ethical farming involves letting the animals express themselves as they would in nature. This goes beyond the parameters of free-range, free-run, farm fresh, born free, naturally raised, or whatever other fancy terminology the corporate egg producers can dream up to make an unwitting public think they are supporting decent agricultural practices or family-run farms. And one of the many benefits of raising a small flock is that you gain a more intimate knowledge of your birds and you can let your hens express themselves as chickens. If mine wanted to become mothers, they were free to do so.

As for the roosters, they got the same treatment as the gals but were soon used for meat as roosters are less than stellar egg layers. Lots of folks tell me that roosters can be stroppy or vicious, but not Pavarotti, our hand-reared "stud-muffin" rooster. He was a keeper and lived out his natural lifespan on the farm. Any new young roosters that challenged him got put in the pot forthwith; those that recognized him as king got to stay and fulfill their biological imperative, adding to the gene pool. As a result, I had very few cock fights, perhaps also because living conditions were pleasant.

In general, my chickens suited themselves. They had free access to as much feed as they wished but mostly foraged for themselves, running, scratching and eking out a living as nature intended them to. Because they were not a hybrid type of chicken, genetically altered or manipulated into growing to meet market demands, they never hung about the entrance to their barn. Instead, they ran all over the farm. In fact, they were even known to leave the property and, on one occasion, neighbours caught them heading for the airport. Where they were planning to holiday without passports, I have no clue! While I want all my animals to have the freedom to be what they were meant to be (not just a food machine for human consumption), letting them get on a plane without me was out of the question.

Cabbage anyone?

One crop that consistently grew well in my garden was cabbage, and this is ironic because I really don't like cabbage. But with a bounty of big, tight, heavy cabbages, I was forced to learn how to eat them. What I knew about cabbage was that my mother used to make coleslaw, so I made coleslaw, coleslaw … and more coleslaw. And I don't even like coleslaw. Next I searched the web for a hundred things to do with cabbage. Nothing appealed, but I finally found a coleslaw recipe I liked that included cucumbers with a mayo, garlic, lime juice and cilantro dressing.

I also decided to try making sauerkraut. I don't like sauerkraut either, but what else can you do when you have several kilograms of the sweetest cabbage you have ever tasted and exactly one good coleslaw recipe? Having made that recipe and eaten it on a daily basis for a week straight already, it seemed to me that learning to make sauerkraut was my only salvation. Besides, cabbage needs to ferment for at least several weeks and up to a couple of months before it turns into kraut, and this would give me some breathing space to figure out what to do with the fermenting beasts!

My mother had given me a beautiful sauerkraut crock for the occasion so I got it ready. This crock goes by the trade name of Harsch Fermenting Crock, and it is designed so that the gases that are produced in the fermenting process can escape but no unsterile air can enter. I searched the web for a recipe and got out my food processor. The directions were vague but basic: shred cabbage, sprinkle salt, pound. Repeat. It was easy and, to be completely honest, shredding the cabbages in the food processor and then pounding salt into their wounds felt wickedly satisfying.

I once stayed in a gorgeous little bed and breakfast near 100 Mile House called Arcona House on the Lake. I immediately hit it off with the proprietor, whose name is Henning, a generous, interesting and kind man. Henceforth, whenever I travelled through the area I would stop in and have a visit. Once, when staying in the area with friends over the Christmas and New Year holiday, I took them to meet him, and he served us a sumptuous German-style dinner centred on cabbage rolls. Now normally I don't really like cabbage rolls. As a child I would unroll the boiled cabbage and eat the filling, leaving the cabbage leaf splayed out like a discarded wet rag on my plate. But Henning's weren't just any cabbage rolls. These had been homemade by a friend who used soured cabbage leaves instead of the boiled leaves my mother had always used. These were the best cabbage rolls I'd ever tasted! So that afternoon as I sliced, salted and pounded bits of cabbage, I suddenly recalled the delectableness of Henning's cabbage rolls. At that moment inspiration took hold of me and I sunk a whole head of cabbage into the mix, hoping this was how it was done.

Seven weeks later the kraut had finished fermenting; I processed all of it into jars and gave most of them away. But the whole cabbage head had fermented properly, and my inspiration was realized. Now all I had to do was make the filling and find some willing friends to act as guinea pigs! I decided to start with an invitation to Darrell, who has a very Germanic surname, and he confirmed that he was a huge fan of cabbage rolls and was willing to sacrifice himself to the cause. My friend Carole was also keen so she too got an invitation. She suggested we really go traditional on the theme and add homemade perogies to the menu. Consensus around the table that night was that they were the best cabbage rolls (not to mention perogies) we'd ever eaten!

The value of heritage

During that first year on the Howling Duck Ranch I grew fantastic zucchinis on an old burn pile. While living in New Zealand, I had learned that the best time to harvest these things was when they are still only about fifteen centimetres long, but despite this youthful harvest time and the fact that I only had seven plants on my burn pile, I was not able to keep up with them. I made tons and tons of zucchini relish only to realize that unless I opened a Heinz-sized factory, I was still not going to keep up with the prolific plants by turning them into relish. Or cake, for that matter. But in light of the fact they are so easy to grow and produce so prolifically, I couldn't not grow them. What I needed was a way of beating them back. Enter zucchini flower recipes.

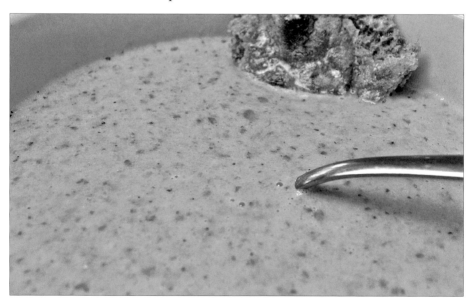

Once a season I indulge in *Flor de Calabaza* soup. The delicate beauty of this soup is matched by its unique but subtle flavour.

From my travels in Mexico I knew there existed myriad uses for zucchini flowers, but I'd never tried any of them. I got out the Mexican cookbook that I'd bought on my first trip there and found the *flor de calabaza* soup recipe. It is a cream-based soup with a beautiful colour and delicate flavour. Not only was

Zucchini flowers ready for soup making. This is one of the best ways I've found to control zucchini plant production overdrive.

it divine but it also did the job of providing a reprieve from the zucchini harvest for a couple of weeks. I look forward to this soup every year, but because of the inordinate number of zucchini blossoms it requires, I make a large pot of it only once per growing season. Consequently, knowing I will only taste it once every three hundred and sixty-five days, I start to anticipate that blossom harvest practically from the minute I finish eating the soup. This is truly in-season eating! One day I mean to have a large row—perhaps a whole patch of garden—dedicated to zucchinis for their blossoms alone.

However, the year I got really serious about provisioning my pantry solely from my garden, I couldn't seem to grow a zucchini plant. I planted early in the spring and nothing sprouted. Maybe it was too cold, I thought, and planted again. And again. Then I bought new seeds and out of a whole packet had only one or two plants come to life. I was aghast. What kind of gardener was I if I couldn't even grow a zucchini?

That's when I asked my neighbours if they too were having problems with zucchinis. Yes, they were. I concluded there must be something wrong with the seed if I wasn't the only one having problems. It certainly was not the weather as the other vegetables in my garden were doing fine. It was then that I finally did some serious research on genetic engineering and seeds. Horrified by what I learned, I got serious about buying organic, non-hybrid, open-pollinated seeds.

Homegrown Sauerkraut

Ingredients
- Minimum of 2 heads of cabbage
- Kosher salt (I use pickling salt)
- Water

Apparatus
- One very large crock, glass or enamel container or a Harsch crock
- Heavy-duty food-grade plastic bags or 2-gallon (9-litre) freezer bags (unless you are using a Harsch crock)
- Wooden spoon (or something to pound the kraut with)

Notes
- Never use aluminum utensils!
- Absolute cleanliness is necessary for a healthy brew. I have one very old 5-gallon (23-litre) crock that I use to make sauerkraut; I cover it with plastic bags and a plate to keep air out. I also have two Harsch crocks that were designed for making kraut and have airtight seals. You can also use a glass or enamel-coated container but you must clean it well and then scald it by pouring boiling water into it and swishing it around for at least 30 seconds.
- When I use a Harsch crock, I follow the directions that come with it. The Harsch recipe uses less salt than the recipe that follows.
- If you plan on refrigerating and not canning your sauerkraut, use just 3 tbsp (45 ml) of salt for every 5 pounds (2.25 kg) of cabbage. If you want to make cabbage rolls with whole fermented leaves, then when preparing this recipe, core 1 whole cabbage and nestle it into the shredded cabbage, covering it as you layer the salt and cabbage. Be sure to weigh this extra head of cabbage and adjust the amount of salt accordingly.

Directions
1. Remove and discard the outer leaves of the cabbages. Wash and drain the cabbages and cut them into halves or quarters, removing the cores in the process.
2. Shred the cabbage. I use my food processor for speed and ease. If you shred by hand, make sure the shreds are no thicker than a nickel or dime.

3. Using a wooden spoon or very clean hands, mix cabbage and salt in the ratio of 5 pounds (2.25 kg) of shredded cabbage to 4 tbsp (60 ml) of kosher salt. Pickling salt will do but it changes the flavour a bit. Do not use table salt. Toss and mix thoroughly until salt dissolves.

4. When juice starts to form, pack the cabbage firmly and evenly into a clean crock or a glass or enamel container. Press firmly to encourage juice formation. Fill the crock to no closer than 5" (13 cm) from the top edge. Make sure the juice covers the cabbage completely. Unless the cabbage is fresh from the garden, this does not always happen so you will need to prepare additional brine by putting 1½ tablespoons (23 ml) of kosher salt into 1 quart (1 L) of boiling water. Dissolve salt and cool the brine to room temperature before adding it to the pot of cabbage.

5. Once the cabbage is completely immersed in the brine, place a large food-grade plastic bag filled with brine water on top of the cabbage. (I use 2 large bags, one inside the other so that if one bag breaks, it will not water down the cabbage into a tasteless mess.) The cabbage must be well sealed all around with the bag, so no air can get in and contaminate the sauerkraut with unwanted yeasts or molds.

6. Now cover the container with plastic wrap and then a heavy towel or cloth and tie securely into place. Do not remove this until the fermenting is complete. Place the crock in an area where the temperature will not be above 75°F (24°C) and the fermentation will begin within a day. If the room temperature is a constant 75°F, allow 3 weeks for fermentation. If the temperature is 70°F (21°C), allow 4 weeks; at 65°F (18°C), allow 5 weeks; at 60°F (16°C), allow 6 weeks. Note that if the temperature is above 75°F or 76°F degrees, the sauerkraut may not ferment and could spoil.

7. Once the cabbage is fermented, taste it to see if it has reached your required tartness. At this stage it can be eaten immediately. However, if you plan to can it, make sure it is a wee bit more tart than you like as this tartness will weaken in the canning process.

8. Canning Methods: If you use the hot pack method, process pint jars for 10 minutes and quart jars for 15 minutes. If you use the raw pack method, process pint jars for 20 minutes and quart jars for 25 minutes. I have tried both and prefer to use the cold pack because it makes a crisper sauerkraut.

The genetically modified threat

Ever since humans took up agriculture they have been using selective breeding to modify plants and animals to suit their food needs. This selective breeding became more sophisticated in the mid-twentieth century when techniques were developed for making changes within organisms by exposing them to radiation or chemicals. But in the late twentieth century it was discovered that genes could actually be deleted from an organism, or a gene from a different species could be inserted to enhance traits that would make the organism easier to grow and harvest. This latter process, which is called transgenesis, has been the most commercially successful process for gene modification, especially with soybeans, corn, canola and cottonseed. The first of these genetically modified (GM) plants appeared on the market in the early 1990s, and now some 93 percent of the US soybean crop and 86 percent of the US corn crop are genetically modified. The importance of this fact is made clear by Stephen L. Hopp in Barbara Kingsolver's *Animal, Vegetable, Miracle,* where he writes that "if every product containing corn or soybean were removed from the grocery store, it would look more like a hardware store." Next time you go to the store, check out the ingredients on that bottle of pop or those chewy granola bars!

While genetically modified foods offer some benefits, such as plants that are disease-resistant, there is also a huge list of potential health and political hazards associated with these products, including increasing dependence on a few seed producers, seed and plant patenting, and the lack of sufficient testing for the long-term impact of genetically modified foods on the environment. For example, in 1970 John E. Franz, a scientist working for Monsanto, which today is one of the world's three producers of genetically modified seed, discovered that glyphosate (an aminophosphonic analogue of the natural amino acid glycine) had herbicidal properties. That is, it could kill a wide spectrum of both broad-leaved and cereal plants, making it ideal for weed control. Monsanto patented it as Roundup, then the company set its plant scientists to work inserting gene sequences from plants *not* affected by this herbicide into food plants such as soy and corn. The result was "Roundup Ready" crops that would continue to flourish when sprayed with the herbicide while at the same time the weeds around them would die, thus eliminating manual weeding. However, cross-pollination between these engineered plants and nearby native plants has already produced weeds that are also Roundup Ready, thus compromising the advantage of the engineered plants. Because antibiotics are used in the transgenesis process to produce Roundup Ready seeds, the resulting plants are also resistant to antibiotics, and the impacts of this unintended result are as yet unknown.

In an effort to prevent "theft or infringement," GM producers, including Monsanto, have also experimented with introducing a "suicide gene" into their seeds. The plants would yield for just one season before literally committing suicide, thus forcing farmers to buy new seed year after year. It isn't difficult to imagine how devastating this could be to developing countries where farmers cannot afford to buy new seed each year, not to mention the fact that we risk turning over absolute control of all our basic world crops to giant corporations.

However, the most frightening concern about this development is the devastating possibility that the pollen from plants grown from suicide gene seed will drift and cross-pollinate with something in nature and cause the seeds of wild plants to no longer be viable. Can we really afford to lose control of our natural crops, too?

Monsanto has gradually taken control of the soy, corn and canola crops of North America by selling Roundup Ready seed to farmers under an agreement that requires a fee payment over and above the seed cost and a promise from the farmer not to replant his harvested seed. In 1999 Monsanto sued Percy Schmeiser, a Saskatchewan farmer, because in the previous crop year approximately 95–98 percent of the canola growing in Schmeiser's ten-square-kilometre field was found to contain the company's patented Roundup Ready gene, although the farmer had never bought Monsanto seed. Schmeiser argued that the patented seed had drifted onto his property and had contaminated his crop. The company insisted that, because such a high proportion of the crop contained the gene, Schmeiser must have selected for it, and in court it was effectively proved that he had collected seed from areas adjacent to his property. The case went all the way to the Supreme Court where the judges ruled in a five to four decision in favour of Monsanto. While they upheld Schmeiser's claim that a *plant* cannot be patented, they sided with Monsanto in regards to the company's bid to protect the gene they had inserted into their *seed*. In response to the Schmeiser case, farmers in Saskatchewan sued Monsanto for making it impossible to grow organic canola without the threat of drift pollination; many countries have also banned GM canola for the same reason. Australia and China have gone as far as banning Canadian canola entirely as a way of preventing contamination of their own crops.

Why buy heritage?

Over the centuries farmers throughout the world have raised many thousands of animal breeds and plant varieties, and in time they developed outstanding heritage plants and animals by selectively breeding for traits that would make specimens that were particularly well adapted to local environmental conditions. In general, these heritage breeds were better adapted to withstand disease and survive in harsh environmental conditions, and their bodies were better suited to living on pasture. As a result, even today they are well suited to sustainable farm operations since they are able to survive without the need for temperature-controlled buildings, continuous doses of antibiotics, and the otherwise sterile environments that factory farming methods attempt to achieve today.

Industrial agriculture breeds have, on the other hand, been developed to produce lots of milk or eggs, gain weight quickly, yield particular types of meat, and thrive in confined spaces. Since these industrial farms rely upon only a few specialized types of livestock and crops, thousands of non-commercial heritage animal breeds and crop varieties have disappeared. A report from the United Nations Food and Agriculture Organization (FAO) in 2006 stated that "within the past fifteen years, 190 breeds of farm animals have gone extinct worldwide, and there are currently 1,500 others at risk of becoming extinct. In the past five years alone, 60 breeds of cattle, goats, pigs, horses and poultry have become extinct, an average rate of one breed a month." Unless steps are taken soon, heritage breeds will continue to disappear along with the valuable genetic diversity they possess.

There are other reasons for maintaining heritage breeds. Some farmers just like to be raising something different from the mainstream—they like a particular animal for its looks or rarity—but for the small farmer the heritage breeds of both plants and animals provide a special niche market because they taste better. Genetic preservationists, on the other hand, have deeper philosophical, ethical and political reasons; they are concerned about keeping options available for future generations. They know that there is a very real possibility of a major disaster in industrial farming that would wipe out the only breed of a species being maintained. Moreover, they know that when that happens, the heritage breeds that have been conserved will provide humans with important genetic resources that can be used to breed new or existing traits into existing livestock breeds. If these heritage breeds become extinct, their unique genes are lost forever.

Heirloom seeds

Defining the word "heirloom" when it is used to describe plant varieties is problematic. Some experts set the year 1945 as the cutoff date for heirloom varieties since industrial agriculture began making widespread use of hybridized plants after World War II. Others insist that plant varieties must have existed for at least a hundred years in order to be legitimately called heirloom; in fact, some heirlooms are known to be much older and probably prehistoric. However, most are agreed that true heirlooms are open-pollinated and evolved through standard agricultural breeding practices, thus increasing biodiversity, while the controlled plant breeding that is used to produce hybrids guarantees that all seeds of a crop are descended from parents with known traits. Industrial agriculture varieties are chosen for productivity, their ability to withstand the rigours of mechanical picking and shipping, and their tolerance to pesticides; heirlooms, on the other hand, are propagated for their suitability to a specific climate and soil. But the seeds will have a wider variety of genetic traits, not all of them desirable in terms of taste, flavour or consumer appeal.

If you, like me, are concerned about genetic diversity, then you will choose to use open-pollinated and heirloom varieties of seeds. The problem then becomes maintaining the variety if you want to save the seeds yourself. You have to make sure they do not cross-breed with other types of plants of the same species, and this means you must understand how broadly the pollen for the plant species you are growing can disperse.

You can overcome the cross-pollination problem in a variety of ways: by only growing one variety of a plant, by making sure that different cultivars are not sexually mature at the same time, by keeping them enclosed in greenhouses or walled enclosures, or by field isolation if you are lucky enough to have sufficient land to accomplish this.

Given that the Howling Duck Ranch did not have enough land for crop isolation, I chose to support regional seed growers such as Salt Spring Seeds and West Coast Seeds. Both companies specialize in open-pollinated, non-GMO, heirloom and organic varieties. If you choose to save your own seeds, just look up the Salt Spring Seeds website and check out the detailed instructions given on the page headed "How to Save Seeds." Another good site to visit is Seeds of Diversity Canada, which is a charitable organization dedicated to "promoting the conservation and use of heritage and endangered food plants, preserving knowledge of traditional seed saving and agricultural practices and encouraging people to actively engage in protecting the diverse gene pool of plants that sustain human civilization." Besides offering an ongoing seed exchange and providing support for community organic grower organizations, this site also allows gardening groups right across Canada to advertise their Seedy Saturday and Seedy Sunday events, at which plants and seeds are exchanged. There is one of these events in Bella Coola each spring and in at least ten other communities within BC. For more information on seed saving and seed sharing see page 271.

Year Two at the Howling Duck Ranch

As the second spring at Howling Duck Ranch began, the chickens and I attacked the grass and weeds in the veggie patch, and about the time we started to win the battle, it was time to plant. To me this is the most exciting part of gardening—next to harvesting, of course. David and I had passionate discussions about what we wanted to eat and what would actually grow well in our climate. Once we had made a list of the plants we wanted to grow, something we later found out can take years to perfect, it was off to the nursery to buy seeds and seedlings.

The beet affair

The previous year a friend had introduced me to Deborah Madison's cookbook *Local Flavours*. I have a cookbook fetish and, consequently, more cookbooks than I need and many more than I have room for. Responding to my husband's dismay at the ever-burgeoning bookshelves, I insisted I needed at least one more cookbook because as far as I am concerned, Madison's cookbook is a must for anyone who takes local eating seriously. It is beautifully illustrated and well written, and the recipes are unsurpassed in inventiveness, presentation and taste. What at first seems an unlikely marriage of herbs, spices and traditional food items is transformed according to her recipes into dishes that give sybaritic meaning to Barbara Kingsolver's phrase "animal, vegetable, miracle!" My mother would concur, not because she's seen Madison's book, but because she fought with me throughout my childhood vis-à-vis vegetables. There were very few I would eat without the threat of the stove timer, beets being one of them! My mother finds the idea that Madison can get me to eat beets miraculous. What my mother doesn't know is that I not only eat them now, I absolutely crave them.

The fact is that one of the vegetables that really grew well in the soil and climate of the Howling Duck Ranch was beets. It happened that I had also found a recipe for pickled beets that is not overly sweet, but more savory and very dilly, and my husband used it to can the last of our first beet harvest. They were absolutely scrumptious and we gave a lot of them away as gifts, to rave reviews, and my husband's pickled beets joined Madison's cooked beet recipes as vegetable-miracle.

In our second year, the moment I soaked my beet seeds before planting them, my mouth began to water and continued to water until those delectable jewels were mature enough to make the ultimate sacrifice. Knowing I was going to want lots of Madison's beet salads, I planted several more rows of them than I had the first year. I was secure in the knowledge that we'd have more than enough for pickling, eating fresh and making borscht, and still have enough left over for winter storage. So with much enthusiasm and admiration I regularly reminded my husband of his success with the pickled beets.

When the day finally came that I remarked, "Hey, the beets are finally ready for harvest," he was primed to leap into action. By the time I got home, he was the vision of Martha Stewart in the kitchen, apron snugged tightly around his waist, hand poised over the water-bath canner, tongs just lifting out the last of his pickled beets. I was thrilled. I love the look of our produce lined up in glass jars, like see-through soldiers on parade, promising the delights to come in winter meals.

"Hey, look at you go!"

"Yep, I've finished the lot," he responded proudly.

"Excellent. Where are the rest of them? I'd like to make that beet salad tonight!"

Pause.

"They're all gone," he said.

"What do you mean, they're all gone!"

"When I said I finished the lot, I meant I canned the lot."

His moment of culinary triumph came to a crashing halt there in our kitchen. Every last one of the beets that I had been so looking forward to had been hung, drawn, quartered and pickled and now stood there, gleaming, in jars on the counter. The vision of succulent salads and savoury soups vanished and all that remained was a cheery line-up of Christmas gifts and appetizer plates for dinner parties to come. Not a single fresh beet had escaped.

I was forced to store-buy beets of questionable merit in order to satisfy my Madison miracle desires. It is a sore spot I carry around inside me, raw and unhealed. I know it sounds ridiculous, but the passion that I feel for growing food is beyond description. I love everything about it: the connection with the natural world, the link to the past through families who have carefully saved seed, crossed continents, created and kept cultural foods and traditions alive. I love my fingers in the earth, the quiet moments alone while weeding, lost in some kind of transcendence.

Building the permanent garden

The first year in the garden had been largely devoted to beating back the grass in order to establish a veggie patch. The second summer I began to look further afield in order to develop my food forests. I had a vision of establishing a self-perpetuating food system that entailed sourcing and transplanting a variety of wild plants from the actual forest around me, such as saskatoon berry plants and strawberry plants, and placing them into my garden and food forest areas, depending on the plants' requirements. I had varying degrees of success with this. Not one of the saskatoon berry bushes survived. I've since read that they are notoriously difficult to transplant, which made me feel like somewhat less of a failure!

That summer I also took a trip to Vancouver and picked up my sister, Jeanine, along with twelve young fruit trees: Italian plum, several cherries, an apricot, a couple pears, and a variety of apple specimens. On the way into the Valley, Jeanine, looking out the window, suddenly exclaimed, "Oh my god, there's a bear!" Indeed, a black bear was grazing in the field of the farm that supplied us with beef. I was about to provide my sister with this

Harvesting fresh peas. In terms of garden veggies, these are the first to produce and delight. Photo David Dowling.

interesting bit of information when a distinctive thud and an unmistakable shudder shook the back end of my truck.

"What was that?" Jeanine said, her eyes searching my face for reassurance.

"We have a flat tire," I said.

"What are we going to do?" she asked, stifling a nervous giggle.

I was worrying about the work it was going to be to unload all the fruit trees in order to access the tire, jack and wrench. I grumbled out loud while Jeanine offered helpful commentary about fruit tree smorgasbords for bears. Luckily, help came along within minutes in the form of a big burly man willing to rescue two damsels who were in the midst of erecting a bear-attracting roadside food forest.

The next day I set to planting the trees, and over the subsequent weeks my husband erected the protective fencing. I arranged the trees according to food forest principles. In other words, I placed them around the yard and then strategically planted other bushes, shrubs and flowers among them. Some of the trees occupied empty spaces in the lawn while others got knitted in among already established flower beds. Still others were put into ground where I quickly established food-providing beds around their bases. It was like having a blank canvas and installing living, ever-changing art throughout the landscape.

Mr. Mallard meets his maker

When you are dealing with animals, you have to face the fact that they are one day, in some fashion, going to die. Animals that you are raising for food tend to die at your own hand—a planned death, as it were. However, there are occasions when they die an unplanned death, and those are the hardest to deal with emotionally. I have lost two dogs to vehicles, many a chicken to foxes (and even a few to my own dogs until I got them trained), and baby ducks to eagles, owls, ravens and crows. It seems that everything is out to eat your would-be food, and this was not something I had counted on or factored into the equation when I first started thinking about personal food sovereignty. In fact, I'd never even thought about the complexities of the food production and distribution systems or how, in order to get a chicken to a consumer's table, a lot of wild space and the critters in it would have to be tamed! Now I was trying to raise all my own food on my own land and everything that moved seemed to think I was providing it with a buffet. It is an uneasy relationship which, it seems, only farmers understand. Consequently, I began sleeping with one ear cocked to the night.

All this was brought home to me in my relationship with Mr. and Mrs. Mallard. It began one spring day when I went for a very welcome appointment with our local hairdresser. In the middle of our six-week catch-up, she casually mentioned that she had told a friend up on the Chilcotin Plateau about my food sovereignty project, and this friend was wondering if I could take her mallard ducks. Though pets, they were muddying her water source too much. "She's offered to pay the shipping costs," my hairdresser urged. At eleven the following night our sole freight connection dropped off two boxes, the second one holding a bonus rooster who couldn't bear to be parted from his avian friends. The arrival of Mr. and Mrs. Mallard certainly livened up the duck pond. The general dignified quietness of our Muscovies was now augmented by the regular raucous complaints and disruptions of the mallards.

The mallards spent several weeks touring the property looking at real estate, Mr. Mallard always a few paces behind Mrs. Mallard, and she regularly ducking her head around to make sure he was still there in his subservient place, commenting all the while in a persistent abbreviated quack about the poor drainage or lack of view or high prices. He would respond patiently with a muted "Yes dear, yes dear, yes dear ..." Eventually, instead of returning to their duck house each evening, the mallards regularly disappeared into the woods just beyond our pond. Although I spent time every evening looking for them to get them back inside, I could never find them. Then just before dawn one morning I heard the mallards' anxious squawking, and I dashed outside with my flashlight and ran all over the lawn, hoping to interrupt the predator and dissuade it from its intentions, but it was still too dark to see or do anything.

As soon as it was light, I went out to the pond to check. Mrs. Mallard was there looking very forlorn, and I could read the night's events in the webbed tracks in the dew. Their little footprints scurried here and there, she had gone one way from their nest, her mate another, and a fox had followed him. The two tracks zigzagged all over the lawn, but there was no sign of the noble drake—not even a feather. I've since learned that a telltale sign of a fox kill is that there is nothing left behind.

That afternoon Mrs. Mallard waddled forlornly over to the Muscovy ducks' pen. As soon as I let her in, she moved to a safe corner and for the next three days she sat there, staring into the forest where Mr. Mallard had been taken and occasionally making a mournful little grunting sound. Over the following weeks and months she slowly recovered from her grief and eventually merged with the rest of the flock until once again she became the gabby boss she had been on arrival. In fact, she assumed the role of general manager of the whole farm with some relish. She let me know when it was time to get up, when it was time for dinner (particularly the ducks' dinner), and when it was time for everyone to go to bed.

Gordon gets into the grain

One day that second summer my husband was alone at home and, filled with a sense of joie de vivre, he decided to declare a free-range day and let all the animals out of their paddocks. While they enjoyed meandering hither and yon, he mounted the ride-on mower and wove in between the flower beds and fruit trees, the chickens, the ducks and the goats. When that job was done, he picked strawberries while the goats nibbled on some comfrey and the chickens and ducks went on weed patrol.

Then, to avoid the noonday sun, he went into the garage to touch up his latest construction—yet another dog/duck/goat house—with the barn-red paint that had become the standard for all structures on the property. When in mid-afternoon he came out to collect the eggs, he was surprised to see Gordon in the chicken yard. Goats sure are sociable little critters, he thought as he shooed him back toward the goat pen. By the time I arrived home from work, everything looked fine: chickens, goats and ducks all at home, present and accounted for and locked in for the night, and dinner in the oven.

"The lawn looks great, honey. How were the goats?"

"No problem. I let them out to range today. They helped mow the lawn and then just hung around their pen."

The next morning when my husband went to feed the animals, Gordon didn't come out to greet him as he usually did. Even the sound of the food bucket being banged drew only Sundown out. Alarmed, David entered the pen and approached the goat house. There lay Gordon on his straw, panting in the warm air and looking if he were expecting triplets. But Gordon was a boy—a castrated male, in fact! Surely he hadn't eaten that much during the night? Gordon barely opened his eyes as my husband crawled in to pull him out and then tried to heave him to his feet. He managed to get the goat to stand, wedged between the structure and a tree trunk. David began to panic. His mind raced: intestinal parasites, worms, cancer ... laundry? (Goats do enjoy clean laundry from the clothesline.) But he hadn't done any laundry yesterday. Running out of possibilities, he sprinted for the house.

"I think there's something wrong with Gordon."

"Why?" I asked.

"He looks kind of ... pregnant."

I knew right away what the problem was and that, if I was right, Gordon's life was in jeopardy. Out I rushed. One glance was enough to confirm my suspicion. "Oh god, he's bloated! You must have given him too much grain yesterday."

"I didn't give him any grain yesterday." Then the incident in the chicken yard burst into his mind. "But I did find him near the chicken shed."

"That'll be it. Corn. This is not good. Look, I know when this happens to horses you have to keep them walking. So get the dog's leash, quick!"

He found a leash, tied it to Gordon's neck and began coaxing and dragging him in small circles. Gordon made it clear walking was the last thing he wanted to do. Several times he fell forward onto his front legs.

"He doesn't want to walk," my husband called out.

"Well, he'll die if he doesn't, so keep him moving!" I dashed inside to phone the nearest vet, a mere five hundred kilometres away.

Once I described what had likely taken place, the vet confirmed bloat. "You've got two choices," he said.

"What are they?" I asked, swallowing hard in an attempt to tamp down my rising panic.

"You can stick a metal tube into the rumen and expel the air."

"You mean through the skin from the outside?" I looked at Gordon's bloated side.

"Yes. But you have to know what you are doing with that because you can kill your goat if you miss or the tube gets stuck inside him," he said matter-of-factly. I tried picturing myself with a metal tube tentatively trying to pierce through Gordon's beautiful grey coat into his rumen. I could see myself wincing as I pushed, blundering the job and making matters worse.

"Is there a less bloody option?" I asked with bated breath.

"Stomach-tubing your goat. Have you done that before?" he asked.

"No. Can you talk me through it?" I asked. Craning my neck to hold the phone, I motioned to my husband to go back to the house and get me a pen and paper. I took the leash from him and continued trying to lead Gordon around the yard, but he was no longer fighting us and had sunk down onto the ground, wedged between two hay bales we'd placed there for him, and looking sorry for himself.

"I can sure try!" the vet said. I thought I could detect amusement in his voice. "First off, be sure to use a stomach tube or other appropriate equipment. You'll need a piece about three or four feet long and quarter-inch to three-eighths-inch in diameter and you'll need to round it off at the end."

"Like a garden hose?" I lifted the phone to relieve my neck, eyes searching the property for something suitable and making mental notes while waiting for the pen and paper to arrive.

"Oh god, no! You can use a garden hose on a cow, but it is too large for a goat. You'd split the esophagus and kill him."

"Okay. So, like, surgical tourniquet-sized tubing?" I probed, trying desperately not to panic. Just then David passed me a pad and pen, and nesting the phone once again, I began furiously scribbling notes.

"That's the right size, but it would be too rubbery to do the job. You'll need to find something that's got some stiffness to it."

I knew I had nothing suitable in my possession. "Any idea where I am going to get a hose that small?"

"No. You'll have to sort that one out yourself. Sorry." I heard him sigh. I couldn't tell what kind of a sigh it was—general boredom, frustration with me, or knowledge of how hopeless the situation was. Not wanting to face the last as a possibility, I focussed on getting the rest of the details down on paper.

"Okay. Tell me the rest."

"The tube must be long enough to reach from the mouth to the distended flank, with some length to spare. And you have to make sure the tube has no rough edges. It needs to be really smooth or it may scratch the esophagus and that could kill your goat. You'll also need a speculum so the goat won't bite down and sever the tube while it's inside him, which of course would also kill him."

"Hold on. What is a speculum?" I asked, again gazing down at Gordon who now had his nose on the ground and looked like a beached whale, ready to die without so much as a last gasp.

"Something to keep the goat from biting down on the tube and chomping it off while it's still inside him. You can use a piece of wood with a hole in it, a piece of one-inch hard plastic pipe or a sheep harp—that's a special mouth gag for sheep and goats. Some nearby farmer might have something suitable. Anyone else keep goats down there?"

I considered his question. I probably had the biggest herd, and that wasn't saying much. I blew the hair from my eye and rubbed the sweat off the back of my neck before answering. "No one who would have anything like that. No one really farms goats here."

"Okay. Once you get all that equipment sorted out, you'll have to figure out how to hold him still so you can get the tube into him. It helps to have two people for restraint and to keep the speculum in the mouth. Measure the length between the mouth and the middle of the abdomen so you'll know how far to put the tube in."

"Uh-huh."

"Insert the speculum into the mouth so that the goat can't chew the tube or your fingers. Pass the stomach tube through the speculum and gently into the back of the throat. Usually they'll swallow it voluntarily. You have to make sure you're not going into the lungs though. Watch carefully for the swallowing action because that's a good indicator it's gone down the right hole. Now gently push the tube down the esophagus while blowing on your end to inflate the esophagus and make the tube passage easier. It usually goes in pretty easy."

"Okay."

"When you reach the stomach opening, resistance on the tube is reduced and, if you're lucky, a large volume of gas will rush out. If not, don't despair, simply move the tube back and forth and around until you find the gas pocket. If you can, let some of the grain and liquid siphon off as well. It's all extra calories he doesn't need right now. Then, once the deflation process is done, pinch the tube and remove it in one smooth, complete motion."

"Okay. Is that it?"

"Well, if you manage that, then while you're at it you should get some mineral oil down him—and milk of magnesia if you can. But when you do that you really have to make sure you're not down his trachea or you'll drown him and that will *certainly* kill your goat. But you know, even if you do get the air out, you'll probably lose him. Goats are pretty sensitive and it's likely he'll die of infection. I'm not sure I'd bother with all this ..." Then just before wishing me luck and hanging up, he told me to call him back if I had any more problems.

"What did he say?" my husband asked as I got off the phone.

"Well, he said there are all sorts of ways and means that I might kill the goat." Pushing all negative thoughts, reason and panic aside, I looked down at Gordon. I couldn't let him die.

Determined not to kill my goat, I phoned Lorri, a local woman who helped a different vet when she made her semi-annual visits to town. Over the phone I explained the problem, knowing she would understand because she is a horse breeder.

"Have you got a suitable tube—smaller than a garden hose?" I asked.

"Come on over and we'll look. I might have something from the Oscars," she said and hung up. On the drive over to her place I wondered if Lorri had a secret life as an animal wrangler in Hollywood. By the time I got to her place, she was standing in the driveway waiting for me.

"I think this hose from my oscar tank should work," she said, holding up a chunk of aquarium tubing for me to inspect. *Oh*, I thought, *oscars must be fish!* She then gave me a plastic syringe, cut the end off, and showed me how she would attempt to de-bloat my goat.

"You mean you're not coming to help?" Since speaking with her on the phone, I had presumed not only that she had done this many times but also that she would actually come home with me and do the stomach tubing.

"No, I've never done it before either!"

When I arrived home with the tube and syringe, my friend Carole had also arrived to help. I asked David to stand Gordon up with his bum against the barn and wedge him between the two hay bales. I tried pleading with Carole to take on the role of vet nurse, reminding her that she was actually a trained human nurse. She in turn reminded me she was actually a *psych* nurse and that she'd only been a guinea pig in her class's stomach lavage exercises. She was, however, happy to be an extra set of hands—opening bubble-wrapped syringes, holding the ends of stomach tubes, filling vessels with water and, whenever necessary, wiping my brow and peeling me off the ceiling. It was clear that I would have to attempt not to kill the goat on my own.

I chopped the end off a syringe, filed the edges down with a nail file, fitted the oscar tube to it, and stuffed it into Gordon's mouth. "It'll go in nice and easy, the vet said."

But two inches in, it stuck. Gordon was squirming and screaming pitifully. Without thinking, I pulled everything out of his mouth just to get him to stop crying. With renewed determination, I knelt down and tried again. No luck. I tried again from a different angle, but again the tube got stuck. What the heck? The vet said this part would be easy. With the perceptibility that only a trained psych nurse has, Carole interjected helpfully, "Maybe he's got something in his mouth."

I looked through the syringe and realized he'd somehow gotten his tongue rolled up to block the passage. This is why I ask skilled friends for help! Using my index finger like a tongue depressor, I wiggled and angled the syringe until it got past his tongue, then miraculously, just as the vet said it would, the tube began sliding smoothly in. For a few seconds there was no sound except the panting of all four of us, Gordon coughing and snorting, my husband heaving and sweating, me praying I'd gotten it down the right hole, and Carole maintaining composure for all of us. I wiggled the tube as the vet had suggested, and suddenly it began filling with a pea-soup-like mixture and pumping slowly out the end.

"Just like siphoning gasoline. Takes me back to my youth," my husband said with relief, watching the liquid pour out onto the cement around our feet.

I wondered how long to let it drain when suddenly Gordon wailed, startling me, and I withdrew the tube without thinking. Oh no! Now I'm going to have to put it back again. Two more attempts saw the ground again covered in a yellowish-white mixture. I went back to phone the vet, triumphant.

"Well, that's a good start," he said, "but even if he survives the bloat, the real worry now is viral infection in his stomach. You've introduced infection and with all the acid damage in there, it's likely he'll get really sick. There's also laminitis, but I doubt he'll get that far. Get the milk of magnesia in there and good luck!"

Doubly determined, I went back to Gordon. "I'll watch him," I announced. "He's just gotta live. I'll sleep in the garage with him and keep him walking."

We turned the garage into an intensive care unit: a cot for me, a blanket on a bed of hay alongside the cot for Gordon. I tube-fed him water and apple juice (for the electrolytes), alternating this with forced circuits of the yard every fifteen minutes through the next three days and nights. Carole was a trooper and came by every day to help, bringing pages of information about goats' digestive systems for me to read. David made cups of tea, stayed out of the way and worked hard at feeling guilty.

At first Gordon's belly seemed no less distended, but by day two the basketball seemed to have deflated slightly, and he was opening his eyes and wanting to connect a little with the world. Then sometime during the next night I recalled the vet saying that another goat's cud could be used to replace stomach acids. However, after stalking Sundown's cud for an hour to no avail, I began thinking about what I'd do if Gordon were human. Yoghurt, of course! It had acidophilus, too! Once again I force-fed Gordon through the tube then had a sudden wave of anxiety—what if goats are lactose-intolerant? Once in New Zealand I'd unwittingly killed a baby possum that I'd rescued from its dead mother's pouch by feeding it cream. But about half an hour after I force-fed the yoghurt, Gordon began burping and I immediately felt relieved. Burping was surely a good sign. The next morning he willingly left the garage with me in tow and took a long pee just outside, and shortly afterwards he dropped a few black pebbles of poop. That was it! Finally, normal-looking goat poop! He was on the mend. On day six he returned to his sister and was soon frolicking in the pen with her again.

When the vet learned of the saga, he congratulated me. "Yoghurt, eh? Never heard of that before. We should write that into the manuals." Then he chuckled and asked, "You ever thought of opening your own practice down there?"

For three nights I slept on a cot in the garage "intensive care unit," keeping an eye on Gordon after his near fatal overindulgence with the corn. Photo David Dowling.

Late in 2006 my job was made redundant, but David and I decided to try to continue with the farm. He was now working full-time and at least for the time being we thought we could make ends meet. My new-found time would be dedicated to the garden.

Egg profits: Keeping it local

The chickens had thrived and were now laying more eggs than David and I could consume. It was time to consider another dream, one of becoming a small-time egg producer. Who knows, maybe I could dodge the need to go back to work entirely? I asked the manager of one of our local grocery stores how many dozen eggs per week he sold: the answer was fifteen hundred. That meant our community was spending at least $250,000 each year on eggs and likely twice that amount, since there is a second grocery store in the Valley.

The Bella Coola Valley is a remote, economically depressed community. Imagine if all that money kept circulating here instead of the majority of it going to an anonymous corporation a thousand kilometres away. It occurred to me that if we could develop a local food system, this money would support small family farmers who use ethical farming practices. Then our community would not be supporting a system that treats animals inhumanely, raises eggs of questionable integrity and pollutes the environment with long-distance egg travel—and let's not even start on the topic of egg freshness!

I began crunching the numbers to see if I could make the Howling Duck Ranch economically viable in the egg business. I was already trying to build my flock up to ninety-nine laying hens, which is the maximum number of hens I could raise before requiring a quota from the BC Egg Marketing Board (BCEMB). Hens only lay well for approximately forty weeks per year, at least when they are living in natural conditions. (Industrial producers might achieve forty-six to fifty weeks by confining the birds in artificial conditions, stimulating them with artificial light, mutilating them, and feeding them antibiotics and hormones.) My calculations worked out as follows:

- 99 hens x 1 egg per day (almost) x 6 days per week = 594 eggs per week
- 594 eggs per week ÷ 12 = almost 50 dozen per week;
- 40 weeks (to give the benefit of the doubt) x 50 dozen x $4 per dozen (average cost based on local grocery store prices) = $8,000 gross income.

That doesn't sound too bad until you factor in the cost of feed, which recently increased dramatically, and the cost of buying the chickens as day-olds, transporting them to the farm, providing electricity for lighting and heating to raise them and keep water from freezing during the winter, providing bedding material (including trucking it to the farm), and paying the occasional vet bill. The producer also needs a constant supply of new egg cartons and labels because, legally, you cannot re-use cartons, which is shameful in this age of "reduce, reuse, recycle." Add in your annual taxes as well—which can only be reduced if you obtain farm status, which is an increasingly difficult thing to achieve. In addition, there may be labour costs. Oh—and factor in mistakes, blunders, ice storms and power outages. (In addition, there are capital expenses to consider if you are to make a serious go of raising chickens for egg production, including the up-front cost of the building to house the hens, nesting boxes, roosts, waterers, feeders, and special lights for heating the chicks as newborns.) It doesn't take a sharp pencil or further detailed calculations to realize you will be lucky if there is anything left over at the end of the year.

If I had chosen to continue developing the career for which I am well qualified, I would have a very good wage, full benefits including life and disability insurance, unemployment insurance, paid leave and a pension plan. Instead, I spent my days checking my birds' feed and water; letting them in and out of their house daily; changing their bedding regularly; collecting and cleaning eggs; putting them in cartons; delivering them to customers; doing the specialty chores (which take an inordinate amount of time) like giving them greens and doing the "poopy-bum patrol" (which I will discuss later!); creating an ecologically sustainable farm; contributing to local food security; practising local economic development; increasing my community's social capital; advocating for food sovereignty through meetings, discussions, educational workshops; and writing a blog after researching, reading and learning from mentors and trailblazers.

However, recently the powers that be in British Columbia have begun to make it harder for someone like me to be a small farmer. They want to up the amount of money that a small farmer needs to make on a farm of two to ten acres from $2,500 per year to $10,000 in order to legally qualify as a farmer. In 2006, according to Statistics Canada, there were 19,844 farms in this province, and of that number 9,466 make less than $10,000 gross sales each year. In other words, nearly 9,500 family farms will be forced out of business if this change is made. This increase in required gross sales revenue, coupled with the BCEMB's ceiling of ninety-nine laying hens, makes it impossible to maintain a two-acre farm by non-industrial egg production alone. Ah, you say, what about economies of scale? Why not get bigger? Why not have more hens? Because I was not allowed to, that's why. The British Columbia government's regulation states that "an egg producer is legally required to obtain a quota from the BCEMB if they have more than 99 layer hens." According to that board—the BCEMB is a producer-managed organization authorized by a 1967 act of the BC legislature to manage all egg sales in the province—there are already approximately 130 registered producers in British Columbia who raise almost 2.4 million layer hens, which in turn produce over 64 million dozens of eggs. In order to buy a quota, I would not only have been required to fork out a significant amount of money but it would also have been necessary for me to make the leap from housing ninety-nine hens to thousands of birds.

This marketing board would have us believe that their system of supply management is the only way to ensure a stable supply of safe, locally produced eggs. I'd like to know what they consider local. Nearly 80 percent of the registered egg producers in this province are located in the Lower Mainland and Fraser Valley, 10 percent are in the Interior, and the final 10 percent are on Vancouver Island. Certainly for many British Columbians the majority of these eggs do not fall within the bounds of the 100-mile diet. When the average BC egg farm raises 17,000 hens, I'd also like to know how they define safe and healthy, let alone ethical or sustainable.

Why would anyone want to try to develop a farm and raise food for the community when the profits are so low (or non-existent), and the barriers are so high? When you cannot grow your business as you wish and build your chicken flock up to a reasonable number—beyond the allowable ninety-nine, but in keeping with your farm size and sustainability—without having to jump through major exemption or special status hoops, how can you make a profit at the end of the year? What is the incentive to farm? How can a small egg producer in British Columbia avoid throwing in the towel and working off the farm? It's no wonder there has been a mass exodus from rural communities and family farms and a concomitant burgeoning of cities with all their environmental issues.

While all of the above only applies directly to British Columbia, every province and territory in this country has a similar board. They are all serviced by an umbrella organization called the Egg Farmers of Canada, which addresses "industry issues of regional, national and international importance," so you can bet that the rules for every one of those boards are pretty much the same. I have been in touch with other small farmers around North America, the UK, Europe, Australia and New Zealand, and most are faced with similarly prohibitive legislation. But as it happens, out of all the places I've contacted, upstate New York seems to have the most supportive legislation for small holders. For example, if you have fewer than three thousand chickens, you don't have to have a licence to sell eggs, nor do you need a licence to sell unpackaged produce. A farmer can butcher and sell chickens and turkeys so long as he raises fewer than 1000 chickens and under 250 turkeys. Not only that, the state allows the farmer to produce and process and sell directly to clients—a crucial right that has recently been taken away from farmers in British Columbia.

Every province in Canada, every state in the USA, and every country in the world seems to have different agricultural rules and regulations. Some are more prohibitive than others and I believe these laws were created to protect corporate interests rather than to protect our nation's—let alone our communities'—food security or our public health. Look into the policies that govern your food: you'll probably be very surprised at what you find. A little research will likely explain why you can't find things like honey or meat or cheese or milk at your local farmers' market or buy them directly from a farmer, unless that farmer has been legislatively morphed into a retail outlet for the right to sell his or her own products. By contrast,

My first flock of turkeys raised in the poultry palace brooder room. The dark ones are the Broad Breasted Bronze turkeys and the white are the Broad Breasted White. Photo Jammi Kumar.

if you find there are policies in your area that work, like those in New York state, then fight like hell to keep them!

It was not that many years ago that a farmer in the US could support himself and his family on the revenue generated from keeping fifteen dairy cows; in fact, across the country there were three million such farmers. It is prohibitive legislation that has pushed these folks out of business and created a monolithic centralized production and distribution system—a system that is not healthy or sustainable nor is it supportive of communities and families. It is a system that allowed the Peanut Corporation of America's peanut butter/salmonella fiasco in the US in January 2009, and killed twenty-three people in Canada in 2008 with a listeriosis outbreak caused by products from a Maple Leaf Foods plant in Ontario.

In light of these events and the bleak economic forecast, it would make far more sense to allow farmer-direct sales and encourage local productivity because no government can make my food safer than my neighbour down the road can. Who better to judge whether or not the food is safe than my producer-processor neighbour and myself? If I know how his animals are fed, see how they are housed, know how well they are treated, watch how the farmer handles his products, and have the opportunity to help slaughter his beef or poultry or milk his cow, why can't I decide for myself whether his farming practices are in line with my own philosophies and/or cleanliness standards? Moreover, since the legislation states that the product is safe enough for the person who raised it to eat, why is that same product unsafe to be sold to me? Clearly the rules have little to do with health and safety.

I don't want to feel scared about the food I bring home, the food I put in my mouth. I want to know where my blueberries, my milk, my beef, and my honey come from. I would like to know where my cheese and my tomatoes come from. I would like to know how all the animals and vegetables that comprise my diet are raised, killed and processed. I would like the right to decide who I buy food from and what goes in my body. I would also like to know that my money is circulating within my community, not going straight back out to some anonymous conglomerate far, far away.

But many farmers are giving up and going out of business, and that scares and angers me. I don't want to have to provide all my food myself because there aren't enough hours in the day. In addition, I resent the fact that we are forced to twist and turn and jump through government hoops in order to stay within the law. That farmers cannot buy a few cows and sell their milk to interested, willing consumers who understand the risks without first forking out for a state-of-the-art, million-dollar dairy plant is ridiculous. And I am even more discouraged by the fact that we get excited if we can still get around the current restrictive legislation. We shouldn't have to "get around" it; we should be supported by it!

Meet the Hen that Feeds You

Because they all look roughly the same on the outside, the only real way to know if you have bought healthy, fresh eggs is to crack them open. However, there are other indicators before you get that far. First, the shell of a fresh egg should be shiny, not dull. Second, the egg should feel strong, not so delicate that regular handling threatens to crack it. Third, if you hold the egg up in front of a light, you can often see through it well enough to check out the size of the air sac inside. It should be small and lopsided or angled.

Of course, the first rule of thumb when you are looking for fresh, healthy eggs is to bypass the cheap, supermarket brand eggs. They are usually produced in vast "factory farms" with upwards of five hundred thousand birds in one facility. They are caged in buildings that are artificially lit and ventilated. Their feed is most likely a mixture of conventionally grown corn and soy—though it will undoubtedly be contaminated by genetically modified organisms and laced with antibiotics, which help to keep disease from spreading among the hens. Unfortunately, the antibiotics fed to these factory farm–raised chickens are passed on to the humans who ingest the eggs, along with the milk, cheese and other animal products that also come from confined operations. There is not much goodness in eggs of this kind.

On the other hand, if you seek out eggs from a small local grower, consider asking the following questions to learn more about the eggs you buy:

What do you feed your chickens?

The ideal feed is a combination of grains, legumes, grasses, greens, worms and insects—in other words, they should be pasture-raised with free access to grains to supplement their range diet. Less ideal, but still acceptable to many, is a diet of organic lay pellets and organically grown corn and soy. At the bottom of the feed heap are commercial lay pellets, conventionally grown cottonseed meal, corn and soy.

Do you use antibiotics?

If the health of a whole flock is threatened by disease, then judicial use of antibiotics can usually be justified as long as eggs from the treatment period are not sold for human consumption. The farmer's answer to this question should not be, "Antibiotics are routinely added to the feed ration."

How many birds do you have?

In this arena small is beautiful. If the birds are separated into smaller flocks—at maximum 100–150—they can maintain a healthy chicken society and a natural pecking order and will thus be less stressed.

What are living conditions like for your birds?

Chickens should have regular access to the outdoors. Their living quarters should not be cramped, and they should be able to express themselves as chickens. In other words, they should be able to run around, scratch for worms and bugs, and have personal space to get away from marauding roosters if they want to. If chickens are given enough space, they are less likely to become stressed and/or diseased.

How fresh are these eggs?

Small producers sometimes store eggs for days or weeks until they have enough to make a delivery. Eggs should be no more than ten days old when they are brought to market and should be labelled with the date of harvest.

Are the eggs fertile?

If the producer keeps roosters, the flocks will better resemble a natural chicken society and the hens will be less stressed. There should be a good ratio of roosters to hens; one to between ten and twenty is a good balance, depending upon the breed and aggressiveness of the individual roosters. Many producers say that if they keep more than one rooster, they will fight, but fighting is a sign that the birds do not have enough space to get away from each other. Multiple roosters in a healthy, happy flock with enough personal space will not fight to the death or pick on another bird and kill it.

What breed are your chickens?

While the breed probably doesn't matter much to the quality of individual eggs, you may want to know for reasons beyond freshness and even animal ethics. For example, do you want your dollars going toward helping a farmer keep a heritage breed alive, develop a breed with special adaptive characteristics for your area, obtain farm status to lower land tax, or increase food security in your neighbourhood by being economically viable? These are not just interesting philosophical questions but are also politically important in that promoting them means increasing food security by keeping the gene pool of chickens varied (which makes them less susceptible to a host of problems), developing regional characteristics in a local flock, maintaining important animal husbandry skills, and helping a local farm to remain viable. These are all interesting, conscientious ways to spend your hard-earned dollars.

May I visit your farm?

While you might never actually visit, the producer's response will give you an idea of whether he or she is proud of the operation or ashamed of it. Ideally a visit will show you that the chickens' feed is organic, the chickens have constant access to fresh pasture, and they roam around a large space, never at the risk of being predated upon. However the farmer has many variables to consider in creating a healthy, vibrant, economically viable, ecologically sustainable farm. How much the market is willing to pay for the end product is a big part of that juggling act!

In the end, it is always better to shake the hand that is feeding you. You will have the confidence of knowing where your food is coming from, where your dollars are going and what they are supporting. You may also develop strong relationships between yourself and the grower and indirectly strengthen your community bonds (this is what academics call "social capital"). Isn't that better than mindlessly funnelling your dollars through chain supermarket check-outs to an unknown conglomerate far, far away?

The Food Sovereignty Project

Do I go or do I stay?

By the time our third spring on the Howling Duck Ranch rolled around I was becoming very discouraged by the lack of government support for small farmers and all the cumbersome regulations besetting us. When I was holding down a decent paying job and viewed my farm work as my "downtime," my hobby, my private passion, I had been able to justify the fact that the farm was costing us a small fortune to maintain. But farming was now a fuller-than-full-time job for me, and still it was costing us to run it, and our savings were dwindling. It was also painful to think that I should be at the peak of my earning power by this time, the height of my career, and saving for retirement.

I decided to temporarily abandon my dreams of full-time farming and return to school. Farming, it seemed, would have to be a hobby after all, one that I could only afford to take up when I had a full-time job. In the summer of 2007 I applied to do a PhD at the University of Regina and was accepted, and not only did I receive a scholarship but I also found a part-time job. For a while I enjoyed being in the city, going to the symphony, seeing live plays, and eating at a variety of restaurants. The job was exciting and challenging and came with good benefits and a certain amount of security.

However, one morning in March 2008 I woke up, stood in front of my closet trying to decide what to wear to work, and had a meltdown. "I do not want to do this anymore. I want to be in my gumboots and overalls in my garden. And if I continue with my PhD, I will end up with a good career where, God forbid, I will have to dress properly every day!"

I was two provinces away from everything I loved—my husband, my garden, my animals. With shocking clarity I realized I was ready to accept my husband's generous offer to support us both on his teaching salary. I was apprehensive about this decision for several reasons: I would no longer be building up my pension, I wouldn't be bringing in a wage so I couldn't save for my future, and I would be completely dependent on my husband's support. On the other hand, if I had what it would take to get a PhD, surely that same diligence would help me become a successful farmer, especially with the resources available to me through neighbouring farmers in the Valley and the inexhaustible resources of the Internet. That night (the "meltdown night" as it has come to be known), I talked to a couple of friends and with my husband, who was very supportive of the idea of me trying to provide for all our food needs. A few days later I gave notice at work.

Planning to provide

It was mid-May and David and I were having a discussion about growing all our own fruits and vegetables, raising chickens and eggs, catching all our own fish, hunting all our own deer, and bartering with the neighbours for other local foods. Now we needed to decide what store-bought items we could live without and what we would include from the outside world. David, I discovered early on in our marriage, was a Marmite fanatic, but I had made up my mind that for the next year we should live without such things. He was not convinced, and the defiant angle at which his head was set should have dissuaded me from exploring the subject further. But I was determined. Surely he wasn't really addicted to that awful stuff? We are, after all, talking about a thick, brown, sticky lump of fermented yeast. You might as well suck on a Bovril cube—actually a Bovril cube first rolled in sugar. Then in the midst of this domestic impasse, I realized that by excluding Marmite from our provisionist diet I was suggesting we expunge the very essence of his being Kiwi. Oh. My. Gawd. What was tightly sealed inside that little brown jar with the yellow label was his deepest sense of self, the origin of his very being, the locus of his creation. And at that moment I realized an important truth: our personal food choices transcend popular whims because they are shaped by personal experience. Their tap-roots extend deep into our social history and are therefore governed by strong cultural traditions. Shaping one's diet is no arbitrary procedure; it must satisfy—or at least not contravene—these traditions. With this fresh understanding of the delicacy and enormity of our plan, I proceeded with a little more flexibility.

We then discussed the project's various pragmatic challenges. I was hoping to reduce our store purchases to things like sugar, salt and vinegar that I called "support items" because we would need them in order to pre-serve our own home-grown produce. So should we buy sugar to make jam with our fruit, and what about vinegar for canning relishes and pickles, or perhaps I should make vinegar from our own apples? Quite soon I realized that we had to decide whether we would be purists or realists and simply accept that some foods are necessary to make other foods last. Eventually our pragmatism prevailed.

We also discussed avoiding foods we could not produce ourselves, such as olive oil, coffee, wine and beer, but unlike Smith and MacKinnon (*The 100-Mile Diet*), we decided not to cut out all off-farm luxuries—not only for those personal historical reasons but also for socio-cultural reasons. Food creates community. Food is culture. Food is a social binder. Once you decide to cut out this or that, you can suddenly find yourself sitting alone on the bench. (If you have ever gone on a strict diet, you will already know this!) In addition, since we would be hiring neighbours to help us fell trees, landscape the property and build barns and greenhouses, I just could not see myself explaining to the guys why I couldn't make them coffee to keep them going at mid-day or offer them a beer after a hard day's work. The compromise we made was to buy regionally roasted organic coffee and to brew our own beer and wine at the local U-Brew.

Despite these allowances, it was a daunting undertaking. In spite of these decisions, it was an almost daily negotiation to figure out where to stop and what my limits were. Someone asked me if I planned to feed our dogs as well as ourselves with our farm's produce. Another friend asked whether or not I would make herbal teas and sachets, and still another whether I would grow wheat, oats, and barley to feed our goats. Yet another wanted to know if I would have a cow.

Overwhelmed with the limitless potential of the project, I realized that if I wanted to have a reasonable life, I had to delineate my project and firmly mark my boundaries. With this in mind, I acknowledged that even the pioneers and cowboys had bought sugar, flour and coffee. In the end I had to let the idea of *rigorous* personal food sovereignty go. It was just too unrealistic: we did not own enough land, and we lacked the funds to buy not only the necessary larger piece of land but also the requisite equipment to work it. As well, the growing conditions in the Valley were not conducive to raising crops such as grain and legumes. Finally, I was only one person, albeit with a helpful partner, and I didn't want to be divorced at the end of the year!

Counting chickens before they're hatched

Once we'd established the ground rules, the real calculations began. We were still relying on the remnants of last year's harvest. I had some canned beef left over from the previous year and we'd traded for several fish during the summer, but I estimated that we needed to make it to Thanksgiving with these remaining supplies before we could butcher our own chickens.

I had decided I would raise all our own chickens for meat, but this would involve gaining control of chicken numbers. The previous year when I realized I could no longer afford to rely on the whims of my gals and wait for them to go broody, I had bought an incubator and set to doing it myself. This way I could purchase fertilized eggs and breed new genetic stock into my flock. I know many people don't worry about such things when keeping chickens, but I don't like the idea of eating inbred meat. However, the incubating results had not been spectacular. On my first attempt only five out of thirty-six hatched. From the second batch I had two live hatchings, but only one survived. In the spring of 2008, before I returned from Regina, my husband had set a few dozen eggs to hatch, but though he had a very successful hatch rate, I had been welcomed home by twenty-five dying chicks. This time round I decided that as well as incubating eggs I would order live chicks from the Rochester Hatchery in Alberta.

But how many should I order? Exactly how often did we want to eat chicken each week? Once or twice? I presumed that one chicken would last the two of us for one dinner with probably enough leftovers for my husband's lunch the next day. However, for the sake of simplicity, I would omit the potential leftovers from my calculations, and as a result, I estimated that altogether I would need at least fifty-two roosters for meat plus a lot more hens to step up the egg sales—we had more people wanting our eggs than we could supply, and I had been relying on the infrequent duck eggs to meet our own needs. So I decided to order sixty chickens from the Rochester Hatchery in Alberta. Some would die while being raised, some might get taken by a fox, and I would have to allow for dinner parties. So extra would not be a bad thing.

Someone living within or near a decent-sized population base can easily get baby chicks just by ordering them and having them shipped or by going to the hatchery and picking them up. In Bella Coola it is not so easy. Many places won't send to a post office box address, which is all we have, and the closest hatchery is more than fifteen hours' drive away in another province.

Are you my mother?

From the literature available on egg incubation one would have to conclude that saving eggs for incubation is an art unto itself. You must collect them carefully so as not to disturb them too much, place them gently in cartons with the small end down, raise one end of the carton to an angle of thirty-seven degrees and make sure to turn this daily so the other end gets raised. The temperature must be kept stable—neither too hot nor too cold—and they must not be in a drafty place, and so on.

Since we lived in a fairly tiny home (under one thousand square feet), our options for setting up an egg incubator were severely limited. I considered putting it in the garage but quickly dismissed that option because it had to be monitored closely for three weeks. Both the temperature and humidity had to be regulated carefully or the embryos would not survive. As well, one had to check regularly that the automatic egg rocker was indeed rocking. All this monitoring, humidifying, and temperature gauge fiddling meant I wanted it in a handy place. If I was going to facilitate these eggs' conversion from ova to baby chickens, it must be easy and stress-free, so I unilaterally decided that the hallway was the best option for my adventure into pseudo-motherhood.

I followed the instructions diligently and took a donation of another half-dozen eggs from a friend until I had enough for a decent hatch. After a week of collecting, being aware that using eggs more than seven days old would dramatically affect the hatch rate, I set up the incubator and hovered over it for three weeks. Then, as luck would have it, the power went out just as the chicks began to hatch!

Eggs and baby chickens must be kept very warm or they will die shockingly fast. I suddenly had to figure out what do with five baby chicks and several eggs. We didn't have a wood stove or any back-up power source, so I was severely limited in my options. With a sigh I stuck them down my bra, closed the buttons on my shirt right up to the neck and lay on the couch, prepared to hang tight till the power came back on.

If you've ever had a baby chick down your top, then you will understand how much it tickles. I hadn't. Also, if you have ever held a baby chick, you will understand just how tiny and fragile they are. When they scramble up inside the collar of your shirt against your neck it is no laughing matter, yet it is ticklish, so I was involved in a very delicate, very squirmy dance. At some point I caught sight of myself in the mirror and saw how ridiculous we looked: their little heads fighting to stick up out of my collar, just under my chin. Fortunately the power was restored after an hour, and I could unleash them from my bra and put them back to bed in their heated cardboard box. Although you won't find it in the manuals, this whole manoeuvre was a great success, and I had baby chicken scratches in the most unlikely places to prove it!

The dedicated poultry barn

Incubating chickens in my hallway and raising turkeys and chicks in the garage wasn't exactly ideal. Our garage had been everything but a place to store the truck: chicken and turkey nursery, Muscovy duck critical care unit, and bloated goat emergency room. However, after three and a half years of developing our homestead, we finally constructed our second barn, the dedicated poultry barn and reclaimed the garage on behalf of our aging Toyota 4Runner. As I wanted to get the birds installed in their new barn as quickly as possible, I needed to clean out their old accommodations and get the new ones ready for the turkeys, which would soon be old enough to move in.

In an effort to avoid having to clean the entire chicken house each week, I had placed boards below where they roosted at night and scraped these boards off each day. I soon found that, while this system worked okay, it was not ideal because it was very labour-intensive and time-consuming. For the chicken's bedding I used hay until one of the contractors we hired to help with the fencing and felling of trees suggested that wood shavings, a by-product of lumber milling, would be better. "Hay gets heavy and difficult to clean," he said one day. This was true. When I switched to the wood shavings, the labour was cut down to cleaning the shed out only once every month to six weeks. I was thrilled. I soon discovered that shavings could do double duty as I also used them to mark out paths in the garden.

Now, while scooping out the bedding, I found myself pondering why shovelling chicken poop didn't bother me. I thought of all the kinds of

This is Joel Salatin's deep bed litter method. The hens have 20–30 centimetres of wood shavings below their feet and turn the bedding in search of corn. This method cuts down on the work of cleaning the shed and produces a rich compost.

poop I've had the pleasure of shovelling—horse, dog, cow, goat, duck, chicken and turkey. Any farm is simply a symphony of poop, but the only poop I seemed to have an innate revulsion for was the dog's. What was it that made it different from the other animals' poop? I noted that I was unbothered about handling the chicken poop as I cleaned out the barn, breathing it in as the dust rose while I scooped it up and moved it to the wheelbarrow, picking up bits and pieces that fell from the shovel with my bare hands, transporting it to the compost pile so it would make its way to the veggie patch come spring and then get turned into the soil—generally handling it in ways I would not dream of doing with dog waste.

During this meditation I realized that ultimately I would eat the chicken poop. Not, of course, before it had completed the cycle of life. Nevertheless, eventually, it would feed me. The poop would be turned into soil by microorganisms and other biological processes and finally be taken up by the plants as nutrients. Gazing at it on the end of my shovel, I realized that it was no longer simply chicken poop, something to be dealt with, moved, composted, cleaned up. Its immortal potential was catalyzed as it began its sacred transformation through the cycle of nature, eventually to nourish my body, feed my soul. It was chicken poop for the soul.

The freshly constructed poultry palace. The left-hand side is a 4-by-6-metre chicken coop. On the right-hand side is the feed storage room at front and the poultry incubation room behind the far right door.

Later that week I arrived home, after being away for a few days, to discover fifty new baby chickens snuggled into the nursery part of the new barn. Before I had left for my trip, I had phoned the postmaster to let him know I might not be back in town before he closed for the day but that I had live cargo on order.

"Can you get someone else to pick them up?" he asked.

"Sure, I could ask Darrell. I'll call you back."

"That's okay," he said. "I'll let him know." And that was all he needed. No last name, no phone number, just the name was enough for the postmaster to entrust Darrell with my fifty babies.

So when Darrell unwittingly went to pick up his mail that Friday, the postmaster gave him the assignment. By the time I got home, the chicks had been picked up, fed and watered, and were all safely nestled in the barn, peeping and pooping happily. When I checked on them once more before going to bed, I noted that two of them didn't look very strong and by morning one was dead, followed by two more later that day. And then there were forty-seven.

One of the things I noticed immediately was that several of them had what I officially called "poopy-bum," a condition where the feces form a pasty plug that covers the vent (anus). The birds will die if it is not corrected quickly, so I checked for this every time I raised baby chicks or turkeys. I shudder to think how many factory-farmed birds suffer and die in this way. Medicated feed is supposed to prevent this, but it isn't 100 percent effective. I discovered that I could significantly reduce the poopy-bum death rate in brought-in birds by feeding them fresh, ground-up weeds from the garden. For the first few weeks of their little lives, however, regular poopy-bum patrol was essential, so the next day I set to addressing the immediate emergency: I took a bucket of warm soapy water, a roll of paper towels and a stool out to the barn and let the games begin. I sat quietly watching the little rear ends as they raced by. Whenever I spotted a poopy bum, I reached out and grabbed its owner and put it in a small box until I was satisfied there were no more poopy-bum chicks on the floor. Then I washed the bums gently, one by one, in lukewarm, soapy water.

The Cure for Poopy-bum

First prepare a bowl of lukewarm water; the temperature should be the same as that you would use to feed a baby bottled milk, lukewarm to the wrist. Then gently take a chick in one hand and immerse its rear end in the water. Rub the poop between your fingers, being careful not to pull on it as you might hurt the tiny bird.

Eventually the water will soften the poop enough for you to clean it off the feathers. Don't pull on the poop because this will tear the skin off the bird or even pull its innards out if the poop is stuck to its colon. Either event is fatal. Be patient: the poop will eventually dissolve, leaving behind a clean behind.

Before putting the chick back with the flock, wipe its bum with paper towel until as dry as possible so the chick doesn't catch a chill. (Don't blow-dry with a hair dryer! This will burn the skin completely. Let the heat lamps in the chick nursery do the rest of the drying.)

Chick poop is incredibly sticky. Whoever invented glue from horse/cow hooves obviously never tried chicken poop first! Thanks to its tenacity, the whole ordeal for one poopy-bum cleaning may take a few minutes, but it will come off eventually and you will have saved a life in the process.

Teach a woman to fish

The next food source to consider was fish. My dad had taught me to fish when I was very young. I was an only child for nearly ten years, so I got a lot of time alone with him. Mum was not a water person so the two of us would head out in our boat to the salt chuck and troll for salmon. Sometimes we were successful, other times not. It didn't matter to me and I doubt it did to him either. I liked being with him and he liked being outdoors. I think he also liked teaching and was good at it—perhaps he missed his calling. Sometimes we'd go down to the river and fish for trout, and on one occasion I recall a crayfish challenging him for territory: the crayfish won, forcing us to move on.

I did not know it then, but looking back now I realize that my dad planted the first seeds of independence in me on those expeditions by teaching me how to gather from the wild. And not only did he teach me how to fish, but on one of those trips I also recall him showing me what huckleberries were. My father was doing what parents have been doing for thousands of years: passing on the knowledge and ability to self-provision.

The first summer we lived in Bella Coola, he came for a visit, though I knew he really came for the fishing. Earlier that year a fellow I worked with, Richard—a keen fly fisherman—had organized a course for us to learn how to build our own fly rods. I had made two, one for me and one for my dad, and when he came that summer, he, David and I joined Richard and a couple of his friends at one of Richard's favourite spots on the Bella Coola River, four-by-fouring to the river from the end of a gravel road. It was a beautiful spot with not a soul around. The day was perfect, the river was flush with fish, and the scenery couldn't be better. The six of us might have been the only humans in existence, for everywhere we looked there were no signs of civilization. We were at the edge of the earth and enjoying its bounty.

Soon everyone was catching fish except me and one of Richard's friends, a visiting doctor. I was thrilled nonetheless because my dad was having the time of his life. But while Dad and the others were catching a fish every now and then, all of us were amazed at Richard's ability to cast and catch, cast and catch, as if he had some sort of contract with these particular salmon. When Dad caught yet another and Richard began heading over with the net to help him bring it in, Dad shouted, "Hold on Richard! I want to let Kristeva have a chance to reel in a fish." Hearing this, I looked up to see my dad, smiling proudly while picking his way across the beach toward me with his rod held out gingerly, taking care not to lose the fish before he got to me. "Do you want to have a try?" He was looking after his little girl. It was a daddy-daughter bonding moment and I felt five years old again.

With the day nearly over, the good doctor, who was still having no luck, had called over to me with a challenge: "Okay, this is getting pathetic. Let's see who can get the next one, eh?" Richard, being the gentleman that he is, heard this and came to my rescue. Unwilling to believe that I wasn't getting any bites whatsoever, he took my rod from me and ... boom! he immediately landed a fish. "You're getting lots of bites," he said. "You're just not feeling them. That fish was the third bite."

"Oh, come on," I said as he was handing me back my rod, "that's got to be a fluke."

Without speaking, he took back my rod, made a beautiful cast and flicked another fish onto the shore and then another.

"How the heck are you doing that?"

Richard stood behind me, grabbed the rod and showed me how to feel what I wasn't feeling. "There, you had three bites," he said as we began to reel in the line. He was right, I wasn't feeling it. I had only trolled or spin-cast before and had been expecting a much bigger, more obvious tug on the line. Fly-fishing was more subtle, an art. I cast again and he held the rod from behind me. "There, two more nibbles." After a couple more casts I realized that what I had thought was the weight bumping along the bottom hitting rocks was actually a bite. Within seconds I too had landed my first fish and left the good doctor in the dust.

That had been our best day of fishing in the Valley. My dad came back year after year for a repeat of that experience, but the fishing in the Valley gradually declined as the years passed. By the time I was into my personal food sovereignty project, even the commercial fishermen were hardly going out because the cost of fueling the boats would be more than their catch. One friend remarked that the declining salmon stock was affecting the air, too. "There's no rotting fish," he said, and I realized he was right. It was August: the rivers should have been smelling to high heaven, full of spent carcasses, the bears getting fat and the eagles cleaning it all up. It used to be that Bella Coola and salmon were synonymous, but those days are sadly gone. However, despite the poor fishing, we still managed over the next few years to get enough to can for the winter.

Now I had to ask myself how often per week we wanted to eat fish. How would I keep it once it was caught? Freeze it? Can it? Drying it was out of the question. Although *sluk,* the Nuxalk version of smoked salmon, is a delicacy where I live, I don't particularly like it, though I'm embarrassed to admit that in public because most Bella Coola people simply swoon over it. My only redemption is that I am more than happy to get involved in the labour-intensive process of making it. And in my defence I have to say that seafood in general is not my thing. Salmon and halibut are about my limit, and even then they have to be really fresh, as in caught-yesterday-fresh.

Planning the Garden for Self-Sufficiency

THE PRAGMATICS OF CHICKEN REPRODUCTION aside, the mathematics of animal products for the table seemed relatively easy: determine how many times per week you want to eat each item and multiply by a factor of fifty-two weeks. However, this plan stalled when it came to fruits and vegetables. We only had a small orchard and between the predators and the fickle climate I didn't have much control over its production capabilities. But how many tomato plants would I need? How many of any vegetable does one family of two people need? I noted the advice of various author-gardeners: one fifteen-metre row of spinach per person, five bean plants per person, fifteen metres of potatoes, and so on. In the end, I figured that because so much of farming depends on an infinite number of variables, there was no hard and fast rule about these things. I was forced back to calculations based on my supposition of our needs.

I knew I shouldn't be surprised at this uncertainty. After all, it's what all settlers contend with. I remembered driving around Saskatchewan and looking out at the vast prairie, trying to imagine the people who had colonized that land. Who on earth was it who stopped and said, "Gee, this looks like a good place to build a community and raise a family"? Now that I was contemplating the realities of growing all our own food, I was thankful that I was not living a hundred and fifty years earlier when one couldn't simply walk to the store and buy much-needed food to supplement imperfect calculations of expected yields or, worse, crops that had failed altogether. I was also thankful to be living on the West Coast where the winters are not so brutal and the growing season is a bit longer, and I had central heating in lieu of a dirt floor.

Planning ahead for our food needs made me think like a pioneer, and I was acutely aware that miscalculations, while thankfully no longer fatal (after all, we had Marmite in the cupboard!), could easily jeopardize my ambition to be self-sufficient. I realized that this project could take years to actually perfect in order to accomplish my goal of food sovereignty—or rather, my version of personal food sovereignty, which takes into account my penchant for chocolate!

The asparagus incident

The day after my arrival home from Regina, I had gone into the garden to take a look at what needed to be done before planting. I was especially interested in the perennial beds where I had planted garlic, strawberries and asparagus—especially the asparagus, which I'd dutifully tended for nearly three years and which would be ready to eat that spring. I was horrified to see that my husband had very kindly rototilled the entire veggie patch, including all my perennials—*including* the asparagus.

I am ashamed to admit that I suddenly blew a gasket. My sister was a witness to this event, and trying to help my husband's cause and return some harmony to the moment, she unwittingly stepped in with, "What are you getting so bent out of shape about? It's just asparagus." I think I gave her an earful. A week later she was dining with friends at a fancy restaurant in Vancouver when one of them said, "Did you know that asparagus takes three years before you can harvest it?" Yes. She did.

On the day of what has affectionately become known in our family as "The Asparagus Incident," I learned that our family, too, carried its own gardening traditions. Distraught and with near-murderous intent in my heart, I phoned my mother. As I relayed my troubles with my husband vis-à-vis our garden, she listened without a word to the symphony of my complaints and the ghosts of trespasses previous. When the orchestra reached its crescendo, my mother inducted me into the folds of our family secrets: "Some of your father's and my worst fights," she confided in hushed tones, "have been in the garden."

The truth is I was no longer interested in using the rototiller at all because I now understood that it destroyed worms and other life, which are important to healthy soil structure. The no-till method does a better job at providing aeration and drainage, thanks to the hard-working worms, and their excretions bind together soil crumbs to encourage the growth of beneficial fungi. There are other no-till benefits such as the fact that weed seeds will lay dormant indefinitely until the soil is disturbed and the seeds are exposed to light, and the soil will hold more water if is not tilled so less watering is needed. In addition, tilling the soil breaks down the carbon-enriched humus and decaying organic matter, which releases nutrients too quickly. It is far better to have a steady, slow release of nutrients as it is more beneficial to both plant growth and root development.

Spring harvesting

It was the first sunny day in late April, and David and I were cleaning up the yard in preparation for planting. Birds were twittering, the iron ground was softening, tulips and crocuses were nuzzling the new warmth, and the air buzzed with possibilities. But there was one thing missing that spring—my dog Tatra. She'd had a great life, a dignified old age, and had died peacefully in my arms three months earlier. But when there are several feet of snow outside and a pet dies, you have a problem, further complicated by the fact that in order to cremate an animal in mid-winter, you need about a cord of wood. So our plan had been to wait until spring, then lay her to rest, like the other farm animals, in one of our farm's several pet cemeteries. In the meantime I had wrapped her in a garbage bag and gently laid her in our chest freezer.

I wanted her to have her own garden plot, but no particular place had suggested itself to me during those long winter months. However, as my husband and I took advantage of the warm snap to clean up the yard and do some burning, I had a vision of Tatra running around the bonfires of other spring cleanups, and I knew it was time to put my good friend to rest. We built up the already smoldering fire to a white heat, knowing that we required a high intensity to do the job satisfactorily. Then, while my husband gathered a good supply of logs, I brought my darling from the freezer, but when we unwrapped her, I almost lost my nerve. She seemed to be just sleeping, still as in life. "I can't do it," I whispered, so my husband placed her gently in the middle of the fire and I instantly knew it was the correct thing to do.

A few moments later our neighbour suddenly materialized in front of us—as if by magic—the smoke from Tatra's funeral pyre billowing around him underscoring the ethereal quality of the moment. He was chewing energetically and holding out a plate of something for our scrutiny.

"Ah-h-h," he began and then in his heavy Norwegian accent continued, "I vas jus' vandering if you'd tried some of dees tings." They lay on the plate glistening with butter, the exact shape and colour of curled-up cabbage moth caterpillars.

"What are they? Fiddlehead ferns?" I asked, puzzled by the absence of leaves.

"Ya. You jus' snap off de tip." His gnarled logger's hand made a dainty twist in front of my face. "Ya godda get dem quick. In dis kinda vedder, dey don't las' long."

The fiddleheads tasted even better than young asparagus, melting in our mouths with no stringiness. That evening I researched them on the Internet and learned, among other things, that one should never eat them raw. Next day we asked our neighbour to show us where we could gather some. He took us out in front of his log cabin, reached down into the brush, snapped off a fiddlehead and stuffed it in his mouth.

"I don't think you're supposed to eat them raw," I said in alarm.

"Yah, vell, I don' tink it matters much." He smiled at us and went back inside to the warmth of his wood stove.

David and I walked out into our own wood lot, the two acres that buffered us from the highway that we called our "Front Forty." There we found a veritable food forest of fiddleheads in a glade once logged by the previous owners and now open to the sun beneath the deciduous trees. We needed baskets to harvest their curly tops regularly over the next few days. We were exhilarated to be gathering wild food from our own property, food that required zero input from us and that was not disrupting nature at all. For the next two weeks we gorged ourselves on them, steaming them and peeling off the outer leaves before dunking them in melted butter. Sometimes I fried them lightly in olive oil or butter with or without garlic. They are much like asparagus in flavour but much more delicate in texture. There is no trace of the fibrousness of asparagus.

After that spring, of all the wild harvested items I gathered, these were by far the most anticipated. But with fiddleheads the harvest has no sooner begun than it is over. We tried to preserve them by freezing but were disappointed to discover that they turned to a brown soggy mess when defrosted. Like so many of nature's delicacies, they have their time and place, and it was our responsibility to be ready to eat them when they were served.

We found that fiddlehead ferns would transplant into the garden just fine. Better than fine, they actually thrived. But thrive as "ferns" is not what you want from your fiddleheads if you are intent on harvesting food from them. Because I'd put them in a sunny location, their productive attributes were diminished—they burst forth from fiddlehead to frond far too quickly. Unless I was perched over them with my paring knife in vigilant anticipation for the moment they raised their furl above the soil, I missed out. But I like knowing that every March, our property and the hillsides around me will continue to produce fiddleheads—with or without my attention.

Fiddleheads, however, were only nature's appetizer. I knew from reading that stinging nettles are edible and would be on their way up through the ground just as the fiddleheads had finished unfurling, so we donned gloves and harvested this unlikely crop as they took over the responsibility of providing the weekly special on nature's menu. But a plate of these steamed greens was a little overwhelming for my palate, so I worked them into other combinations—like using them with the last of the frozen spinach in spanakopita. I came to love anything I didn't have to tend all year long or think about replanting, fertilizing, watering and weeding, but I had to run to keep up with nature's pace.

Anthropologists have conducted studies on time and have concluded that hunter-gathering groups actually had much more time on their hands than agriculturalist groups. Instinctively, it is difficult to imagine. One would think that being in control of our food sources would free up time, but once I became a serious food provisionist, I understood first-hand why it doesn't. It is so much easier to simply be observant and harvest when nature provides than to do all the planning, weeding, seed starting, transplanting, compost making and so on that has to be done in order to grow things to an artificial schedule.

Cougar capers

When I first came to the Valley I did not own a gun and did not want one. I had the citified belief that if I did not bother the bears, cougars and foxes, they would not bother me. However, this was not true no matter how much I wanted to believe it. Everything out there was trying to make a living, just as I was. Unfortunately, when you are trying to make a living by raising all your own food, you present a farmyard feast of delectable options to a host of predators. Not only that: if you do as I was doing—letting an area of the lawn "go back to nature," as gardening magazines for city slickers suggest—in order to create habitat and lessen one's carbon footprint and so on, what you end up with is just that: habitat.

While this is a great idea for urban folk and for those living in less wild areas than rural or remote British Columbia, I soon came to understand that this idea cannot be applied universally, and certainly not in the conditions in which I was living. What I had managed to create with my reluctant mowing, my garden and my fruit trees was a wonderfully rich and diverse cover for large predators as they found their way to the sumptuous smorgasbord I was providing.

One gorgeous sunny day I was quietly minding my own business, head down, planting strawberry runners into a new patch quite close to the area I had set aside for nature to have her way with. I was building raised beds so that the strawberries would come on earlier when suddenly I got the feeling I was being watched. At first I thought I was just being silly and tried to shake off the sensation, but after a few minutes the hairs on the back of my neck began to stand up and I finally paid attention. *Cougar,* I thought. *I am being watched by a cougar.* I took a look around to see if I could spot anything. Nothing. *This is just paranoia creeping in,* I told myself. *You are alone on the farm and feeling vulnerable.* I went back to what I was doing. But the feeling persisted. *Okay, that's it. Don't risk it. For the love of God, listen to your instincts and head inside. It's a good time for lunch anyway.*

In the kitchen I decided to put on a pot of coffee while I considered my lunch options, and as I stood at the sink filling the kettle and admiring the strawberry patch through the kitchen window, out from the long grass crept a full-grown cougar. It looked magnificent with its pulsing muscles, huge erect tail and, I noted with alarm, a body mass that easily outweighed mine. I called the conservation officer right away and he came running, literally, because I was lucky enough to live right across the street from his office. He brought another man who worked for a different ministry and together with his dog they tried to track the cougar.

"Grass is too long," he said when he returned after a few minutes.

That perfect cover for the cougar also meant he could not be tracked! After lunch, soothed by a bowl of my own chicken soup and some crusty bread, I was feeling a little less agitated. I decided to make a pre-emptive strike and abandoned my Martha Stewart aspirations. This was a job for my Husqvarna brush cutter.

The power saw, along with some of our other power tools, was stored at one end of the big red barn. I picked up the machine and attached the chainsaw, then collected the requisite protection gear—glasses, hard hat complete with earmuffs and face screen, gloves and boots. As I left the barn, I caught the eye of the model in my Driza-Bone poster. "When a woman's gotta do what a man shoulda done!"

As I mowed down my beautiful mixed grasses, wildflowers and lilies, I sensed the presence once more and realized that for the second time that day I was under the watchful gaze of the cougar. That's it! I'm done! This time I didn't hesitate and immediately went inside the house. Again, within a minute of my getting inside, out jumped the cougar, heading back toward the conservation office. Sure enough, a few seconds later the officer's dog was barking excitedly and the chase was on. Unfortunately, the officer and his one dog were no match for the cougar and it got away again. I say unfortunately not because I want to kill cougars, but because I wanted that particular cougar killed!

The pie plants of penchants

Of all my perennials, rhubarb is the first to see the sun, and fortunately my rhubarb plants had not suffered the same fate as the other perennials in my veggie patch.

Rhubarb most likely originated in Mongolia or Siberia. It was used for medicinal purposes by the Chinese for thousands of years and appeared in *The Divine Farmer's Herb-Root Classic*, which was attributed to the Yan emperor Shen Nung and compiled around 2700 BC. There is also a long history of it being grown along Russia's Volga River, and it is known that the Russians in Alaska used it to keep scurvy at bay. Ben Franklin is credited with bringing rhubarb seeds to North America in 1772, but it did not become a popular pie ingredient until cane sugar became accessible to the masses in the late nineteenth century. Suddenly, with the simple addition of sugar, sour fruits and vegetables like rhubarb (yes, it is officially a vegetable and not a fruit because you eat the stalk) were made palatable. By the 1930s rhubarb had become firmly entrenched in North American food culture for pies, jams, jellies and wine, and that's when its nickname was born: the pie plant.

Rhubarb is a welcome change from canned, dried or frozen fruits of winter, but the challenge is figuring out what to do with all that bounty. You have to get creative because on the West Coast you can have two harvests—April and May and late June and July or sometimes as late as September—if you have really healthy plants. The good news is that in spring you can concentrate on recipes for dishes to eat right away, such as pie. But you either like rhubarb or you hate it. One of my friends, who happens to be a hunter, says, "God got it all wrong when he created moose and rhubarb. Moose have got to be the ugliest critters on earth and rhubarb the most unpalatable. But he made up for both of them when he made moose liver." My friend Darrell, on the other hand, is crazy for rhubarb custard pie. His birthday and the first crop of rhubarb in our area usually coincided, so each year he practically foamed at the mouth, staring at the fresh stalks in our garden while waxing lyrical about the best rhubarb custard pies he'd ever eaten. Yet, for all his lyricism, not to mention all that he had done for us, I had never managed to make him a rhubarb custard pie. However, we were planning to build a turkey barn that would double as winter goat housing, and this was going to require more fencing, so I asked Darrell—whose thumb had recovered nicely—if he would help with the fencing. As payment for services above and beyond, I would provide dinner and the long overdue rhubarb custard pie.

Because we were fencing and had several other projects on the go, I didn't have time to do anything too fiddly. I just wanted to be in the garden, not in the kitchen. I had envisioned having to make custard from scratch then a separate rhubarb pie filling, which sounded like a lot of work, but on the Internet I discovered that rhubarb custard pie was a much simpler creation. I didn't even have to make a pie crust. Instead, I opted for the pre-made tartlets that we had in the freezer. I wasn't sure if this would work or not but out of necessity decided to try it. My rhubarb custard tartlets were scrumptious and, more importantly, they finally fulfilled Darrell's fantasy. Thank you, Ward Street Bistro!

Ward Street Bistro Rhubarb Custard Pie

Ingredients

9" (23 cm) pie shell or individual tart shells, chilled.

Topping
- 1/2 cup flour   125 ml
- 1/2 cup demerara sugar   125 ml
- 1/4 cup butter, melted   60 ml

Pie
- 4 cups diced fresh rhubarb 500 ml
- 1 cup sugar   250 ml
- 1/3 cup flour   75 ml
- 1 cup sour cream   250 ml

Directions

Preheat oven to 450°F (232°C).

1. To make the topping: mix together the 1/2 cup flour, brown sugar, and melted butter. Set aside.

2. In a large mixing bowl, combine the rhubarb, sugar, 1/3 cup flour and sour cream.

3. Transfer the pie filling to the prepared pie or tart shells.

4. Sprinkle the topping over the pie filling.

Bake on the lower-middle rack of the oven at 450°F (232°C) for 10 minutes. Lower the heat to 350°F (177°C) and continue baking for 35–45 minutes more, until the filling starts to bubble and the crust is browning.

5. Cool completely before serving. Serve chilled or at room temperature.

To brassica or not to brassica

While talking to a friend in Vancouver about my aspirations for the summer's garden, I listed off all the veggies I planned to grow. At the same time I was mentally making preliminary calculations about how many of the larger plants, like broccoli and cauliflower, I would need to grow and freeze to make it through until next year when they would be fresh in my garden once again. Brassicas being at the top of my friend's list of favourite veggies, she interrupted my thoughts to tell me of her dismay while on a recent trip to Cuba with her boyfriend. Throughout their two-week stay, she had found neither broccoli nor cauliflower in any of the markets they visited there, and she began to suspect a conspiracy of vegetable merchants or perhaps some kind of US trade embargo on the objects of her desire. Describing the lengths to which she had gone to find them, she ended her colourful account with a question: "What's up with that?"

The answer—which would have stumped me, too, had I never taken up the plough—was simply that brassicas are *cool*-weather crops, and farmers must work within the limitations of their climate. While people in the Bella Coola Valley can compensate to some degree for the lack of heat there by erecting a greenhouse, you can't reasonably make it colder in Cuba. Brassicas are not ever going to grow well there, so the farmers don't grow them. But it is a lesson that I struggle with each year in my garden: coming to terms with my geographically induced climatic limitations. What my heart (and stomach and imagination) wants me to grow and what, in fact, will grow are often a long way apart.

"Indeed the tears live in an onion ..."

Shakespeare had it right when he wrote *Antony and Cleopatra*. I use the humble onion every day in practically everything I cook. Onion and garlic are the bra and underpants of the cooking world, the necessary underpinnings though hardly ever considered. The onion is such an unsexy vegetable that I just presumed it would grow while I was lavishing my attention on eggplants and sweet peppers. Nevertheless, in twelve years of eager vegetable gardening, I had not once grown a decent onion. My first garden in New Zealand had been in heavy clay soil so I had the respectable excuse that nothing beyond the jackhammer daikon radish could burrow into that earth. Since then, I had had good soils and myriad excuses: poor drainage, diseases, bugs and the unexpected. One year my husband assiduously weeded all the onion seedlings and left a weed that looked like a carrot, proudly declaring that he had rid that area of the garden of couch grass.

For no discernible reason gardening is a hit-and-miss affair. The first year of my Valley garden, I had bought some cauliflower and cabbage seedlings and heeled them in wherever there was a patch of earth: beneath trees, at the edge of flower beds, on an old burn pile. They grew fantastically with huge, heavy heads, tight and dry. The next year, between cabbage worms, slugs and rain, the only brassicas to survive were red cabbage, despite the fact that we had a cool summer that should have favoured the whole brassica family. Since it is an early crop, I enjoyed putting radish in at the last frost, but I soon learned that here the early ones get attacked by mealy worm. The second year, therefore, I waited until June and planted five or six successive crops. We enjoyed the four or five radishes that the summer-long mealy worm deigned to leave to us. The same mysterious, capricious behaviour was exhibited by my beets, spinach, peas and zucchini. I had been deeply embarrassed by the last, the one crop that every gardener complains about having too much of, even stealthily leaving them in parked cars and on doorsteps.

I had been more scientific in my determination to grow peas, planting different varieties from different seed companies in different years, but for all this effort the peas didn't happen in the second year or the third. But what a gardener does and what a serious self-provisioner does are very different things. As a hobby, vegetable gardening is unpredictable and can be frustrating, but for someone determined to survive on the crops she grows, there are lessons that must be learned. One must husband one's resources, energy and garden space. Accordingly, I changed my game plan to concentrate on vegetables that were suitable to our property or those that tasted awful when bought at the supermarket—like tomatoes. I resolved not to waste my time planting several varieties of eggplant in my greenhouse and instead concentrated on planting large quantities of reliable crops like potatoes. In fact, I had acquired a renewed appreciation for my Irish ancestors and their love of that reviled crop.

With this reduced repertoire the focus turned to the kitchen where I spent a lot of time and energy dreaming up or researching new things to do with my staple or vigorous crops. The previous year I had grown nasturtiums, enjoying their pretty flowers and insect-repelling properties, which contributed to my handsome cabbages. We had also enjoyed the colour and peppery flavour of the leaves and flowers in our summer salads. When the plants went to seed, I harvested the seeds and pickled them to use instead of capers in my recipes. This took an inordinate amount of time but was well worth the effort. I used them in salads, in rice dishes, and even on pizza. In fact, several friends had liked them better than true capers!

This year, however, was a different story. I had to conserve my gardening energy for the work of a subsistence farmer. Choosing what to grow in the garden became an ongoing tango, a dance in which I tried my best, planted diligently what grew well in my area and what I like to eat and hoped it survived the wild foragers. Then I had to adapt and work with what was left to be harvested. The possibilities are unpredictable, endless and ever-changing, so one is never bored.

The new tomato patch

Some unexpected help for my vegetable patch came in the form of my neighbour Colleen. She had come over to visit and we were quietly sitting on the front bench having our morning coffee. After surveying the property, scrutinizing every corner with a critical sweep of her knowledgeable eyes, she looked sternly at me over her coffee cup and suddenly burst forth with, "Aren't you sick of looking at those cedars and juniper bushes covering the front of your house, Krissy?" There was a short pause while she considered my reaction, then she added, "I mean ... come on! Wouldn't you like to see the front of your house?"

Colleen often spoke in question format, but she rarely wanted an answer. She had opinions and was not afraid to voice them. Knowing she was probably not done and curious about her grand plan for the Howling Duck Ranch, I said nothing and waited for her thought train to pull into the station. "I mean, that would be a good place for tomatoes ... you know ... something important." Her arm punctuated the sentence with a semi-disgusted sweep of her hand in the general direction of the cedar trees. I had been thinking the very same thing since we moved in, and we laughed when I told her so. There was just so much to do with this place and with only David and me to do it, some things had to wait ... like clearing cedar trees and making way for tomatoes.

"I could just bring my truck over here and we could haul them things outta there. It wouldn't take long." She paused and, with lowered eyebrows and defiant chin aimed in my direction, challenged me to prove her wrong.

When I didn't respond immediately, she softened, laughed and then leaned toward me. She put her hand in front of her mouth and, like a child hatching plans in opposition to house rules, continued in a hushed voice, "We could probably have it all done before David gets home." Her own wickedness made her voice peal with laughter. When Colleen was on a roll, resistance was futile!

"Okay," I said.

She tipped the last of her coffee into her mouth, made one great gulping noise as she placed the cup on a nearby stump and headed back toward her place, her little Scottish terrier, Winston, trundling along beside her. He, too, thought it was a good plan. Within minutes her green Mazda truck was in front of my house, Winston on the dash, body wriggling with excitement. She attached a long rope to her bumper and turned to me.

"Here, take this and wrap it around that cedar."

With Colleen back in the driver's seat, I signalled to her to go forward. The rope tightened and the roots groaned in protest, then finally admitted defeat and gave way. The cedar bush had been transformed into a big, fat, conical fallen soldier and was unceremoniously hauled over to what was to become its funeral pyre. Within a couple of hours there were three large cedars, several juniper bushes and one lilac tree in a pile waiting to be burned or—in the case of the lilac—replanted. The front of the house was revealed and a new veggie patch took instant shape. Colleen was right. We were all finished before my husband got home.

"You know, I was thinking last night that I gotta stop being so opinionated around here," Colleen said the next morning as we sipped our coffee and she surveyed her handiwork. "I mean, who the hell am I to have so much to say about what you're doing or not doing?"

Then, although we both laughed in acknowledgment of her trespass, without missing a beat she renewed her lecture, telling me exactly how to plant the tomatoes into the newly established bed, what varieties to buy and the spacing requirements. "And by the way," she instructed, "you had better gather chicken poop and place it around the base of each plant, just like so, but be careful not to burn the roots. Then you should sprinkle some Epsom salts here ... and here and here ... oh, and some oyster shell wouldn't go amiss either, and while you're at it, pound in some stakes for them to grow up, and don't forget to keep on top of pinching out the laterals, and for god's sake don't wet the leaves when you water ..."

People who want glass houses

Since the moment we bought the Howling Duck Ranch, I had wanted an addition to the house and a greenhouse, but the greenhouse was the bigger priority. Our first attempt to find one was answered by a local fellow who thought he'd invented a simple, cheap structure involving two-by-threes and heavy plastic. He was going to build the prototype for us and then build them all over the Valley. Interested in fostering local entrepreneurial spirit, we gave him the go-ahead but ended up regretting it: his greenhouse design didn't have a proper foundation and the walls were held together with an elaborate guide-wire system. Before we even got the siding up, a gust of wind collapsed it.

While I was away in Regina, my husband tried his hand at building one. He consulted several knowledgeable people, then he and a friend poured the foundation piers. He phoned to tell me about the progress, and I fantasized about basil and tomato salads, dripping with olive oil and balsamic vinegar that I would sop up with my crusty sourdough bread. Then one evening the phone rang.

"I have bad news," my husband said.

Preparing for the worst, I held my breath.

"It's the greenhouse. I just finished putting up the north wall last night." Pregnant pause.

"Uh-huh."

"Well … the wind came up just as I was putting up the last sheet of clear-light, so I came inside."

"Yeah … so?"

"Well, while I ate dinner, it fell over."

I exhaled with relief and then blurted, "Christ, I thought someone had died!" Then I told him I was glad he was still alive and things sure could have been worse. "Look at it this way," I said, "I could have come home to find just your gumboots sticking out from underneath the greenhouse like some impersonation of the Wicked Witch of the West."

He felt very badly that there was now no way he'd have it done before I got home, and we discussed looking for help again. Unfortunately, all the builders we knew were busy with bigger housing projects, so I told him not to worry and that I'd look into when I got home.

A few months after returning from Regina, I went to visit a friend, and as serendipity would have it, just as I was describing my greenhouse woes, another of her friends, a contractor named Terry, dropped in. She made the introductions, and within days Terry had kindly worked our greenhouse project into his busy schedule. It wouldn't be ready in time for a contribution to my year in provisions project, but I could look forward to the following spring when I would be able to start tomatoes early enough for them to actually produce something. Terry worked a day job that sometimes required him to leave on a moment's notice, but for the next several weeks whenever he wasn't at his day job, he could be found in our backyard working hard to get the structure completed, salvaging what he could from the wreckage of the two previous models. He became part of the family. We had morning coffee together and then an elaborate lunch in the shade of the gazebo, and often a cold drink together before he went home at the end of the day. I enjoyed cooking for more than just the two of us, and he seemed to enjoy the change of pace from the meat and potatoes of his bachelor existence.

Since I had been vegan for many years, beans, lentils and other pulses made regular appearances in my culinary efforts, but the first time I brought out such a dish, Terry eyed it with suspicion.

After a number of tries I finally got my dream greenhouse, complete with a seedling starter bench and winter heating.

"What's that, hippy food?" he blurted unceremoniously.

Worried I might lose him to his regular fare at home, I asked him if he wanted something else.

"No, no. I eat anything. I just don't eat like this. What *are* them things?" he said, eyebrows gesturing up and over the pot rim at the lentils. But when a little later he asked for seconds, I relaxed. The following day when he asked for the recipe and an ingredient list, I knew I'd be able to keep him satisfied enough to stay on the job. As the summer passed, we traded recipes and canned foods while the greenhouse slowly went up.

Not only was Terry eminently capable of putting our greenhouse together, he was also a limitless resource for salvaged material. He made it his business to bid on demolition jobs and haul home any scrap of salvageable material, so we went shopping at his place for extra windows, wood and other goodies that were then incorporated into our greenhouse plan. Parts of the old Hagensborg Store held up our walls, windows from other historic demolition sites furnished us with selective views from inside the structure, an old schoolhouse provided the outside finishing for the back walls, and remnants of the Bella Coola Fair Grounds' huts were worked into nooks and crannies as well.

The finished greenhouse was four by twelve metres with raised beds along the outside walls. We insulated the north wall and covered the east, south and west walls with clear corrugated plastic with some framed-in windows that

New seedlings soaking up the spring sun.

provided views to the outside. In one corner, without prompting, Terry built a table so I could pot up plants and start seedlings (he had heard me tell my husband that I'd like one). Often he came in the morning full of ideas, revealing that he'd been thinking about the job during the night. He impressed me with his ability to listen and figure out what would work well for me. I had always wanted to build a stone wall and talked to him about leaving a space for a rock hearth where I could put in a small wood stove for winter heating. He obliged by inserting a chimney flue in the roof and placing tin around it. Now I just had to find the time to build the hearth.

With the greenhouse at last completed, I realized I had to learn about a whole new aspect of gardening. Greenhouse growing sounded so easy and yet I knew it wasn't. Along with all kinds of new possibilities came a host of new problems: venting the heat out, insulating the heat in, getting rid of white fly, keeping out spider mites, learning when to plant, when to transplant, what to plant for wintering over, what will grow in the heat and so on. The learning curve in gardening and farming is endless and steep, but the limitless creative potential is ripe with possibilities.

Beans, beans, the musical fruit

Becoming self-sufficient in meeting our protein needs sounded easier than I found it to be. At first I had only been thinking about animal sources of protein such as chicken, beef and fish and, if we were lucky and I managed to learn to hunt, wild meat such as grouse or deer or moose. However, I had also become accustomed to cooking with all sorts of beans. Years earlier when I had converted to vegetarianism, the only experience I'd had with beans was from a can—baked beans at that—and I hated them. So I'd had to learn how to cook them. Luckily, I love Mexican and Indian foods so it didn't prove to be difficult once I set my mind to learning how. But now it was a different story: the difficulty went beyond reading and learning. If we were going to continue to eat the way we'd become accustomed to eating—and I was reluctant to give that up—then I was going to have to learn to grow as well as cook beans. Lots of them.

Having read that beans take a long time to mature to the shelling-out dry stage, I made sure to plant them early. I ordered several kinds of bean seeds and planted them, marking the rows carefully, watering as needed (which in the case of that particular spring was not often), and then I waited. I waited and waited some more, but nothing happened. By June I had replanted beans several times, all to no avail. Finally, not knowing what I was doing wrong, I decided to consult my local master gardener and good friend, Clarence Hall. One cannot visit Bella Coola without meeting Clarence because he is a Bella Coola special feature, a fixture, as it were. He can be found having breakfast each day at the Coop Café. If he's not holding forth at the round table then he will be wandering the room looking to greet unsuspecting visitors to the Valley, a one-man self-appointed welcoming committee. It's a tough job and not one for the faint-hearted, but Clarence is not one to shirk a task. In the world according to Clarence, all tourists must be welcomed personally—preferably over breakfast. It is, after all, the most important meal of the day. If you do manage to get into the Valley and out again without his official welcome, then you really haven't lived. In fact, I would dare say that you really haven't experienced Bella Coola!

Clarence had welcomed me to the Valley within days of my arrival in the summer of 2003. I had been sitting in the Chinese restaurant having a pancake breakfast when he came over to my table. "My dear," he said, reaching out his hand to grasp mine, "I don't believe I know you!"

We exchanged pleasantries and I dutifully answered his questions about who I was and where I came from. He sat down, ordered himself a coffee and renewed the interview with increased intensity. Once he was satisfied with my answers, he proceeded to reveal a bit about himself. I learned that Clarence was originally from Pennsylvania, and now at age eighty-three he was a great-grandfather several times over. He had lost his thumb end to a dynamite mishap at the tender age of five, endured 295 days as a POW "guest of Mr. Hitler," as he liked to put it, outlived his wife (but they had enjoyed their fiftieth wedding anniversary together), survived the deaths of two children, and hunted countless troublesome cougars, even getting the better of one that attacked him in 2000 (when he was at the tender age of seventy-five).

After providing me with this brief verbal résumé, he reached into his breast pocket and pulled out some photos. Not, as one would expect an old man to carry around with him, photos of his wife or his children and grandchildren, but photos of a dead wolf.

"I shot it just this morning. Um-hum. Right there in my backyard."

I was horrified but he didn't register my reaction.

"It was after my dogs!"

Instantly I categorized him as a redneck. He obviously had no respect for wildlife. I would soon learn I was very wrong.

Clarence is a complex and yet simple man. He has simple tastes and enjoys the things you can't buy: the beauty of a sunrise, the way a chicken might peck him while he's collecting eggs, the fact my dog recognizes him and doesn't bark when he comes to visit. Indeed, he comments on that fact nearly ever time he visits. He is also a fantastic gardener and each year grows the largest garden in the Bella Coola Valley. Clearly visible from the road and a visual delight come July and August, it is about a kilometre or so west of mine on the south side of the highway. From early spring to late fall he can be found there tending his vegetables, and this is where I found him when I needed help with my beans. For Clarence, the answer to why none of my beans came up was simple and obvious.

"My dear," he said, reaching a solicitous hand out to clutch my fore-arm. He then paused to look me straight in the eye before proceeding, as he often did when he was about to make a serious point. "It is much too early to start beans." His tone, which teetered between sympathy for my situation and grandfatherly admonishment, made me feel at once both heartened and foolish.

He went on to tell me—perhaps more precisely, implore me—not to plant anything before the third week of May and listed various convincing reasons. Taking Clarence's advice, I waited until later in June and tried again. After this attempt at leguminous sovereignty also failed, I again consulted Clarence.

"Oh, I know," he said. "Mine are the same." This time his familiar mid-eastern-American drawl held a purely sympathetic note. "My dear, this spring is a disgrace. It's much too cold for beans."

That spring was indeed the wettest and the coldest that anyone could

Clarence's favourite highly utilitarian potatoes, the Yukon Gold. Notice his direct composting method of burying the tops of the potatoes where the golden tubers are harvested.

Although the dried shell-out beans were a miserable failure, the heritage purple beans were a delight, both visually in the garden and on the plate.

remember. So I waited another week, planted more beans and again waited patiently. Few beans came up and the ones that did quickly turned yellow, wilted and looked pathetic. Frustrated with the whole process and at the end of the window of opportunity for sowing seeds in our area, I went to the local organic food store and bought quantities of the various kinds of beans that we typically ate: adzuki, black turtle, canelli and pinto as well as lentils, both de Puy and brown.

Then, just as I was accepting the idea that I simply would not be able to grow beans at all that year, I had an idea. What if I sprouted some of the newly purchased beans from the organic food store indoors and put the sprouts directly into the ground? After all, I had been successful at sprouting legumes for salads that way. Waiting for them to sprout in the ground could take up to two weeks while sprouting them indoors brought forth signs of life within days. Because time was of the essence, I didn't want to wait to see which ones might come up. I read that the adzuki beans needed the longest time in order to get to the shell-out stage, so I struck them from the list of contenders for that year. I also read that the canellis have a long maturation time, but as they were the most expensive to buy, I planted some of them and reasoned that, if successful, they would provide the most cost savings for our budget. I took a selection from the other beans I had bought, folded them into wet paper towels, labelled them, put them in Ziploc bags and wrapped them neatly in a tea-towel. Because beans need warmth in order to sprout, I set them on the kitchen counter on the electric heating pad. After several days, I had little sprouts of black turtle beans inside the bags.

I made the rows for the beans and set to planting them out and marking the rows. I decided to plant the garbanzo beans despite the fact they hadn't yet sprouted because, unlike the black beans, they are supposed to be a cool-weather bean. In addition, they are said to have the shortest maturation date, so they were the most likely to be successful that year.

After about a week of scanning the rows for signs of life, I noticed that the black beans were poking their first leaves above ground, proudly displaying their beauty. These first leaves were a very dark green with an almost black outline. The garbanzos, which I had planted right beside them, had still not made an appearance, and I decided that perhaps they are the ugly ducklings of the bean world, too timid to grow next to the supermodels.

The black beans had taken just ten days to raise their heads above ground and, with this success, I decided to try my luck with some more varieties. Even if they amounted to nothing, it would be a great learning experience, and I was curious to see how shelled-out dried beans (as distinct from green beans) would grow. I didn't know if they were bush beans or runner beans, so would they need staking or stand up on their own?

In the end I managed to sprout and plant pinto, canelli and black turtle beans and lentils. The garbanzo beans row became a path between the peas and the black beans. Interestingly, all these seeds came from the health food store with the exception of the garbanzo beans, which were from a seed packet!

This was also my first year trying to grow peas to dry for the winter, but I wasn't really sure when to harvest them. Then one day a flock of Steller's jays arrived and began gobbling them up at an alarming rate, and I knew I had better get at them if I was going to have any for pea soup and dhal that winter. I took the vines down, picked them clean, then heaped them into a garden corner to form the beginning of my new compost pile. By that time, having been up since 3:30 a.m. (I enjoy the early quiet hours alone with a dog at my heels), I was too tired to face shelling them out. The next morning I spent an hour and a half shelling peas. Earlier in the season I had been shocked to see that a big basket of fresh pods would shell out into barely enough for the two of us for dinner. It was even more of a shock with the dry peas! After a diligent hour and a half, I'd barely produced a cookie tray full of peas. Either the jays had taken more than I thought or next year I would have to plant more peas. If I was to save any for planting, this harvest would only be enough for a few good meals.

However, I'd had great success with my Alaska pea crop. I had planned to let some of them go to seed and had already marked a few exceptional plants for seed saving purposes for next year's crop. Now, although I couldn't find any information on the subject of letting regular garden peas go to the dried stage for soup and dhal-making purposes, I threw caution

Howling Duck Ranch's Pea Soup

Ingredients

- 3 tbsp olive oil   45 ml
  (Any oil will do, and if I had access to beef or pork tallow or lard, I would use that)
- 1 large onion
- 1/2 cup diced carrots   125 ml
- 1/2 cup diced zucchini   125 ml
- 3 garlic cloves, sliced thin
- salt, to taste
- fresh ground pepper, to taste
- Herbs to taste: thyme, savory, sage, parsley, oregano
- Spices to taste: allspice (if using spices, cut back on pepper)
- 3 cups dried peas   750 ml
  (soaked in 6–8 cups or 1.5–2 L of water for several hours and drained)
- More water as needed
- Soup stock: ideally use boiled salt pork or a ham hock.

Notes

If you don't have access to salt pork then substitute with ham-flavoured stock or a bouillon cube or homemade stock from pork bones. (In a pinch, I have even cooked bacon and used the drippings as the stock base.) You can also make your pea soup vegetarian if you wish.

Directions

1. Caramelize the veggies, cooking the onion first in oil, then adding the carrot, garlic and zucchini.

2. Add salt and pepper and cook until veggies are soft.

3. Add the drained peas and pour in enough water and stock to cover by an inch. Bring to a boil.

4. When the peas reach a steady boil, turn the heat off and cover for 10 minutes. At this point, you can transfer the soup into a slow cooker and cook on low for 6–8 hours. Alternatively, keep boiling the soup until the peas turn to mush. Add desired herbs and spices, salt and pepper to taste.

This soup demands to be dipped into and dredged up, so serve it with good, hearty, homemade bread—preferably made with your own sourdough culture! See the directions on how to catch a sourdough culture in the Yeast Wrangling 101 section page 172. The Ricotta cheese recipe will leave you with whey which, when used in bread recipes, makes the loaves flavourful and light.

to the wind and decided, "Why not?" So I let some of the regular fresh pea crop go to the dry shell-out stage because the food value versus time relationship must be better than at merely ripe picking time. They may not be the right pea for habitant pea soup, but in terms of local eating, food security and self-provisioning, they were going to have to do!

Becoming sovereign in legumes turned out to be an extremely educational experience—an utter failure on the one hand and a completely enlightening experience on the other. Not only were most crops of beans an early failure (several varieties barely made their presence known in the garden, thanks to their penchant for warmer climes), but some that had through sheer will and determination tried to participate in the project had been unable to go the distance before the rotting rains of our fall pounded them into a pulpy mess. Despite these miserable failures, there were several key learning points along the way: I learned the growth pattern of lentils and why I wouldn't attempt to grow them again—too small, too difficult to hand-thresh, too little food value in return for the work involved. I also learned which legumes I would try again. For example, black beans turned out to be particularly flavourful at their green stage. This discovery was a mixed blessing. I had hoped to grow them for dried black beans. However, over dinner one night I asked David where he had found the particularly tasty green beans that we were eating, knowing I'd never before grown such tasty morsels. I was really not terribly happy when he described the row of what with another month's growth would have been my dried black beans.

The King of Wheat's wheat comes to Bella Coola

Each year since we bought our farm, I had expanded my veggie garden. Now I knew that if I wanted to grow all our own food, I'd better get an even larger veggie patch established. The solution was to remove all the flowering shrubs and expand the patch to a twelve-by-fifteen-metre area that encompassed the blueberry and cranberry bushes that had originally bordered the plot.

Once I had enough land, I decided I would try and fulfill a fantasy that I'd had for many years: baking bread from my own wheat had been on my bucket list for years. Back in 2003, while living in New Zealand, I had got as far as sourcing the seed, sowing it and getting it growing. I even had it timed so that I would be back from my visit to Canada in time to harvest it, but I never returned so someone else enjoyed the fruits of my labor. Now, with an expanded garden patch, I decided to search my kichen for the bag of wheat kernels I had stored away after a trip to Saskatchewan in 2006.

Before the trip, neither of us had been to the prairies as conscious adults, and we wanted to see this unknown part of the country. We found some wonderful farms and concluded that Saskatchewan was ahead of British Columbia in its awareness of organic farming practices. Later we learned that Saskatchewan has the highest percentage of organic growers in Canada. We visited many farms, always on the lookout for ethically raised food and opportunities to see good farming practices first-hand. I enjoyed talking with farmers and hearing their stories, their plans for their farm, the passion in their voices. I kept my ears and eyes open for systems that I could employ back on our own plot, things that would make the farm more efficient and the work easier or more sensible.

But the farm that I was most interested in seeing was the one that had belonged to the King of Wheat, Seager Wheeler. I had read about him before leaving for Saskatchewan and knew that he had come from England in 1885 when he was just seventeen, had walked from Moose Jaw north across 290 kilometres of virtually barren country to take up land on the bank of the South Saskatchewan River. There he taught himself to farm, and for many years he won international awards for his wheat, being crowned World Wheat King an unsurpassed five times between 1911 and 1918. The wheat that he developed, Marquis 10B (a cross between Hard Red Calcutta and Red Fife), extended the prairie growing area 160 kilometres farther north, opening up the Peace River Valley to wheat growing. By the 1920s Wheeler's Marquis wheat accounted for nearly 90 percent of the wheat grown in North America.

Today there is a growing interest in Red Fife among heritage seed savers and enthusiastic bakers, though I'm not sure why they're overlooking Marquis or its inventor. At one time Wheeler's wheat varieties made up 40 percent of the world's wheat exports and thus made a significant impact on Canada's economy. Wheeler also wrote books on progressive farming techniques and invented various farm implements. He established what was then the largest orchard on the prairies through the use of windrows and atypical planting in order to create micro-climates, which supported the fruit and conserved the soil. In addition, he introduced unusual horticultural species to the region, such as the Siberian silver leaf willow, the Saskatchewan crabapple, Prolific and Ruby cherry-plum hybrids and the Advance sand cherry. In 1920 he was given an honorary degree from Queens University and he was made a member of the Order of the British Empire in 1943. Now that is an impressive résumé!

I asked myself, if I was going to go to all the effort of growing my own wheat, what better wheat to grow than that developed by the most influential wheat grower of his day in North America? So his farm north of Saskatoon became one of our major destinations. Although I was keen to see the farm and his techniques, my interest went beyond the historic to the gastronomic: I wanted to see if there was any of his wheat seed for sale that I could take back home with me to cultivate and—if luck was on my side—even bake with. Thankfully, Seager Wheeler's Maple Grove Farm is now a Canadian National Historic Site, and the people maintaining his farm still cultivate his wheat and have samples of it for sale. Without missing a beat, I bought 750 precious grams—all that was available on the day we visited.

Now two years later, after some rummaging around in the kitchen, I found the precious cargo in the baking drawer. Once I had the new garden bed prepped, I took 500 grams of seed out of my precious bag of Seager Wheeler wheat, holding back a tiny bit of it—just in case. Then I consulted local farmers as to the best way to proceed and was glad I did. I had imagined just throwing the seed over the ground, raking it in and watering, but the farmers all said the same thing: you'll have to tamp it down after sowing. I would not have thought of this nor did I come across this advice when researching wheat sowing on the web. The consensus was that otherwise, the strike rate would be very low and the stalks would blow over in the wind before the wheat ripened. So tamp I would—but how?

Several people suggested that I get hold of one of those heavy rollers used for golf greens and cricket pitches. It is true that such a roller would have been perfect because my row of experimental wheat was less than a metre wide by about fifteen metres long. However, the Bella Coola Valley is not exactly overflowing with golf courses or cricket pitches. In the end, I raked and prepared the ground, then took the wheat and threw it over the ground—though perhaps casting it would be a more precise description. Next I went over it lightly with a hoe to get it somewhat covered with soil. I was a bit concerned about how much seed I could still see bare on the ground, but I wasn't about to make myself crazy trying to hand hoe in each berry.

My first organic gardening mentor in Wanganui, New Zealand, had taught me the 80/20 rule of farming. One day while watching me fastidiously weeding a bed of carrots, he criticized my diligence. "You're taking far too long!" he said. He then introduced the 80/20 rule: I should go for an 80-percent weeded bed instead of 100 percent because the 20 percent of extra effort doesn't yield a 20 percent return and so isn't worth the time you put in. So in keeping with the 80/20 rule, I left the uncooperative wheat berries exposed.

Looking around the farm for a suitable implement, my eyes wandered over a stack of plywood cut-off pieces left over from building the greenhouse. *Voilà!* I found one the width of the bed and took it to the garden. I laid the plywood on the ground, carefully lined it up on top of the wheat bed and jumped on top of it with all my might. Then I moved the plywood along the bed and repeated the process. After this less than delicate process, there was nothing to be done but water and wait. Seven days later I had one-inch-tall wheat growing. I was thrilled. It was June 20. I marked it on my calendar and counted out 107 days, which would bring me to its maturation date, September 28. With luck, I might just get to harvest my very own wheat. All of that should take place just two weeks after harvesting the beans! Of course, September could go either way: it could be a wonderful month of extended summer, or could be bitterly cold with frosty nights. But for the moment I was thrilled because I had wheat and beans growing in my garden.

Eating with the seasons

The idea of buying in-season foods is in need of definition. After all, in today's global marketplace it's always five o'clock somewhere, and our global food production and distribution systems allow those with the means to buy foods grown virtually anywhere in the world all year round. Therefore, somewhere out there the fruit that we want to eat right now is "in season." Moreover, for those of us living in Canada, it is likely already in our local grocery store. All that is required of us is to drive there and get it.

So why should we buy in-season local food? In the first pace, we can lessen the environmental damage caused by shipping foods thousands of kilometres. Some argue that the amount of energy consumed by more people driving to their local farmers' market is equivalent to the kilometres put on by, for example, getting tomatoes into cans in Italy and flying them to North America, but I'm not convinced. In any case, even if it were true, buying local has the benefit of keeping jobs local and supporting our own farmers. Moreover, there is also the food security issue. I agree with Evan Fraser, the Canada Research Chair on Global Human Security at the University of Guelph, when he says, "Countries must have the right to control their own food. They cannot be at the mercy of the rest of the world. Everybody has to develop their own infrastructure" ("Global Food Part Two," CBC, February 8, 2011). What he means is that we should be focussed on building capacity at home—nationally, regionally and communally. Being dependent on imported food is not a good position to be in because any country that imports a high percent of its food is not food secure.

A Statistics Canada report issued in 2004 said that Canadian food imports increased from $8.1 billion in 1995 to $12.6 billion in 2002, a 57 percent increase. Imports of processed food products grew steadily during that period. The largest increases were in imports from the United States, which rose by $3.2 billion (67 percent) between 1995 and 2002. Canada also increased imports from Brazil by $201 million (79 percent) in those years, China $183 million (60 percent), Thailand $139 million (46 percent), and France $59 million (68 percent). But the same report also boasted about our increased exports.

Cherries are a local crop in Bella Coola. They grew so abundantly on our farm that I canned, dried and froze them and still gave many away.

What's wrong with this picture? Canada imports vast amounts of food while exporting vast amounts of food? With all this food travelling back and forth around the globe, I can't help but wonder, "What if all that food just stayed home?" While the economics of the above are no doubt highly complex and I don't pretend to understand them all, I do know that our farmers—and farmers the world over—are struggling to make a living at home, our foods are largely imported, and we are no longer living within the seasons. I also know that within my lifetime, there was a time when we Canadians survived—even thrived—without having strawberries, mangoes, and pineapples in January from New Zealand, Chile and Hawaii.

When you buy locally and in season, more of your food dollar goes directly to the farmer. This is most obvious when you are involved directly with a farmer or farming family—for example, when you join a Community Supported Agriculture (CSA) group or shop at a farmers' market and get to know the hands that feed you. Not only that, you and your family will be able to enjoy the health benefits of eating fresh, unprocessed fruits and vegetables. Another significant benefit to buying local is that you can eliminate the guessing game with respect to herbicides and pesticides by asking the producer what, if any, sprays are used to grow your food.

Buying seasonal, locally grown produce also provides an exciting opportunity to try new foods and to experiment with seasonal recipes. Some will argue that local food doesn't necessarily taste better (I think it does) but what they can't deny is the fact that it is fresher! Once you control your food sources, you can plan ahead and save money by filling your freezer with fresh fruit for winter consumption. Finally, even if you don't want to change any of your eating habits, you can become a conscientious buyer and demand your local food store provide local produce when it's available rather than bringing in the same type of food from three thousand kilometres away.

Milk

Ruminants with a view

IN 2007, AFTER TWO YEARS with just the two goats, Gordon and Sundown, another unplanned addition came along. One summer day my husband had gone to the liquor store for two flats of beer and came home instead with two more goats: not what was expected but that's how things are done in the Valley. We named these gals Fatty-Fat (or Fat-Fat-Fatty-Fat to be precise) and Shiraz, and they really were fat—obese actually! They didn't just eat like pigs, they had been eating *with* pigs on another farm in the Valley. The farmer wanted to get rid of them because they kept jumping on his tractor. (And we can't have that, now, can we?)

Malcolm X joined us after I came back from Regina. He was born at Darrell's place in town, and when he had outgrown his home there, he and his mother and a few other goats had been moved to a neighbour's place. All went well until over the course of two or three nights a cougar killed his mother and all the other goats. While Malcolm hadn't come out of the cougar attacks unscathed, he had come out alive—no one knows how. Not wanting him to be alone, Darrell asked if he could live with us, so we took him in.

Any time you are worried about what your goats might be doing, they are usually doing it. Of course, if you are not worried at all, then they are even more likely to be doing the unimaginable. They wreck trees, shrubs and basically anything edible—your roses, your kitchen chive patch, and the grapevine you planted close to the house to keep it away from the grizzly bear—even inedibles like laundry fresh off the line. But I wanted goats because I harboured plans to breed and milk them so I could make cheese. I also think that a milking animal is integral to a "real" farm—not unlike that other essential, a big red barn. But making cheese would require investment in milking equipment, not to mention finding a potent buck—both Gordon and Malcolm were wethers (castrated bucks)—and then I would have to dredge up the will to kill and eat the kids because I could not expand the herd indefinitely. I was not sure I could ever slaughter the kids. That word itself makes it even harder!

Over and above these problems was my lack of time: between expanding the garden and maintaining the animals, there was simply no time for sourcing another goat and adding to the barn, let alone for regular milking. Every day when I fed the goats, I wished I had more time for them so I could train them to pull a cart. Sometimes we took them for walks with the dog, and they loved the attention, but they were not easy to walk with because they stopped and started and pulled and tugged. The other problem was that, for goats, life is a smorgasbord, and they viewed these walks as gastronomic adventures; exercise was secondary. When they didn't get to come for walks and saw us leaving with the dog, we could hear their bleating halfway to the airport.

Malcom X came to us after being the only member of his family to survive a cougar attack.

One typical West Coast September morn—it was pouring rain, of course—I went out to do the farm chores, squish, squish, squishing my way across the sodden lawn. Chickens are hardy and the wet weather doesn't seem to bother them at all. Ditto for the ducks—in fact, they seemed to relish all the extra water, delighting in bathing and showering loudly in their pond. In fact, the sound emanating from the pond was that of pure bliss, whoosh, whoosh, whoosh, flap, flap, flap, and it was the only thing I enjoyed on days like this while I moved on to the next beast on the list: goats.

Having observed the goings-on in our newly completed dedicated poultry barn, the goats—who never missed a thing—now had aspirations of their own and were determined that I should know about them. They were lined up along the fence like little tin soldiers all in a row. Goats in the rain, I thought. Not quite as romantic as *Gorillas in the Mist*.

Goats hate everything about wet weather. "Our f-e-e-e-d is w-e-e-e-t. Our t-t-t-oes are c-o-o-o-ld." Normally I put their hay into a wire rack—which they would spend the day kicking around the yard because (God forbid!) their hay might get some raindrops on it. Looking for where the hay rack ended up became a daily Easter egg hunt. In this weather, however, if I wanted the goats to eat the hay and not just stomp it into oblivion, I had to spread it out on the floor of the three dog houses, which had become the goats' day-beds. So on wet days like this they spent their time jockeying for position in the best one—the one with the window in it that was built for the puppy Tui—meanwhile reminding us that we had yet to build a barn suited just for them. At night they made do in one end of the big red barn that had actually been built to house, among other farm implements, the ride-on lawn mower. However, we had moved the lawn mower outside under a tarp, installed a wall and front door and let the goats call the space their own each night.

The raw and the cooked

I had hoped to start milking my goats and making cheese from their milk by the late spring, but I'd had to relegate this goal to my list of dreams to come. I realized there simply weren't enough hours in the day (or resources in my pocket book) to accommodate the expansions necessary to fulfill my goat dairy dream. So when the opportunity to access local cow's milk arose, I jumped at it. I went to meet our cow and the farming family who looked after her. There she stood, staring out at me from the confines of her shelter. As I got out of my truck, she began to make the formal introductions: "Mooooooo, mooooooooo, moooooooo," she crooned at me until I leaned against her shelter gate. She came over and bathed me in her attentions—licking my hand, sniffing my hair, nudging my arm if I let my hand slip out of her tongue's reach.

After several minutes I dared to walk away from her shelter to talk to the farmer. Not ready to be snubbed, she lowed again, "MooOOOO, MoOOOOO, MOOOOOOO." I was thoroughly chastised. Laughing, I said to the farmer, "She seems friendly."

He shook his head. "Too darn friendly. She never shuts up." Registering my amusement, he added, "No, really! If I go to work and get out of her sight, I don't hear the end of it!"

Though he was concerned, an affectionate smile spread across his face as he looked in her direction, obviously smitten with her and his life's work.

I returned to Buttercup's shelter. She began to relax and, keen to finish her ablutions, immediately resumed bathing me with her tongue. Obediently I held my hand out and let her sniff and lick to her satisfaction. Having never been so up-close and friendly with a cow before, I enjoyed basking in her sweet bovine attentions. Eventually I needed to take my leave and get on with my daily chores, but as I moved away, she renewed her effort to convince me that I should stay longer. I found her neediness "udderly" charming and chuckled at the brassiness of her personality, although as I got back into my truck, I thought, *But then you don't have to live with he*r!

After that, once a week we collected wonderfully rich, extraordinarily fresh, sweet-smelling milk from the farming family who worked hard to provide it for us. We were fortunate to be able to see our cow working, eating, or generally basking in the loving attentions of the farmers who work with her (not to mention some of her personal fans). We could see how she was kept, how her stall was cleaned, how much care the family lavished on her. Not only that, Buttercup let us know when they were neglectful in their attentions and would bellow for us to take up the slack, stay on a while and visit with her. Some days she even let us stop fawning over her and talk to the family farmers! They love their work (if you've ever kept a milk cow you will know that it is work and you'd better love it) and we were thrilled to have the resource available. Together, our farms became better off, each supporting the other in what we did best and had time for. While we were not close socially, I had a conscious awareness of them and how tightly their work knitted into mine by relieving me of the burden of having to do it all myself, as well as providing us with a high-quality food source that I could then turn into other delicacies.

For access to four litres of Buttercup's milk, we paid six dollars (the equivalent of eighteen eggs or a variety of my fresh produce). Each week I skimmed off the raw cream, refrigerated it and put the milk into our pasteurizer. I kept the fresh cream for our coffee (and if you have never had fresh, raw cream in your coffee, you are missing out). In the beginning I made most of the pasteurized milk into yoghurt, but over the year I got better at utilizing it in more creative ways, and I began alternating weeks between yoghurt and ricotta cheese. Finally I set a whole week aside to make six batches of hard cheese. It took a whole week's worth of work but in the end I had almost three kilograms of cheese aging in my bar fridge.

Got milk?

Although the sale of raw milk is legal in twenty-eight US states (and if you include the states that permit the sale of unadulterated raw milk for animal consumption, that number is thirty-five) and all other G8 countries, Canada's federal Milk Act of 1938 made it illegal to sell raw (unpasteurized) milk. This prohibition was bolstered by the Food and Drug Regulations of November 30, 1981, which said in Section B.08.002.2 (1) that "No person shall sell the normal lacteal secretion obtained from the mammary gland of the cow, genus Bos, or of any other animal, or sell a dairy product made with any such secretion, unless the secretion or dairy product has been pasteurized by being held at a temperature and for a period that ensure the reduction of the alkaline phosphatase activity so as to meet the tolerances specified in official method MFO-3, Determination of Phosphatase Activity in Dairy Products."

Humans have evolved alongside milk-bearing animals since antiquity,

Sharing the Crop

Community Supported Agriculture or Community Shared Agriculture (CSA), as it is called in Canada, is a program that allows individuals to purchase a share of a farm's crop or annual harvest. It began in the early 1960s in Germany, Switzerland and Japan as a response to concerns about food safety and the urbanization of agricultural land. In Europe, many of the CSA-style farms were inspired by the agriculture and economic ideas of Rudolf Steiner, the father of biodynamic agriculture, which was an ecological and sustainable farming system that anticipated the development of organic farming.

Through the marketing structure of the CSA, supporters share the risks as well as the benefits of the farm operation with the grower. CSAs are different from buying clubs and home delivery services because the members are only able to purchase what the farm successfully grows and harvests. If a certain crop is not successful then the members receive less of that product or perhaps a lower quality product for the season.

A key feature of the CSA operation is that the members are more actively involved in the growing and distribution process. They visit the farms they belong to and get to know who is producing their food and what production methods are used, and they are often called upon to participate in farm workdays to provide labour for activities such as fence repairing, crop harvesting or even developing the farm's newsletter.

yet pasteurization has only been around since 1862 when Louis Pasteur made his discovery. It was another thirty years before the technique was applied to milk and even longer before it was applied on a national scale. Thankfully, taking home the unpasteurized product of your own property is not illegal, so Canadians can have access to *real* milk (people who want unadulterated milk straight from the cow make a distinction between real milk, a.k.a. "raw," and store-bought, pasteurized and adulterated milk) if they possess their own cow or herd. For many, this is an impossible dream, because of where they live and the difficulties of the dairy legislation. However, the recent introduction of a five-centuries-old British tradition called *agistment* has allowed Canadians to gain access to fresh, pure, unadulterated, "hundred-mile" milk without breaking the law. Agistment is rather like daycare for your kids: you leave your cow in the care of another person (farmer) and just collect its milk. So following this long-standing tradition of agistment, people have bought cows (or a share in a cow or herd) to circumvent legislation geared to favour large corporate dairies and based on the contemporary fallacy that raw milk is dangerous.

When I first took Buttercup's milk home, I was cautious and went through the labour-intensive process of pasteurizing it on the stove. I wasn't raised on a farm, had never drunk raw milk and was acculturated to believe it was unsafe. I then bought a pasteurizer, which made the process much simpler: pour in milk, plug in, wait till "cooked," cool, store in fridge, enjoy. Unfortunately, the space this machine took up in our small kitchen was not justifiable, the soldering that held the pasteurizer's handle in place broke, and it leaked, so after a while I gave up, began risking it and have never looked back.

Because I had never had access to raw milk before, I decided to do some research to find out if all the hoopla around the need for pasteurization was real or (like so much food legislation these days) just scaremongering for the benefit of a centralized distribution system. Reason told me that raw milk had to be safe because humans have been drinking it for between 8,000 and 10,000 years, at least in Europe, the Middle East and parts of Africa.[1] Practically every ruminant the world over—yak, caribou, reindeer, ass, camel, bison, goat, sheep, mare—has been milked by its human caretakers. And with the advent of more sophisticated agricultural techniques and animal domestication, milk became more widely available and humans evolved the ability to digest lactose into adulthood.

Milk's virtues are embedded in western culture and religion. For example, God tells Moses from the burning bush that he will lead the Hebrews into "a land of milk and honey" (Exodus 3:7). So what went wrong? According to Joel Salatin and many other sources (Schmid 2003),

---

1   *A History of World Agriculture: From the Neolithic Age to the Current Crisis* by Marcel Mazoyer and Laurence Roudart (2006).

milk-related illnesses did not exist before the industrial revolution when populations began to congregate in cities. Even then, raw milk was often used and endorsed by doctors, including the 1906 American Federation of Medical Milk Commissions, as a cure for such diseases as tuberculosis; in fact, I recently read of several Americans living healthily for fifty years on raw milk and nothing else.

Claude Lévi-Strauss (1908-2009), the great anthropologist, argued that food is equal to language in importance when it comes to maintaining a culture. In Canada we preserve languages and venerate multiculturalism, even using cultural preservation as a legal weapon, while at the same time outlawing this central practice of most world cultures. Raw milk is shared or legally sold and safely consumed all over the world on a daily basis, yet our authorities have convinced many people that it is unsafe, including many of our public health officials who believe that even a farmer should not be allowed to drink his or her own cow's milk. Though I have never seen a legal argument for the sanctity of cultural practice in the production and distribution of food, surely it could be made.

Until January 2010, Michael Schmidt, owner of Glencolton Farms in Durham, Ontario, was in the midst of a legal battle for the right to sell raw milk (*National Post*, January 2010, and others) that brought the question of constitutional rights into the equation. Schmidt has been providing raw milk to his large customer base since 1983, and not once in those years have any of his customers fallen ill due to the milk. Recently, however, the Canadian authorities, who turned a blind eye for many years, decided to shut him down. In an interview in *Harper's Magazine* ("The Revolution Will Not Be Pasteurized," April 2008), Schmidt revealed that twenty-four officers from five different agencies searched the farm, many of them carrying guns. Aside from the puzzle of why twenty-four officers were needed to deal with one lone farmer, it would seem that with the increase in the problems of gang violence, drug use, homelessness, and so on, assigning twenty-four officers to a case of raw milk and preoccupying five agencies with the associated paperwork is an egregious misappropriation of taxpayers' money.

In September 2008 Schmidt appeared in court charged with refusing to obey a court order that he follow a York Region public health directive to stop selling raw milk. When he was found guilty of contempt of court, he asked the judge to give him the maximum penalty, and in January 2009 began a challenge to the court ruling based on his constitutional and charter right to liberty. It is understandable that Michael Schmidt's Christmas 2008 message began, "The current state of the world teaches us once again that we have no control over so many things we thought we would have."

However, in January 2010 Justice of the Peace Paul Kowarsky of the Ontario Court of Justice found Michael Schmidt not guilty on nineteen charges relating to the sale of raw milk because Schmidt argued that he was not actually selling raw milk but rather making it available to its true owners who had purchased shares in his dairy herd and therefore owned the milk. Because Schmidt had made diligent efforts to keep his cow-share program operating "within the confines and the spirit of the legislation," Mr. Kowarsky concluded that the alleged offence fell into the category of "strict liability"; that is, criminal intent could not be proved. The Ontario government could have let the ruling stand and lived with the reality of cow-share arrangements since the existing cow-share system is a public response to restrictive legislation. However, the province chose to appeal the verdict. That appeal was supposed to start before a provincial court judge on February 8, 2011, but the Crown asked for more time to examine new motions that Schmidt filed in support of constitutional arguments that were not heard in the original trial. A new hearing date was set for April 2011.

The Canadian Constitution Foundation (CCF), an independent, non-partisan, registered charity, has come out in support of Schmidt on the following grounds: (a) consumers have the right to choose what they put in their bodies, (b) freedom of contract, and (c) freedom from government regulation that is "arbitrary, unreasonable, unnecessary, and unfair." After the government's notice of appeal, the Foundation offered Schmidt its pro bono legal services to defend the appeal, which should definitely raise the question of whether the ban on raw milk violates Canadians' constitutional rights. Meanwhile, the more people learn about Schmidt's plight and educate themselves on the scientific and potential health benefits of consuming raw milk, the more they seem to want unrestricted access to it.

Since he was charged in November 2006, the herd he manages has doubled in size and there is a waiting list of consumers wishing to participate in his cow-share program.

Schmidt is still pressing the Ontario government to develop a regulatory procedure that would facilitate the sale of certified, safe, raw milk for interested consumers without requiring a cow-sharing arrangement. He and Ontario raw milk advocate James McLaren have offered to work with government officials to help develop the certification process. Karen Selick, the CCF's litigation director, was quoted in the *National Post* on January 10, 2010, as saying that "Michigan is doing it right now. Why shouldn't Ontario?"

This entire case has presented Canadians with a conundrum. This country regularly endures meat recalls. Glass fragments were found in the ground beef from a licensed and inspected slaughterhouse in Kelowna. Maple Leaf Foods—a company whose plants are federally inspected—made deli products that killed twenty-three people. Have either of these companies been found criminally guilty? Not when they are able to pay an army of lawyers. In the case of Maple Leaf it was recently decided that the going rate for a human life in Canada is now $120,000, the amount the court settlement paid out for each of the Canadians who died (their immediate family members received additional amounts), while those with sustained, long-lasting and serious physical injuries got $125,000. For just $27 million, Maple Leaf Foods was able to continue food processing as usual. Why does the government turn a blind eye to what it calls a "mitigated risk" that killed twenty-three people while prosecuting Mr. Schmidt, who has sold raw milk safely for years to a willing and knowledgeable consumer base?

However, the number of jurisdictions where selling raw milk is legal is decreasing. In California where raw milk sales are legal, fierce pressure is being exerted by the powerful $6 billion commercial milk industry to stop the availability of raw milk to consumers. Recently a farmer who was supplying hundreds of customers in Michigan and Illinois with raw milk was busted by state police for transporting 453 gallons of it on the interstate; he had been "fingered" by an undercover agricultural investigator. Michigan officially prohibits raw milk sales for human consumption, while in Illinois people can buy it at the farm gate if they bring their own containers. Interestingly, it is legal in Washington State and since Canadians are allowed to bring dairy products across the border, there's nothing to stop British Columbians buying raw milk there and bringing it across the line. In fact, there exists a great business opportunity here for all American dairy farmers living close to the border. How ironic it would be if raw milk dairies were set up all along the border to serve Canadians whose government won't serve them directly, but allows the product to be imported!

Hopefully the International Slow Food movement can put raw milk into its Ark of Taste, a list of disappearing foods, because it should be listed as an endangered, if not threatened, comestible.

Before the fall: Raw milk pasteurizing

To pasteurize milk, you can either buy a home pasteurizing machine, as I eventually did, or do it on the stove. To do this safely on the stove, bring the milk to 145°F and hold it at that temperature for thirty minutes, then cool it quickly. (Some sources say you can bring the milk to 165°F for just a few seconds and then cool it immediately.) To cool it quickly, remove the pot from the stove and immediately transfer it to a sink full of cold water and ice cubes. Stir the milk until the temperature comes down significantly, then put it in a clean container and store in the fridge as you would any milk you buy from the store.

If using a home pasteurizer, follow the directions that came with it. With my pasteurizer, I first poured the milk into the container that fit inside the pasteurizer, then placed the container inside the pasteurizer and filled the machine with water. I then placed the lid on top, plugged it in, and waited until the buzzer let me know it was done. The first few times you use your pasteurizer, you should check the temperature of the milk once the cycle is complete to make sure that the machine is calibrated correctly. Once it has finished the pasteurization through temperature process, sluice the container with cold running water until the milk is cool, much the same as the above process. Then transfer the milk to a clean container and store in the fridge.

What to do with Raw Milk

Making yoghurt

Yoghurt is the easiest thing to make when you are first starting out in your journey of self-sufficiency because the process is immediately rewarding.

Ingredients
- 1 gallon milk   4 L
- ½ cup live yoghurt culture   125 ml
- 1 cup skim milk powder (optional)   250 ml

Equipment
- Stainless steel pot (large enough to hold 1 gallon or 4 L of milk)
- Thermometer
- 4 clean quart jars (1 L) for storage
- Electric heating pad
- 2 bath towels

Notes
If you use the skim milk powder, you will attain a thicker product.

Directions
1. Place cold milk in pot. (If using dry milk powder, add it and stir it into the milk.)
2. Carefully heat milk to 195–200°F (90°C–93°C). Do not let the milk boil! Stir gently and hold at this temperature for 10 minutes.
3. Place the pot containing the milk in cold water to cool the milk rapidly. Once it is at 116°F (47°C), remove pot from the cold water.
4. Distribute the yoghurt starter equally among the four clean quart jars.
5. Gently pour about ½ cup (125 ml) of warm milk into each jar and stir well to blend the starter with the new milk.
6. Pour remaining milk into the quart jars, leaving ¼" (6 mm) head space. (The yoghurt will not grow in volume.)
7. Place the 4 jars on top of a heating pad set on low. Wrap the jars well with 2 towels and forget about them until the morning.

8. Unwrap the jars from the towel and place jars of yoghurt in refrigerator. If the yoghurt is not thick enough for your liking, decant it into a jelly bag or tightly woven sieve. Place it over a container that will catch the whey, then place the jelly bag and the container in the refrigerator to drain for a half-hour (or up to several hours) until desired thickness is achieved.

Ricotta cheese

There is simply nothing like homemade ricotta cheese, and there are so many things you can do with it: eat it with a spoon, put it in lasagna, stuff cannelloni, make piggies in blankets and make bread with it. I have even found an easy, flavourful ricotta doughnut recipe. The list is ever-growing, thanks to inventive minds. Ricotta is easy to make and provides an almost instant treat. I like to eat it as the Greeks do: with a drizzle of strong espresso coffee, a sprinkle of cinnamon and a dollop of honey—simply divine!

Ingredients
- 1 gallon milk   4 L
(fresh from the cow if you have access, but store-bought will work fine)
- Lemon juice or vinegar (apple cider or white)

Notes
Save the whey to make bread, muffins or pancakes. I always use it to make my Italian whey bread—fantastic! See recipe page 170.

Directions
1. Put milk in a large pot.
2. Heat the milk until it reaches 200°F (93°C). Do not let it boil. It will be very close to boiling as it approaches this temperature, so be careful.
3. Add a few tablespoons of lemon juice or vinegar and stir gently for two minutes.
4. Turn off the heat and let the pot sit for 10 minutes while the milk curdles into cheese. (What will be in the pot at this point is Little Miss Muffet's curds and whey! So now after all these years of wondering, you know what she was eating.)

5. Strain through a jelly bag or cheesecloth to catch all the curds. Tie an elastic band around the jelly bag, hook it over a cupboard handle and place a bowl underneath to catch the whey as it drains from the cheese. Leave it draining until it stops dripping, about a half an hour.

Fresh Mozzarella

According to the historian Monsignor Alicandri, mozzarella cheese was first made in the twelfth century by the monks of San Lorenzo di Capua in Italy. Originally it was made with sheep's milk, but in the sixteenth century, water buffalo were introduced to Italy and the cheese-makers soon discovered that this animal's milk was rich enough to make cheese with. Henceforth, making mozzarella from water buffalo milk was the norm and a new tradition began.

Note

When making young (unripened) cheeses, it is recommended that you use pasteurized milk. If you have access to raw milk, step 1 should be to pasteurize it.

Ingredients

2 tbsp vinegar or lemon juice	30 ml
1 gallon pasteurized milk	4 L
⅛ tsp liquid rennet	0.625 ml
diluted in ¼ cup of cool, non-chlorinated water	60 ml
1 tbsp cheese salt	15 ml
(salt without iodine; I use canning salt)	

Directions:

1. Pour milk into a large pot, add the lemon juice or vinegar to the milk and mix thoroughly.

2. Heat the milk over a low flame on the stovetop until it reaches 88°F (31°C). The milk should start to curdle. If it doesn't, add another tablespoon of lemon juice.

3. Stir in the diluted rennet with an up and down motion. Continue heating the milk until it reaches 105°F (41°C). Turn off the heat and let the curd set until you get a clean break. This will only take about 5–6 minutes. At this stage, the curds will look like thick yoghurt.

4. Scoop out the curds with a slotted spoon and place them in a microwavable bowl. Press the curds gently and pour off as much whey as possible, being careful to save the whey for bread-making. (Or feed the whey to your chickens. They love it!)

5. Microwave the curds on high for 1 minute. Drain the accumulated whey and quickly work the cheese like bread dough. You can wear rubber gloves if you wish as the cheese will be quite hot to the touch.

6. Microwave the cheese for 35 seconds, working the cheese into a ball and draining the excess whey, and repeat once.

7. Knead quickly like bread dough until it is smooth, sprinkling it with salt as you work. When the cheese is smooth, it is ready to eat.

At this stage the cheese is bocconcini and quite unlike the mass-produced mozzarella of the grocery store. Use it right away. It is traditionally used on pizza napoletana, though I have found it doesn't melt the way mass-produced mozza does. (Of course, this could mean I'm not doing it correctly, and you may have a different experience. So much of cheese-making is about precision.) Instead of using it on pizza, my favourite way to eat it is to slice it thinly and layer it between slices of tomato. Drizzle pesto sauce over the top, then sprinkle the whole thing with toasted pine nuts, a drizzle of olive oil and some cracked pepper. Serve with a crusty loaf of bread or plain crackers. If you have pesto on hand, this is a quick and easy yet still elegant appetizer.

Hard cheese

When I first started fantasizing about making cheese, it was the hard cheeses like cheddar, Gouda, and Romano that I envisioned on the shelves of my refrigerator. While fresh cheeses are much easier to make, they are also much less flavourful and lack the pungency of aged hard cheeses.

I had once watched friends in New Zealand make cheese and had eaten their cheeses many times, but I had been put off attempting to do it on my own by all the dire warnings in cheese-making literature about how scrupulously clean everything must be in order not to kill yourself. Finally I came across *Home Cheese Making* by Ricki Carroll. Interspersed with stories from other home cheese-makers, her descriptions of the process and simple recipes made the art of cheese-making attractive rather than off-putting. The contents of her book are ordered from easiest to most difficult, from soft cheese to hard cheeses and beyond into the world of bacteria-ripened cheeses like brie, Camembert and Gorgonzola. Some-where in the middle of the hard cheese section I came across one of my favourite "dining out" cheeses, *haloumi*, a brined cheese not unlike feta but from the Island of Cypress. Carroll's book described it as a good cheese to make in hot weather so, since it was August, I immediately mustered up the courage (and the implements) necessary to make it. After all, it could be brined up to 60 days before eating, offering dinner party flexibility, but it could also be eaten fresh, and that appealed to my impatient taste buds.

I decided to make *haloumi* to kick-start a Greek-themed evening. I made my signature Greek salad (dressed with just lemon juice, no oil or vinegar), prepared a large bowl of tabbouleh with vegetables and herbs from my garden, marinated chicken in lemon and garlic and baked cumin biscuits. Then I roasted peppers and peaches and drizzled them in olive oil dressing with cumin. For the starter, I prepared fresh pita bread to serve with hummus and *haloumi* cheese.

Once our friends arrived, I put on Greek music, poured glasses of wine and offered them around. My friend Carole, who rarely drank wine, pre-ferred a soda. Not long into the evening, I wondered if people were ready for appetizers, so I turned to my teetotalling friend and asked if she would like to try some of my *haloumi*.

"No thanks. I don't want to get a headache," she replied.

I thought it odd that she knew specifically that this kind of cheese would give her a headache, so I asked how she knew. "Oh, red wine always gives me a headache." She has to this day never lived down the fact she did *not* know what *haloumi* was!

After that first successful attempt, I broadened my repertoire and tried my hand at various kinds of hard cheeses—feta, Romano, cheddar, Gouda, parmesan, a goat cheddar, a traditional cheddar, and a Leicester wrapped in lard and cheesecloth—and left them to ripen in my cheese fridge. Of course, one of the joys of cheese-making is the mystery of how each cheese will taste when you finally decide it has ripened enough to cut into. So far I've had some really tasty successes, while the dog has

Never waste the by-product of cheese making. Here I have ricotta cheese draining. It is a delightful ready-that-day treat when sprinkled with espresso coffee, brown sugar, and cinnamon—the way Tony the Greek likes it.

benefited from my failures. When I opened a three-year-old Romano cheese, it was unlike the Romano you would buy at the store in terms of texture. Instead, it was more like an aged cheddar and equally robust in flavour. To give it its full due, my husband and I enjoyed it on its own alongside a homemade shiraz, then we placed it on top of my homemade bread, and finally I grated some over a pasta *al fresco* dinner I created with capers and roasted red peppers in garlic and olive oil. It was divine!

Summer Harvesting

The best laid plans

IT WAS THE BEGINNING OF JUNE, I had all my major crops in but I was chomping at the bit for more gardening space. I'd had a good look around the yard and begun to formulate a plan, so I called my neighbour, Mitch. He is, among other things, a man who has a lot of useful machines and under-utilized talent. What he doesn't have is enough time. So although I didn't have a fully developed idea when I picked up the phone, I knew I could trust him to help me develop my plan *in situ* and, knowing how busy he is, I wanted to book him as soon as possible.

"What do you want done?" he asked casually.

I rattled off a half-baked plan while he calculated how much time my job would take.

"You're twelfth on my list," he let me know. "I should be able to get to you on June seventh. Will that do?"

I looked at the calendar: two weeks from now. I wondered how he could be so specific about when his twelfth-on-the-list job could be done, but without questioning him I marked the calendar, happy to have made it onto his list at all.

I don't recall how we first came to know Mitch or what we even asked him to do on that first occasion. What I do recall was that I liked him right away and it's why I chose him over others for that first job. Quite apart from the fact that he is talented and useful, he is an organizer. If he couldn't do the job himself, he was happy to do the legwork and find the right person for whatever we wanted done. But what clinched the deal for me was the way he spoke about his wife: he was all respect and admiration. Not only did he have nice things to say about her, but in his storytelling he also managed to make himself the brunt of jokes between them. That is the mark of a secure man and a man who respects women—and that's the kind of man I hire. When Mitch was on the job, David and I managed to maintain matrimonial harmony. It was something I had noticed but hadn't really thought much about until my husband brought it to my attention one day.

"You know," David said, "Mitch is predictable when he shows up."

"How so?"

"Well, the conversation between me and him amounts to this: 'Hello,' followed by a few pleasantries and then, 'Where's Kristeva? I gotta talk to her about the job.'"

"So?"

"Well, he obviously knows who he's really working for!"

As the summer work piled up and I became embroiled in growing fruit, I almost forgot my appointment with Mitch. The property came with six established fruit trees—two cherry, two pear, two apple—and one not-so-established peach. The first three produced wonderfully but the peach, being much younger and probably not really suited to this climate, had a yield of six peaches for two years running. A winter storm proved too much for the little tree and snapped it off brutally at its base, and worse, I couldn't source a replacement. There would be no more peaches on the menu at Kristeva's Kitchen.

Other established food sources included our two highbush cranberries and three blueberry bushes. The blueberries provided us with masses of the dark blue, sweet fruit, which I not only like but know what to do with, unlike the highbush cranberries. What could I make them into? I knew they were in theory edible, but I had never in my life eaten cranberries. Much to my mother's chagrin, I had turned my nose up at her cranberry sauce each Christmas. Fruit with turkey just didn't fit, no matter how pretty it looked against the white meat. Then came the Christmas when I searched the Internet, made a rum and highbush cranberry sauce, and took it to my mother's house for dinner. It is amazing what you will eat when you have gone to the trouble of growing and preserving it. Now that it was mine, this humble berry sauce had taken on special meaning and taste.

I had bought several more fruit trees and shrubs and was busy planting them the day Mitch showed up. "I'm a day early," he said, walking toward the gate to unlatch it so he could get his Bobcat machine into the yard. "I hope that doesn't put your schedule out too much." I put down the plants and told him it was fine, my mind struggling to switch gears from orchard planning to property development and fence-post pounding. I had been planning to clear the work space later that day, but now, knowing I might get bumped to fourteenth on his list if I let him go, I mentally shuffled some of my tasks around and began rattling off a list of things for him to do.

First up, we needed to prep the site for the new building that would be our turkey pen by summer and goat pen by winter. There was an unspoken understanding between Mitch and me: he had the grace to ask me what I

Dave teaches me how to run his backhoe while clearing our front forty.

wanted done, wait politely while I went on at length and then let me know what really needed to be done while still managing to let me think it was all my idea. He did this by asking a question that revealed something that I hadn't thought of but should have been thinking of.

On that day it was which trees he should fall. I had decided upon three, and if absolutely necessary, four. "So where are you going to put your gate?" Mitch asked, and—knowing he was going to have some time on his hands—he lit a cigarette and began my reorientation class.

"I guess over there," I said, pointing to an area in front of where the building would eventually be sited.

"Okay." He paused. "There's quite a slope there." He motioned back and forth with his cigarette-wielding arm at an angle that matched the slope of the ground. When it was obvious that I wasn't catching on to his subtle attempt to point out what was wrong with my idea, he posed another question: "How will you seal off the gate so the chickens can't get out?"

"Uh ... well ... um ..." Though the light bulb was on, my mind was slow to filter through the various possibilities in search of an intelligent solution to the gate problem.

He took a long drag on the cigarette, placed it between his first two fingers, and then through his exhalation made a sensible suggestion as to where to locate the gate, listing the merits of the choice.

"Okay, done," I agreed. But we weren't done. There were several more decisions that "I" needed to make, and Mitch gently led me through each one. He somehow always managed to get the answers he needed from me in less time than it took him to finish a cigarette and without much resistance—now *that* is a skillful man.

In the end he took out seven trees, levelled the ground, chose the location for the gate and prepped the site for the foundation work. As Mitch began falling trees, I went back to work in the garden and every now and then looked over to see what he was doing. It was amazing what he could accomplish with his little machine, but it was even more amazing that he could do it all without losing the cigarette that seemed permanently nestled in the left corner of his mouth.

As the last few trees were crashing down around him, my husband, unaware of our plans, suddenly came running from the house. "Does he know when to stop?" he asked.

I tried to calm his alarm because stop Mitch and his machine I would not! But I noticed that he had very nearly accomplished his tasks, so I figured that while he was in the mood for whacking down trees, I'd ask him to deal with a couple more in the front yard. They were mostly dead anyway and quite ugly. Happily he agreed and the Bobcat began its slow but steady march across the lawn.

Within minutes the two ugly willows were down, bucked into moveable pieces, roots dug up and set around the fire pit. "Anything else?"

Now I was on a roll. "Well, can you flatten out this lump of dirt?" I asked, pointing at a sizable mound that had always bothered me but I could now see a use for.

"It's good dirt," he offered. "If you cover it with fertilizer and then wrap it up, it will be great garden soil by next year." I told him to go for it and within minutes the lump was repositioned and ready to be put to bed until next year. "Anything else?" he asked again.

"Well, could you dig out those willow roots from the edge of the pond?" Done. "How about those ones over there in the stream?" Ditto. "While you're at it, can you just move that fence post a wee bit? Oh, and that cherry tree, can it be moved over here?" Within a few hours, the landscape of our yard was completely transformed. I now had a site for the future turkey barn prepped and ready for the cement pad. I also had a future veggie patch nearly as large as my first veggie patch—I was thrilled.

Mrs. Mallard meets a mate

Each spring the Muscovies mated and the female ducks sat on eggs, so each spring we had a couple of hatchings of little baby ducks. But the Muscovy ducks were, in general, hopeless mothers. They might hatch ten or fifteen ducklings and be lucky to see four or five to adulthood. One year only one of the ducks successfully sat on eggs but she hatched fourteen. Within a couple of weeks she was down to one duckling. Between the ravens, the crows, and a saw-whet owl, and despite our elaborate fishnet covering, the poor little things didn't stand a chance.

Mrs. Mallard, having watched one of the Muscovy gals hatch out thirteen ducklings earlier in the spring, no longer having a mate but wanting desperately to become a mother, finally started courting Renaldo. Not sure whether this mating was even possible, I asked a veterinary friend of mine if such a cross-mating would be viable. He said it was unusual but possible, although he warned that the offspring would likely be infertile. I was excited by the prospect of seeing little cross-breeds running around our yard, but it was not to be. Despite the fact that Mrs. Mallard's amorous attempts became more and more obvious, Renaldo would have none of it.

Mrs. Mallard was undeterred. She troopered on with her maternity preparations as if to prove she didn't need a mate around to help. She was certainly off to a much better start than the other ducks because her nest was inside the duck house where it was safe, while the Muscovies' nests were scattered here and there around the pen. I began to get hopeful that she might just prove to me that ducks can be good mothers. She continued to feather her nest as if an arrival of fertilized eggs was imminent, and as it grew in height, she became more and more proud and protective of it. Eventually she practically breathed fire and shot laser beams from her eyes whenever I came to change their water and so much as glanced in her direction.

With Renaldo uninterested, Mrs. Mallard had to get creative and began looking further afield for a mate. She would march to the middle of the pen and call loudly. Before long, several wild mallard ducks would fly overhead, but they wouldn't land in the yard because our farm activities were just too much for them. However, one day when she called, I heard an unfamiliar response coming from the slough. She had managed to convince a wild mallard courtier that it was safe to land behind the duck pen! Unfortunately, each time I tried to get a good look at him, he bolted guiltily from the slough and Mrs. Mallard scolded me in no uncertain terms.

Finally, fed up with her suitor's lack of gallantry, she took matters into her own wings and flew the coop—she was off for a dirty weekend! She didn't return for three nights, during which time, like the mother of a teen-aged girl, I was both thrilled for her and worried at the company she might be keeping. Three days later she showed up and asked to be let back into the pen. Her nesting efforts were renewed with relish and within days she had installed a few eggs. Because they were different colours, I wondered if she'd been gathering from other nests in her desperation to start a family. In any case, nothing came of it. Thirty or so days later she dismantled the nest as if to erase all evidence of her maternal efforts, and I determined that none of the eggs was fertile. Perhaps she didn't understand that a wild weekend and perfectly prepared baby's room didn't guarantee a family.

The twenty-mile community feast

Each year I looked forward to the Bella Coola Valley Garden Tour as it was a reminder that there were other farmers in the Valley and I was not alone in my endeavours. It was also an opportunity to learn that so many beautiful things were possible with a little ingenuity and patience. That year the tour took on a more pragmatic aspect: the emphasis was on self-sustaining food production, and the climax was a Feast of Fields featuring all-local produce.

On a bright Sunday afternoon in July 2007, a school bus driven by a community volunteer set off from the farmers' market with forty agro-tourists. Our first stop was Putliixw (which means "something budding") Gardens, the community garden recently developed by teachers and a Nuxalk horticulture student at the Four Mile and Acwsalcta School. Community donations of hay and manure and timber milled off the site had helped them to create raised beds and a potato patch. Junior students had cleared rocks, rototilled, planted, watered and weeded until the end of the school year. Bug control had been accomplished through a combination of all-natural fertilizers and the flicking of fingers, and everything looked extremely healthy and almost ready to eat. My husband was scheduled to teach a course there in the fall called "Agriculture in the Classroom," and he arranged for these gardens to supply some of the food for the lunches provided to students.

We then toured a dozen private gardens, each featuring something for all of us to learn from. One of the local U-pick places had a large corn patch and orchard. The owners were particularly inventive and demonstrated the plough they had designed and machined to make their raised beds; when attached behind their tractor, it rototilled and created symmetrical beds effortlessly. These folks paid tribute to their grandparents for building up the garden's ten feet of topsoil! They also honoured the support and honesty of locals. Each year they put out a stand full of fresh produce with what in New Zealand was called an honesty box. The farmer told us that at the end of the day there was usually a jar full of money. He had learned a lot about marketing over the years, too. "Carrots," he observed, "that are washed and packed in a plastic bag don't sell nearly as well as unwashed carrots tied with string, with their tops still on!" One of the tour visitors noted that these particular gardeners had kindly donated pounds and pounds of cherries to the Community Kitchen Program so they could make jam.

It was a short walk from that farm to another innovative garden where a half-sunken greenhouse with electrically heated soil had our tourists sketching and taking notes. Again there was a sense of history, with the owner responding to a question about the poppies dotted randomly through her vegetable garden by saying, "My mother loved poppies, so now I let them volunteer themselves."

Dodging the rain showers, the magic bus then headed up the Valley to another large garden above the highway. The owner, who came from Niagara Falls, Ontario, said he had been born into market gardening. Generosity was again the order of the day here, as each cherry tree had a sign hanging on it identifying it as belonging to a friend who would pick it that year. He too noted that history was all around us, and he pointed out a Spartan apple tree planted by Jean Hammer's father in 1894 and still bearing. On this farm we also saw a pile of horse manure lying under a black tarp while it cooked and sterilized, and beside the house a roped-off area of lawn was reserved for the mason bees who make their home in the soil and help pollinate his garden and orchard trees.

Grapes were the focus at the next gardener's place. His home was surrounded by thirty-year-old grapevines and grafted apple trees. The tour group was very interested in the nearly lost art of grafting.

Then the owner of Edlyn's Nursery gave us a tour of her successful greenhouse operation, including a unique heating system that utilized two recycled fuel tanks from the gas station to pump heated water through both the greenhouse and her home. She said she started the business by selling herbs and then moved into flowers when another woman in the Valley who used to run a nursery retired. Now she was exploring the idea of growing tomatoes, cucumbers and eggplants.

The owners of the Co-op Restaurant had worked with a friend to build a greenhouse on their property and were busy turning the adjacent wood-land into a vegetable garden so they could supply their restaurant with fresh organic produce. To solve their irrigation problems, they planned to use a diesel engine, run on fat from the restaurant, to pump water around their garden beds. At this garden stop there was much discussion about soils, natural fertilizers, nitrogen, chicken manure, the need to build up potassium and magnesium, and the origin and population density of earthworms in the Valley. An informed contributor on these matters was Dr. Terry Lewis, a soils ecologist from Courtenay, who was in the Valley to map the soil.

With heads full of facts, figures and ideas for their own gardens, our busload of agro-tourists arrived at the last stop, our own Howling Duck Ranch. Here the unique feature was not so much the vegetable garden as the livestock. Our visitors were treated to the antics of the goats, turkeys, ducks and chickens, and were especially taken with our "chicken tractor," a chicken run on wheels that transported and confined our workers to a chosen patch of the garden. When the "tractor" was moved along after just three hours, the tourists could not believe the way the grass had been turned into soil. I explained that I let our band of tireless workers free-range as much as possible because I enjoyed their company and their ridiculous antics. But the part I liked most was that for a handful of corn, I employed a tireless workforce to turn over and fertilize the soil, and most of them threw in an egg as well. Our tour guide, Professor Art Bromke from the University of British Columbia's Faculty of Land and Food Systems, was really impressed by my chickens, who put on the best demonstration of free-ranging and soil-turning he'd ever seen. "The chickens at UBC cer-tainly don't work that hard," he said, astonished at their vigorous efforts.

The culmination of the tour was the Feast of Fields. We had lined up tables on the front driveway in full view of the goats, ducks and chickens, and we ate glorious, home-grown, locally prepared food, while the members of the volunteer *a cappella* chorus sang softly in the background—cock-a-doodle-doo, mmbaaa-baa-baa, gobble-gobble, quack-quack-quack.

My contribution to the feast was duck. The first time we butchered one of the ducks, I couldn't bring myself to eat it and ended up feeding it to the dog. From that experience I discovered that I needed to have a decent amount of time between when my husband killed them and when I got around to cooking them. I was also getting better with preparing and eating our chickens if they spent time in the freezer before gracing my roasting pans.

But finally it had become necessary to do in a few of the ducks because the males were maturing and I didn't want in-breeding going on. I worked up the courage to do the deed myself, but then I needed to figure out how to disguise the meat enough that I could eat it. I knew it was about time

Professor Art Bromke from UBC was really impressed by my chickens' demonstration of free-ranging and soil-turning.

I got over this it's-too-cute-to-eat fetish. For me the answer lay in Indian cooking. Chicken biryani has always been one of my favourite dishes, and a friend from the city of Hyderabad, where it originated, had taught me how to cook it. Traditionally it is made with goat meat, but I figured the herbs and spices would provide enough of a disguise for the duck that I could get over my reluctance to eat it! The first time I cooked duck this way for guests, it garnered rave reviews, so when the Feast of Fields committee asked me to host the event, I decided to contribute this dish. It became the Howling Duck Ranch's signature meal!

Around eight in the evening the guests reluctantly began to leave, slow to break up informative discussions, slow to leave the huge, delicious variety of food all created and processed by themselves and their Valley neighbours, and slow to bring to a close this celebration of local industry, initiative, hard work and healthy living.

A Feast of the Fields sample menu

- Beets, green onions and lettuce from Putliixw Gardens
- Sopalali (traditional aboriginal ice cream)
- Baby carrots, lettuce, radishes and onions
- Chicken, beef and turkey
- Strawberries, frozen Concord grapes, Queen Anne cherries
- Elderberry drink, apple juice, and mint sun tea
- Flowers
- Early Girl, Husky Gold and grape tomatoes plus green bell peppers from Edlyn's Nursery
- Muscovy Duck Biryani, cherry pie, strawberry-rhubarb-mint pie, and aged cheese from the Howling Duck Ranch
- Spring and chum salmon from Bella Coola Seafoods
- Salmon pâté, spinach and strawberry salad from Bella Coola Valley Restaurant
- Two pizzas from Palm Garden Restaurant
- Garlic scape and herb focaccia bread from Cook's Cuisine Artisan Bakery
- Salad ingredients from the Bella Coola Valley Inn restaurant
- Asian noodle salad from the Bay Restaurant

The Howling Duck Ranch Muscovy Duck Biryani

Ingredients

- ½ cup canola oil — 125 ml
- 1 tbsp ghee (or extra oil) — 15 ml
- 5 medium onions, sliced thin and chopped
- 4 garlic cloves, chopped
- 2–4 dried red chilies
- 3" (7.5 cm) piece ginger, peeled and finely chopped or grated
- 1 tbsp whole garam masala, ground in a coffee grinder or by hand with a mortar and pestle — 15 ml
- 1 cup fresh cilantro, chopped — 250 ml
- ½ cup fresh spearmint, chopped — 125 ml
- 1 tsp allspice — 5 ml
- 1 tsp turmeric — 5 ml
- ½ cup coconut milk (or sour cream) — 125 ml
- ½ cup yoghurt — 125 ml
- meat from one Muscovy duck (or two chickens), skinned and cubed
- 4 cups brown basmati rice — 1 kg
- ½ cup oil — 125 ml
- 1/2–1 cup water — 125–250 ml
- 1–2 lemons

Directions

1. Fry the onions in the oil and ghee for 10 minutes until browned and slightly crispy.

2. Divide the fried onions between three bowls, reserving one for topping. Place 1/3 of the onions in a blender with half each of the garlic, chilies, ginger, garam masala, cilantro and mint, as well as the allspice and turmeric. Blend and add yoghurt and coconut milk.

3. Marinate the duck in this yoghurt mixture for 6 hours or overnight.

4. Cook rice in rice cooker according to instructions.

5. Heat ½ cup oil in large frying pan. Add 1/3 of the onions, the remaining garlic and remaining ginger. Crush and add remaining chilies and fry for 1 minute or just until the spices are aromatic, then add the meat and water. Cook on low heat until the meat is done.

6. Squeeze lemons over the meat mixture and add the rest of the fresh cilantro and mint.

7. Place half the cooked rice in a casserole dish or lasagna pan. Remove the meat mixture from heat and layer over rice. Then add the last of the rice mixture. Sprinkle the final third of the fried onions over the top and garnish with more cilantro and mint, if desired. Cover with aluminum foil and place in oven at 350°F (175°C) for 15–30 minutes until heated through.

Serve with naan and yoghurt raitha.

The running of the chicks

It was August and suddenly I was out of feed for the baby turkeys and the local store didn't have any in stock. It would be another two days until the next shipment would arrive from Williams Lake. At such moments I liked to quote Lord Rutherford: "We don't have much money, so we're going to have to think." The solution would have to be found on the farm or in the garden.

I went out to the garden and began pulling some carrots and potatoes to give to the turkey chicks. As I did this, I weeded those areas I was harvesting and carried the weeds to the chicken coop. Then it struck me: why am I doing this extra work? Why not close this circle and feed the chickweed to the turkeys, too? Of course neither poultry nor turkey chicks can eat weeds wholesale, especially if the weeds are not rooted to something that they can pull against. To compensate for this, I decided to take the weeds into the house and put them through the food processor.

It worked like a charm. At first the turkey chicks were a bit skeptical, but once they caught on, they enjoyed the greens. In fact, it wasn't long before I began calling the turkey nursery "Pamplona" because taking the mixed greens in to them was like participating in the running of the bulls: I was lucky not to get trampled in the stampede to get to the front and secure a prime position relative to the plate I was putting down for them. That was how the weeds in my garden and the brush alongside the road became a resource that supplemented my feed costs. A side benefit of giving the chicks greens was that they grew really well and did not have as much "poopy-bum" as they did when raised solely on chick starter ration.

A potato party for one

It was getting close to the end of summer and I was helping my friend Clarence harvest potatoes. Each year he planted one of the largest gardens in the Valley, and people flocked to him for goodies as they came to fruition. In fact, Clarence's garden was quite the food security resource for our community, with many people relying on his harvest each year to stock their pantry shelves. Of course, his immediate family came first and were duly provided for, but the rest of his harvest he sold or, more often, gave away to those less able to pay. His garden was also a wonderful feast for the eyes each spring, largely due to the bright and cheery red tulips he grew in the middle of it. They were often the first true signs of spring in the Valley and I always kept my eye out for them.

Clarence loved to talk about farming and pass on his farming knowledge, and one year he had the opportunity to teach a nine-year-old girl who had moved to the Valley with her mother. As soon as she met Clarence, they struck up a friendship and she asked him to teach her how to garden. A large crudely painted sign sprouted beside his driveway announcing: "Tiffany's Garden. Aged 9."

I, too, tended to go to his garden to harvest knowledge and take home his stories by the bucketful. Today we stood chatting amidst a sea of potato tops while he was harvesting potatoes for someone who would soon arrive to pick them up. Then quite abruptly he turned on his heel and took off across the garden. Apparently he had decided I needed to test out a fingerling potato that did not impress him. Leaping rows in a single bound, he called back to me, "I don't know what to make of it." When I caught up to him, he was already unearthing some small, light golden-coloured tubers. "See how they are too small," he said, holding them out and looking at them with mild disdain. "They call them the Indian potato. I don't know why." He then listed off their various conformation faults—he didn't like the fact they were "knobbly," they were difficult to harvest, they weren't easy to clean, but mostly he was unimpressed with their size. Clarence was big on *big* vegetables, and each year hunted for the largest of each item in his garden, which he then showed off to everyone. Once, while he was displaying a big potato at the local Co-op store, it was inadvertently scanned through the check-out and Clarence ended up paying for it!

"I want you to try them," he said, loading a bunch of the fingerlings into a bucket.

"Are you going to keep growing them?" I asked.

His hand came up in front of me and paused there as if to punctuate the moment. "Question," was all he said, and his finger traced the shape of a question mark, echoing the announcement through the air. His personal jury was still out. My assignment, according to Clarence, was to take these little "twisty, turny, knobbly" things home, cook and taste them and report back with the final verdict. He was unsure whether or not he was going to bother with them again.

"I had them in my garden years ago and got rid of them," he told me, "but now they're back." He shrugged helplessly, staring down disdainfully at the wrinkled fingerlings in his hand as if they had decided on their own to recolonize his garden. The pressure was on. The future of these potatoes rested on my experience with them. Clarence outlined the set of parameters that I was to judge them by. How were they to clean? Were the eyes too deep? Were they, as he suspected, too much bother for the amount of food value they contained? In his list of guidelines I noted there was nothing about taste, heritage or pedigree. Here was a utilitarian gardener, a man who obviously had a different value system than mine, but then this did not surprise me, given the more than forty years and generations of experience that separated us.

"Well, while I'm at it, Clarence, would you mind if I took home one of each variety?" That year Clarence was growing four kinds of spuds: the Canadian heirloom Kennebec, Red Rose, Yukon Gold (another Canadian variety) and the fingerling potato of questionable merit. If I was going to do the experiment, I thought, I might as well make it worth my while and pit the fingerlings up against some other varieties. I wanted to really "put them through their paces," as it were.

"By all means. Help yourself," he said generously and began helping me harvest a bucket of each variety. I took the four varieties home, washed and chopped them up and then added my own organic red potato of unknown pedigree to the pot. Wanting to keep the testing simple and really taste the potatoes in as undisguised form as possible—in order to even the playing field, I reasoned—I simply boiled them in salted water. Once they were cooked, I laid them out on a plate and began the taste testing. Surprisingly, there was a riot of colour and shades on the plate in front of me, and I began sampling them in turn. They had remarkably different textures as well as flavours. Not surprisingly, I liked each of Clarence's varieties better than my own. Even his Yukon Gold outclassed my own Yukon Gold—which said a great deal about consistent soil management, among other things. But although I thoroughly enjoyed my personal potato party, as ironic fate would have it, the winner in terms of flavour, aroma and texture was the knobbly little fingerling. Clarence was not going to like my final verdict.

After searching through various websites and photos of potato varieties, I found not only the pedigree of Clarence's Indian potato but also the reason behind the name. It is an ancient variety brought to North America by the Spanish explorers in the 1700s and given to the Makah Native people of Neah Bay on the Olympic Peninsula in Washington State. Called the Ozette, it gets its name from the area where the Makah still grow it after all these years. In the late 1980s the seed was obtained from Anna Cheeka, a Makah of Neah Bay, and introduced to the market by David Ronniger of Ronniger Potato Farms. According to their website, "the Ozette is one of the tastiest of all fingerlings. Classic in appearance with pale gold skin and creamy yellow flesh. The slightly earthy, nutty flavor comes through beautifully when lightly steamed or sautéed. Late variety."

Now I was armed with knowledge, with a history, with a name. Having tasted the potato and fallen in love with it, I felt a personal responsibility toward it and knew I would feel guilty if I let it down now. Why, Clarence might even stop growing it! It was as if the future of the fingerling in the Bella Coola Valley lay in my hands.

The next day I returned to help harvest the little beauties and report on my findings. (I also admit that I wanted to ensure I would have some for next year's seed.) When I told Clarence that the fingerling had come out on top in my taste-testing venture, he looked disappointed. The fact that I raved about the texture and flavour of the Ozette did nothing for him, but as I described the long and distinguished history of this hardy little potato, his face finally softened. "Oh. Well then ... I suppose I'll have to keep some for seed." The down-turned corners of his mouth told me he was torn between two philosophies. He liked growing big, utilitarian items (he was an alpha male through and through) yet the acquiescent shrug revealed his commitment to keeping the heritage alive. Grudgingly he concluded, "Well, you can take as many as you like." I was almost certain he was hoping I'd take them all off his hands and rid him of the burden of keeping the seed going. I happily dug in and took a five-gallon bucket-load home—probably about twenty-five or thirty pounds—along with the others he'd harvested for me.

Clarence was doing something in his potato patch that was foreign to me—placing the potato tops and rogue weeds back into the hole where the harvested potatoes had come from. Having just harvested all of my own potatoes and carried the potato tops, along with the weeds, to a compost pile inside my garden, I asked him about it. "I've just always done it this

My favourite potato: the Ozette from Clarence's garden.

way," he said, and then shrugged. "It's what my dad taught me." Then he added as an afterthought, "It feeds the worms, too." By spring, he explained, he would have rich soil while my compost might not be completely biode-graded. I had thought that I was being clever by having my compost pile inside the garden, thereby saving myself two steps: heaving the weeds and garden waste out onto the pile and then in the spring heaving it all back again as composted material, which the chickens would spread for me. But what Clarence was doing eliminated both steps and produced a better result.

Clarence paused in his potato digging to pick up a small rock. "You know that soil scientist who was here last year? He told me I had the best soil in all the tests he'd done in the Valley." Clarence worked with a three-bucket system: one bucket for the keepers, one for the rogues, and one for the rocks. The keepers he stored for his family, the rogue potatoes he gave away to those who could not afford to buy, and the rocks he disposed of. He had been maintaining this system in his garden for longer than I'd been alive. "You know, people say their gardens are too rocky for vegetables," he said, while continuing to hoe, "so I ask them, 'Have you ever thought about digging them out?'" He went on to tell me about the thousands of rocks, small and large, that he'd taken out of his garden over the years. "One of them was too large for removal so I spent nearly two hours digging a hole beside it, you know, and tipped it in." He stopped hoeing then nodded toward an area in the garden. "It's still in there, you know ... under the soil deep enough for my rototiller to pass over unscathed." This diligence in rooting out even small rocks made his soil deep, rich and friable.

He's like the Ozette potato, I reflected as I drove home. He came north when young and flourished in a new climate. He, too, was a master survivor. No wonder he had the best soil in the Valley!

Hi-ho, hi-ho, it's off to work experience I go

I passionately believe in what I'm doing in general, and in ethical farming in particular. So in September when I had the opportunity to have some junior high school kids come and spend the day with me doing work experience, I jumped at it. One of the high school classes had come to tour the farm a few weeks earlier, and when the class was asked where they would like to be placed for work experience day, I was thrilled to learn that two of the boys had chosen Howling Duck Ranch for their placement! Both were interested in becoming farmers and keen to spend some time working on the farm and playing with my animals.

I picked them up from school in the morning and we got straight to the ugly stuff. I gave them the choice of mucking out the chicken coop or fixing the fence. They chose the mucking-out job. Before setting them to it, I explained how it should be done, where to pile the muck, and where the replacement bedding was. They went at it heartily and seemed to enjoy the work. The chicken coop was four by six metres and the bedding was about ten centimetres deep so it was a big job, but I was impressed with how they worked without complaint. Even so, it took a while to get it all hauled out and into the compost pile.

While they worked, the boys asked me all sorts of questions about farming in general but chicken keeping in particular. They were obviously engaged in the task at hand as the questions they asked about the chickens were very thoughtful. "How often do you have to change the bedding? Why are the nesting boxes that big? How often do chickens lay eggs? Can they lay eggs without a rooster? What do you feed them?"

Once all the old bedding was out, we began to barrow in the new stuff. Again, I had to field their questions as they arose. At the time I was experimenting with deep bed litter. I had read about this a long time ago but had not had the right conditions to actually try it out. Now that I had my new deluxe barn, complete with a fifteen-centimetre pony wall, I was enthusiastic to try it and shared my research with the boys. According to Joel Salatin of Polyface Farm, if you keep the bedding deep—twenty to thirty centimetres—the composting action will keep the smell down and add heat to the building, cutting down on your heating costs. (See *Pastured Poultry Profits* by Salatin.) This system cuts down on my work time as well because I didn't have to clean out the chicken house as often as I had been. Salatin also claims that if the bedding is closer to fifteen centimetres deep, bugs will grow in it and can actually contribute to the protein needs of your chickens. To me it all sounded good, with no downside.

The boys began to place bets on how many wheelbarrows of bedding it would it take to fill the coop again. "How deep do you want the litter to be?" they asked, and then the serious calculations began. I was impressed— they were within one barrow-full of their estimation.

At one point during the new bedding refill work, one of the boys quite unselfconsciously started to sing "I've been working on the railroad." I'm not even sure he was aware he was singing out loud!

While they were bringing in the last of the new bedding, I spread it evenly inside the coop and was surprised to find a rogue egg. It must have been laid in the outside pile of sawdust by one of my chickens and had survived the shoveling into the barrow by the boys, then the trip by barrow into the coop, and even the dumping onto the clean coop floor. One of the

A pretty little Rhode Island Red hen foraging in the garden.

boys asked if he could take this one home, and I told him he was welcome to it though I was not sure how he was going to keep it from breaking. I asked if he knew how to check if the egg was fresh, as we had no way of knowing how long it had been hidden. He didn't, so I explained that he should put it in water, and if it sank, it was still fresh.

After lunch, when I made hot chocolate and brought out cookies, we moved on to the fencing job. The boys walked the fence line and decided where upgrades were needed. We got to work digging down into the grass so we could place boards and other barriers where there were gaping holes. Again they had a raft of questions that showed me they were engaged with what they were doing, but they also made suggestions for how things could be done better and we tried them out.

While mending the fence, the boys got distracted by the chickens who quite easily convinced them that it was very important to stop digging each time a worm was discovered and feed it to them. Production came to a grinding halt as the boys fed the greedy girls by hand. But chickens are extremely serious about maintaining social order and the question of which one gets fed first is not to be taken lightly, so they gave the boys a first-hand lesson in chicken pecking order. The boys quickly picked up on the chickens' social graces, or apparent lack therof, and named one of the more boisterous chooks Miss Piggy.

When the day's end finally came, we washed up before I took them back to school. But they had one request before leaving: to play with the goats. Of course, the goats were always eager to welcome them into their paddock, to nibble at new people, their jackets, their hair, their ears, or to have a nice scratch from a human playmate. I was surprised that the boys remembered all the goats' names from their class trip to the farm a few weeks earlier, and they even got some correct when trying to identify which one was which. My husband couldn't even do that!

Preserving the Harvest and Generally Persevering

The pantry

ONE WAY TO MAINTAIN VARIETY in our diet was to process our own food more elaborately. The following list of our pantry's contents will demonstrate this. This list may seem exhaustive as well as exhausting—it was. This is partly because we in the pampered West have grown accustomed to a global diet and my husband and I wanted to maintain a certain level of *haute cuisine*, but it was also because I enjoy cooking Mexican, Greek, and both South Asian and West Indian foods. As well, I want things to taste just right. I found myself thinking about Helen and Scott Nearing, the famous American pioneers of organic gardening. Their first book, *Living the Good Life* (1954), is generally considered the major spur behind the American back-to-the-land movement of the 1960s. They were a great example of people managing to achieve personal food sovereignty even in the agriculturally unwelcoming climate of New England, but it occurred to me that they probably never thought of making lavender jelly. And I know for certain that they didn't have homemade bread or gouda cheese!

Pantry contents (Winter 2008–9)

- pickles: sauerkraut, dilly beans, pickled beets, dill pickles, dilly carrots
- relishes: zucchini, Coney Island
- chutneys: spicy gooseberry chutney, chili piccalilli, apricot-apple, apricot
- salsa: tomato, zucchini

A full pantry represents hours of work as well as many days of good, healthy eating.

- jams: raspberry, raspberry-rhubarb, raspberry-lavender, strawberry, strawberry-rhubarb, tayberry, blackberry, apricot butter
- jellies: red currant, blackcurrant, lavender, grape
- syrups: blueberry, cherry
- canned preserves: pears, apricots, peaches, rhubarb, apple pie filling, apple sauce, salmon, chicken, turkey, beef, spaghetti sauce
- frozen foods: basil pesto, cherries, strawberries, blueberries, red currants, black currants, gooseberries, blackberries, cherry pie filling, basil, dill, cilantro, peas, snow peas, green beans, carrots, zucchini
- schnapps: redcurrant, blackcurrant, rhubarb and lemon juice concentrate
- wild crafted foods: red and blue huckleberries, salmonberries, stinging nettles, fiddlehead ferns. We could also have harvested mushrooms—pine, shaggy manes, morels, chanterelles—but as I don't like mushrooms, I didn't bother. They were part of my if-I-absolutely-had-to list.
- dried foods: zucchini, carrots, cabbage, jalapeno peppers, red peppers, tomatoes, apples, pears, cherries, mint, oregano, dill, thyme

Our dried cherries were worth their weight in gold.

- dairy products: yoghurt, ice cream, sour cream, cheese (Leicester, cheddar, cumin-Gouda, Gouda, parmesan, ricotta, haloumi, mozzarella, feta)
- frozen bread: true sourdough culture, whey bread (bread made from the whey leftover from cheese-making), and various breads in general
- lard: I learned how to render down the beef fat and froze it for future use—I planned to make soap with it.

While preparing all these foods, I learned that you cannot achieve personal food sovereignty on a shoe-string budget until you have established the infrastructure. For example, we invested $1,500 in two more fridges and freezers. We built a second barn to raise turkeys, which cost more than $20,000, and even then it was still not completely bear-proof! On top of those costs was all our home processing equipment, including:

- water bath canning equipment
- pressure canning equipment
- jars and lids
- milk pasteurizer
- crock pots for sauerkraut
- cheese-making inoculants and equipment (moulds, molds, thermometers and presses)
- gardening equipment (a never-ending list of necessities and/or replacements due to loss and breakage)
- fencing rails, posts, and wire
- hunting course, hunting licence, guns, bullets, gun-cleaning gear
- fishing rods, flies, tackle, waders, nets, boots

We also bought two Excalibur dehydrators to augment our food preservation options as I planned to dehydrate more food than I had in previous years. For one thing, it cut down on the need for storage space, which was at a premium in our small home. Perhaps more importantly from a preservationist point of view, in the long term dehydrated food would make us less dependent upon electricity for our sustenance. It is all well and good to keep things in a freezer, but if you lose power for more than a few days, you may lose a lot of your food as well.

Our first drying adventures were with fruit. We sliced apples and pears into rings and dehydrated them without sugar. I used the dried apples when making muesli and enjoyed the dried pears on their own, often scarfing them down while watching a movie. I found them to be a really sweet snack that kept my hands, at least, fooled into thinking I was eating potato chips.

As much as I loved our fresh black cherries, we simply could not eat all that our two old trees provided during their short ripe season, so I made cherry pie filling, froze some cherries fresh, and dehydrated the remainder until my fingertips were stained purple and I was sick of pitting them and listening to the dehydrator at work. This produced Ziploc bags brimming with wonderful instant cherry pie potential and several quarts of dried cherries to be enjoyed all winter long. A trip to the local health food store made me feel even better about these wizened wonders because I learned there that they were worth their weight in gold: a one-hundred-gram package fetched nearly $18 before tax. I decided that the way the stock market was going at the time, I was better off having my holdings in organic dried cherries than banking on the Dow to rise. And with prices like that, they really were fit for a queen—only a royal could afford to eat them!

I dehydrated zucchinis and carrots, and then realized that the addition of cabbage, peas and green beans would make a nice soup or stew mix. When I was feeling lazy or exhausted, I found it handy to reach for the dried veggies and toss them into a meat curry or stew while it cooked— no washing, chopping or slicing required. I barely needed to plan dinner with these bags on hand; I just needed to invent a soup or sauce to throw them into. What is more, they plumped up in the soups, stews and curries so well that anyone would have been hard pressed to tell (particularly with the carrots, tomatoes and zucchinis) that they were ever dehydrated.

Canned pears. I use these straight out of the jar for desserts as well as grinding them in a food processor to put into bread when making breakfast loaves.

I found my dehydrated vegetables to be some of the most rewarding of my processed foods. They made life and cooking easy, they looked fantastic in jars sitting on my counter, and every now and then I could be caught lovingly caressing them, stirring thoughts of summer!

When we first moved in, I thought that having meandering mint was a good idea, but it soon became a riotous spearmint grove among our blueberry bushes, so coppicing and dehydrating it became a time-consuming but necessary job. Still, the smell was nice while I picked blueberries, and the same aroma filled the house while it was processing. The resulting mint tea was much richer and fresher than any I had bought in stores, and the sealed plastic bags made great, light Christmas gifts for sending through the mail. One of my friends drinks green tea because it's good for her but looked forward to our Christmas package to sweeten the taste. Now if only I could convince the goats to eat it. Pre-seasoned meat, anyone?

Oregano is another herb I dried. Compared to store-bought, it was a different beast altogether. Mine retained so much colour and pungency that I was shocked at the difference when I put the jar up against the pallid, wheat-like colour of store-bought organic oregano. I wondered what had

Lavender jelly fit for a queen and pretty enough to sit in the window on display.

been done to the poor plant in processing to leave it so undernourished, and despite the fact it was organic, I immediately threw out the store's oregano in disgust.

The dehydrating machine came with a package of jerky seasoning, so in the interests of diversifying our food stores, we dehydrated some of our own chicken meat, trying three different strengths of seasoning. But the length of drying time was difficult to get right. Our tendency was to overdo it because I was concerned about food safety and spoilage. The meat texture of the first couple of batches was almost brittle, and only the dog appreciated them, but once we began to calibrate it more carefully, we began to enjoy the fruits of our labours.

By late autumn we had collected wild alpine strawberries, red and blue huckleberries, alpine blueberries, salmonberries and thimbleberries. We relied on our Norwegian neighbour to announce the berry seasons. "Dem burries are r-r-ready," he would proclaim at regular intervals, not once providing details about which of "dem burries" he was referring to. I was never sure whether he simply liked to draw out a conversation or whether he thought he was stating the obvious. Needless to say, I would have to probe further to see which he meant and if he would reveal a secret location where they might be found growing in abundance.

Saskatoon berries are also rumoured to grow wild in the Valley though we never found our own local patch and instead gathered them up in the Cariboo when we stayed at Arcona Haus Bed and Breakfast on our way to Williams Lake. Not being a fan of hiking for the sake of hiking, I began to plan our bush excursions around a season and a purpose: as the various berries came ripe, we became gatherers. But picking enough huckleberries to make a couple of pies takes ages because, not being bred for abundance like the garden varieties, they are spread very thinly on the bushes. I soon began to recognize the foliage and surroundings much more intimately, which as it turns out was a good thing because I also learned that the local bear population shared my interest in berries.

Once when we were picking red and blue huckleberries on the lower slopes of the Valley, I caught a movement out of the corner of my eye. It wasn't my husband. A black bear was approaching his berry patch, occasionally stopping to glean berries with his big black snout along the way. I started moving slowly downhill toward our truck, calling out to my husband as calmly as I could, "You might want to stop picking about now." Being from New Zealand, he had never seen a bear before, so I had no idea how he would react to it.

"Why?"

"Because I think we've got enough now," I said, still intent on not startling him. "We should start to move downhill from this patch—now."

"Why?" He sounded a little annoyed. "I haven't finished picking yet."

There was no way to soften the blow, so I said as calmly as possible, "Because there's a bear about twenty feet away and he's moving toward you." I don't know if it was his inexperience with bear behaviour or his phlegmatic self-control, but amazingly he did exactly the right thing.

"Oh," he responded quietly, and then began walking slowly toward me. Together we climbed into the truck, each still clutching a full pail of berries, and vacated the area. Once safely back home, we picked through our loot, painstakingly separating stems and bad fruit. I had always wanted to make a huckleberry pie, maybe from the association with Huck Finn or from its iconic value as the ultimate symbol of self-sufficiency, so I made a delicious huckleberry pie whose delicate taste we shared with enthusiastic friends. We froze the rest to make into a mixed wild berry jam some time in the fall when we had enough other varieties to warrant the process.

Whatever the product we made from wild berries, this wild gathering process had its own satisfying qualities: no input, no back-breaking stooping to the ground as we weeded, fenced, dug, fed and watered—just the readiness to observe, answer nature's call, and work with her rather than wrestle against her. Gathering like this, I could glimpse the truth of the anthropologist's observation that hunter-gatherer societies have an unusually large amount of free time to pursue activities other than survival. Many anthropologists also argue that evolving into agriculture was a wrong turn for humanity because we have not only lost this leisure time but have also been forced to clear forests and endlessly work and adulterate land in order to coax food out of it in the form of crops or domesticated livestock.

My first attempt at making salsa. The lid says Old El Paso but the contents are all mine.

Haute cuisine–style fast food

Often—and especially in late summer—by the time dinnertime came along I was too bushed to bother, so I decided I needed to have some "fast food" on hand. For me, that meant something that I could take out of the freezer, pop in the oven, and within half an hour or so be eating in a satisfying meal. Now when I say "satisfying," I do not mean some tasteless slog that will satisfy hunger, be incredibly nourishing and sit like a brick in my belly, the sort of food my grandmother would say "sticks to your ribs." That did not appeal to me. Instead, like Goldilocks, I wanted food that was just right, which meant leaning toward nouvelle cuisine. Since I'd had a good potato harvest, on the first too-wet-to-go-out day, I decided to make samosas for the freezer. As I found the time, I would later make perogies and cabbage rolls and freeze them, too. I also had two more five-gallon crocks of sauerkraut on the go and one of the crocks had a whole cabbage sunk into it.

This may sound like pretty stodgy fare but it's not, and here's why. The ingredients in my fast food were actually "slow food" fare: heritage vegetables, chickens and eggs, as well as beyond organically grown veggies (by that I mean original, un-co-opted, non-industrial organic) that were grown from open-pollinated seed, and home-fermented foods. For example, the potatoes that I used for the samosas were the Ozettes, the ancient variety of uniquely flavourful fingerling potato that I had harvested from Clarence's garden, and I used the fermented leaves of my sauerkraut cabbage for the cabbage rolls. That's the haute cuisine part of what could otherwise be quite stodgy fare because it made a world of difference in the flavour. All who have ever tried my cabbage rolls claim they are the best they'd ever had, and I have served them to some self-proclaimed experts. (We have many Germans, Swiss, Austrians and Norwegians in this corner of Canada!)

I had also been hoping to make spaghetti sauce from my own tomatoes, but that didn't happen, thanks to a late start on the construction of my greenhouse and an unprecedentedly poor summer. If I was going to have my own spaghetti sauce, I would have to admit defeat and order tomatoes. This was not how self-provisioning is supposed to go! Nevertheless, there were many uncontrollable variables to deal with, and I was at the mercy of Mother Nature and the whims of my soil.

In the late spring I had planted twenty-four tomato plants, some in the greenhouse and some outside, and sadly I had harvested exactly one ripe tomato. Gone are the days when I ever take a tomato for granted again! After going to the effort of clearing the sunny space in front of the house to plant tomato plants early, I was frustrated (to say the least) when they amounted to nothing. They were perfectly located in the sun, the soil was warm, and I had built a raised bed for them. They were well-fed (tomatoes like soil that is slightly acidic—around 6.0 to 6.8 pH), and they were well mineralized. Before planting I had looked up the needs of tomatoes and hand-catered to their every penchant: calcium delivered via ground oyster shell, magnesium through carefully doled out portions of epsom salts, well-rotted manure dug deep into the soil before planting. I diligently picked out the laterals, watered without getting their leaves wet, and yet still they refused to develop. It really wasn't their fault, I told myself, or mine—the summer was the wettest the Valley had experienced in sixty years.

Because I did not have a harvest of tomatoes and did not want to live without spaghetti sauce for the entire winter, my friend Jessica and I decided to buy seventy kilograms of tomatoes from our sole supermarket and make salsa and spaghetti sauce together. Jessica, however, got waylaid for a couple of days and some of the tomatoes began to go off. Knowing that tomatoes wait for no one, I decided to start the process myself: drying, roasting and making lasagna with on-the-spot-sauce. I got through about twenty pounds of them before being sick of slicing, preparing them for dehydrating, and catering to what seemed like each tomato's special needs in the dehydrator.

Over the course of a very long weekend, I prepared another fourteen kilograms for saucing by blanching, peeling, coring and chopping. On Sunday morning at eight I began cooking the prepared tomatoes. As this was my maiden voyage with our Back-to-Basics food strainer and sauce maker, while the tomatoes were boiling, I read the instructions, put the thing together and began saucing the cooked tomatoes. My friend Jessica joined me at mid-morning to take over the saucing job while I worked on the first pot of spaghetti sauce: washing, chopping, slicing, dicing and then sautéing the veggies. Once we got that first pot on the stove, we began dealing with the other three eleven-kilogram cases of tomatoes: wash, blanch, peel, core, slice, boil and strain through saucing contraption.

Several hours later, with two large pots of spaghetti sauce reducing on the stove, we found ourselves facing the last box and a half of tomatoes: blanch, chop, core, slice, blanch, chop, core, slice, breathe in, breathe out, blanch, chop, core, slice, rinse and repeat. As these last boxes were to be made into salsa, the saucing step was thankfully omitted. By 8:30 that night I was exhausted, and we still had not started the canning process. Jessica made two double batches of the salsa mixture, still uncooked, put it into pots and took them home to finish the processing job there. Meanwhile, I put a double batch of salsa on to boil and turned back to the spaghetti sauce, which was finally reduced enough to be transferred to jars and processed in the pressure canner. By midnight I had one lot of spaghetti sauce processed and one double batch of salsa water-bath-canned, and they were all now cooling on the counter.

The second lot of spaghetti sauce, sufficiently reduced at last, was still waiting to be processed so I put it in the pressure canner and turned on the stove timer. Exhausted, I collapsed on the couch and managed a few hours of sleep, hands still on fire from the hours of chopping jalapeno peppers. As I drifted off to sleep I made a mental note: *use gloves next time!* At 3:00 a.m., when the canner had cooled enough to be opened, I took the second batch out and set it on the counter beside the other batch.

The next morning I still had a single batch of salsa in the fridge waiting to be cooked and canned, and the dehydrator was still working away noisily on the kitchen table. The uncooked salsa, however, would have to be put on the proverbial back burner because I still had to deal with the fresh milk collected from Buttercup on Sunday, as I intended to pasteurize it and turn it into cheese. Then I had to get ready for a group of high school students who were coming to tour the farm at eleven. They were eager to see the animals and wanted to pet a goat or maybe catch a chicken.

Altogether I had seven 750-ml jars of spaghetti sauce as well as eight 650-ml jars of salsa sitting on my counter and three waiting to be processed while Jessica had the same. In addition, I had three quart jars of dehydrated "sun-dried" tomatoes on the counter and two quart jars of slow-roasted tomatoes in olive oil in the fridge. I had also made one batch of fresh spaghetti sauce for lasagna and ... that was it. This is what seventy kilograms of tomatoes had been reduced to!

When you buy a jar of fancy spaghetti sauce at the store, it will cost you $3 or $4, so those seven jars of sauce on my counter were worth between $21 and $28, yet at $1 a pound, I had spent about $30 just on the tomatoes that went into them. In the economic sense, I hadn't broken even on the tomatoes, and I hadn't even factored in the cost of the other ingredients or the propane used in the cooking process, let alone the hours of labour we put into the job. As I looked at my beautiful jars of spaghetti sauce and contemplated what it would take to grow sufficient tomatoes to keep us in sauce alone, I was overwhelmed. If I had to do it over, I thought, I would use Roma tomatoes (or any dry type of tomato) to shorten the reducing time. I might even try dehydrating them slightly before beginning.

It was a great lesson in time management and I began rethinking the idea of delegating some of the work. In future I would grow just a few plants with the intent of producing enough tomatoes for fresh use. I realized that fresh tomatoes, like zucchini flowers, were not something I was destined to have access to year-round, and I would cherish them accordingly when I did. If and when I needed tomato sauce, I would leave the bulk efforts and canning to other producers. After all, like giving away the milking job to an area farmer, it would free up my time to concentrate on other tasks. Not only did I not have enough land to do the job or the growing conditions to produce decent tomatoes easily, I certainly didn't have the energy to keep up that kind of canning marathon in order to look after our tomato sauce needs in perpetuity.

Calling for reinforcements

As the end of the growing season approached, I came to the realization that I had probably planted my wheat crop a little late in the season. It was September 23 and snow was beginning to creep relentlessly down the nearby mountainside toward my precious Seager Wheeler wheat. When the weather started to turn sour and rain was in the forecast—something wheat does not like in its later stages of development—rather than risk it all to the elements, I decided to run an experiment: cut some of it and see if it would ripen up as it dried. I hoped that if I hung the wheat stalks, the seed heads would mature a bit more and form viable seeds, just as mature tomatoes will ripen if you uproot them and leave them on the vine.

Since the wheat patch was an experiment to begin with, there was not a vast field to harvest, and instead of a combine harvester the size of a small restaurant, I took my scissors and bucket out to the patch and began to reap. I decided to cut half the patch and let the rest go in the hope that the weather might clear. My wheat was soon drying (amidst several other items needing attention) on my kitchen bench. Although the year's experiment yielded somewhat less than enough for a loaf of bread, I was better prepared for the next spring, and I felt happily connected to another part of Canadian agricultural history two provinces away. Mr. Wheeler's success had once been used to lure immigrants to Canada, so I felt I'd inherited a precious family jewel, and it was satisfying to replicate it and carry on that pioneer spirit. But because my wheat harvest had been minimal (to say the least), I realized I was going to have to buy flour if we were going to enjoy bread, muffins and pancakes during the winter. I was disappointed that we wouldn't be milling our own wheat, but we decided we could still have the opportunity to learn how to mill flour by buying whole wheat kernels.

An important aspect of food security and personal food sovereignty is having access to seed. Obtaining my wheat kernels was, therefore, important in terms of securing sufficient seed for the next year's planting. Since I had used the Marquis 10B from the Seager Wheeler farm, I began my search by contacting them via their website and asking if they might sell me some more of the heritage wheat. When I had no response, I began looking further afield for a source of Red Fife, another Canadian heirloom wheat, organically raised if possible. Surprisingly, it did not take long to find a supplier on the Internet. The Loiselle Organic Family Farm in Vonda, Saskatchewan, grows it organically on their biodynamic farm, and through a link on their website, I found a source in British Columbia. True Grain Bread in Cowichan Bay Village had whole wheat kernels in twenty-five-kilogram bags. I phoned to see if I could order some.

"Of course! Just come on down to the store," said Bruce, the owner.

"Well, that's easier said than done," I told him. "It's a thirteen-hour drive from here to Horseshoe Bay, never mind the drive to Cowichan from the ferry dock on your side of the strait!"

But this was only a minor obstacle to Bruce, the owner. He not only shipped me the wheat but also did all the legwork for me. He contacted the post office, advised me of the cost of shipping, put the wheat in the mail and didn't cash my cheque until I confirmed that I had received the wheat! This sort of over-and-above-the-call-of-duty service is warmly appreciated. I was also pleased by Marc's email response from the Loiselle Organic Family Farm because, despite getting the wheat from an entirely different source, he revealed its contemporary pedigree, adding another welcome layer of knowledge and an additional thread of personal heritage to the wheat I now owned. Marc wrote:

> That wheat [you have just bought] is part of the Red Fife we grew. It is actually a blend of five different lots of Red Fife from Saskatchewan ... from members of our Prairie Red Fife Organic Growers Cooperative. [Fifty] percent is 2006 and 2007 harvests from our farm, 24 percent is from the Wyatt farm at Canwood, 14 percent from the Schriml farm at Bruno, and 12 percent from St. Peter's Abbey (Benedictine monastery) at Muenster.

For me these layers and links to other farmers, friends, families and the "ghosts of farmers past" added a cultural, even a spiritual, dimension to farming. Now I was a part of those farms' living heritage.

The question now was how much wheat I would need for my family for a year. I had no idea. All I knew was that a loaf of bread takes four to five cups of flour—but how many wheat kernels does that take? And how many kilos of wheat does one need to sow over how much land for how much yield? Marc Loiselle again rose to the occasion:

> Sounds like a great project you have going! I've never had such a question about growing a certain amount for a year's supply. But, presuming that you want to grow enough for your food needs and have enough left over for a subsequent year's sowing, and are able to sow and harvest adequately, I suggest you could purchase a single 25 kg bag for example. If you sow half of it in good fertile soil with adequate spacing (30 lbs would sow about one quarter acre ... and save the other 30 lbs in case of need to resow due to natural disaster such as hail) and it grows well, you could anticipate harvesting up to approximately six bushels (360 lbs) and that is based on a good yield of twenty-five bushels/acre. A single bushel of harvested and clean wheat kernels would make seventy to eighty regular-sized loaves of bread. So you could do the math and sort of figure out what that would mean for you, especially if you had a family to feed, too.

So I did the math. Six bushels times seventy-five loaves equals four hundred and fifty potential loaves, which would be more than one loaf per day. As it happened, I had bought exactly twenty-five kilos from True Grain Bread, which according to Marc's calculations was about double what I needed for sowing the next year. That meant I could use half of it for bread-making purposes. Of course, this would likely not be enough to get us through to next year's harvest, so I would have to order another twenty-five kilograms, or maybe two, for our winter's supply for bread making.

The staff of life

During the long winter months that followed, I had time to do some baking and I broke open the bag of Canadian Heritage Red Fife Wheat sent to

Howling Duck Ranch's Whey Feather Bread

This recipe was inspired by the Italian Feather Bread with Whey from the book *Home Cheese Making* by Ricki Carroll. It is my favourite bread to make for everyday sandwiches and for soup, stew or curry dredging. The whey seems to give it a feather-like texture (hence the name, I suppose) even with the whole wheat flour, which is unusual. It is also extremely tasty. Make this bread the same day you make ricotta cheese (or any other cheese) and use the leftover whey.

Ingredients

• 2 cups lukewarm whey	500 ml
• 1 tbsp white sugar	15 ml
• 2 tbsp dry yeast	30 ml
• ¼ cup olive oil	60 ml
• 2 tsp salt	10 ml
• 3 cups organic whole-wheat flour (home-milled if possible)	750 ml
• 3 cups organic white flour (home-milled if possible)	750 ml
• cornmeal for sprinkling	
• one egg, beaten lightly	

Directions

1. In a large mixing bowl, combine the whey, the sugar and the yeast. Let stand until the yeast is dissolved and starting to bubble on the surface of the mixture.

2. Pour in olive oil and salt and stir.

3. Add the flours, one cup at a time, stirring vigorously and alternating the two types.

4. When you cannot stir any longer, turn the dough out onto a floured surface and continue mixing and kneading the rest of the flour into it until it is a nice dough consistency. Note that the amount of flour will vary depending on the flour textures. Some hold more water than others, so vary amounts accordingly.

5. When the dough is soft and smooth, cover with a cloth and let it rise for about 30 minutes.

6. Butter a baking sheet (or if you prefer, 2 loaf pans) and sprinkle it with cornmeal.

7. Place the loaf on the sheet (or cut in half and place in pans), brush with beaten egg, slash with a knife if a free-form loaf, and let rise until double in bulk, about 1 hour.

8. Preheat oven to 425° F (218°C).

9. Bake for 30–45 minutes, or until the loaf is a rich, golden colour and makes a hollow sound when you tap the top with your fingers.

10. Cool on rack and serve warm.

me by Bruce at True Grain Bakery in Cowichan Bay. Since I did not yet own a wheat grinder, I had to improvise so I talked my coffee grinder into doing double duty. It would only take about a third of a cup of wheat berries at a time and needed frequent breaks in order to make up the two or three cups of flour I needed for the recipe. I ground the wheat roughly and then put it in a loosely woven sieve, repeating the process with the leftovers from sifting (the tailings, I like to call them) each time until something akin to flour was left in the bowl. The consistency was much coarser than the stone-ground whole wheat you buy at the store, but I used it anyway.

I almost always use a bread maker and set it on the dough cycle. It keeps the majority of the bread-making mess inside the machine, makes for an easy cleanup job and has the added benefit of making dough while I continue to write or address other items on my ever-burgeoning to-do list. I made three loaves, each with a different amount of the freshly milled flour. For the first I used only 1 cup of the fresh grind and three cups of white; for the second I beefed up the amount of the whole wheat to two cups with two cups of white, and for the third I used three cups of whole wheat to only one cup of the white. When David got home, we did a taste test and agreed that the best of the three loaves was the half-and-half one made with two cups of the white and two of the fresh-ground wheat flour. It had risen nearly as high as the first loaf but had a much more interesting texture and robust—yet rustic—flavour.

The third loaf was decidedly heavy. It had a nice flavour, to be sure, and was really good for dredging the final depths of our soup bowls, but it didn't pass the "butter only" test as well as the second loaf, which had a gorgeous crusty outside and generous chewy inside. It was the best loaf of bread I ever made and possibly the best one I ever tasted. Now if only I could be guaranteed to replicate it every time!

I couldn't get over how different the fresh wheat tasted. I had been told by others that there is nothing like milling your own wheat and baking bread with it, but I had no idea. If you are a bread fan, then you owe it to yourself to give it a go. Like me, you may never go back.

Yeast wrangling 101

Several years earlier, while I was still living in New Zealand, I had wanted to learn more about bread so I took virtually every bread-making and bread baking book out of the local library. One stood out: *The Bread Builders* by Daniel Wing. Its exquisite illustrations provided tantalizing glimpses of faraway places and evoked the smell of baking breads and the heady aromas of wood-fired ovens. But while that book got my mouth watering and my imagination travelling, the book that intrigued me the most was called *Classic Sourdoughs: A Home Baker's Handbook* by Ed Wood because it taught me the basics of yeast wrangling. Wood skilfully describes the art of developing a true sourdough culture, how to feed it, ways to preserve it, and how to use it artfully. Unlike today's more popular version—the

Bread making involves waking up the yeast by bringing the brew to room temperature and feeding it some fresh flour and water.

kind that begins with store-bought yeast and adds sugar and vinegar—the true sourdough culture dates back to ancient Egypt, and Wood explains that back in 1993 he had collaborated with Egyptologist Dr. Mark Lehner to determine how the first leavened bread had been made by the ancient Egyptians. Then, having become a passionate collector of sourdoughs, he founded Sourdoughs International, a company that collects, maintains and sells sourdough cultures from around the world.

His book contained a host of wonderful recipes to work my way through on my journey to becoming a bread builder. "Once you have caught your true sourdough," Wood explains, "you need never go to the store to buy yeast again." That kind of knowledge is a cornerstone in the foundation of true independence—I had to try it.

It turned out to be shockingly simple. Mix water and flour in a bowl, cover with gauze to protect from flies, set near an open window, keep warm, feed often. *Voilà*! Within days I had a bubbling concoction that smelled exactly as you would expect a yeasty brew to smell: like yeast, with light undertones curiously reminiscent of a beer burp. A couple of weeks into this mild-mannered process I had a viable sourdough culture.

My next step, of course, was to see if it actually raised bread. Wood warns his readers that it may take a few weeks, sometimes several months, of keeping the culture alive before it will make a good bread. In the meantime, he advises, use the part of the product that you pour off when feeding the culture to make pancakes and muffins. So I did. If you like sourdough pancakes but have never caught a true sourdough culture, then you have never truly had sourdough pancakes. These pancakes were fantastic, the tastiest I'd ever made. And it was not long before I was brave enough to try making my first loaf of bread with my own sourdough culture. I started with a focaccia because if it didn't rise really well, perhaps no one would notice. I need not have worried because it worked beautifully. It was gorgeous, the air pockets well-formed and uneven just like the better bread from bakeries. I was immediately hooked.

I began to scoff at the regular store-bought yeast for bread making, and I resolved to use my own yeast to make everything—breads both sweet and savoury, muffins, pancakes, even chocolate cakes!

After about a year of using my own culture, I contacted Ed Wood from my home in Rotorua, New Zealand, and let him know how much I appreciated his book and how wonderful my culture was. He was intrigued enough to ask me to send him a sample, which he subsequently put through his testing kitchen in Idaho. He was very happy with the results and said he

Howling Duck Ranch's Rotorua Sourdough Bread

You will need some Rotorua Sourdough Culture, which you can purchase from Sourdoughs International. (See their website at www.sourdo.com.) Of course, you can catch your own sourdough culture by following the directions in Ed Wood's book, *Classic Sourdoughs: A Home Baker's Handbook*, which not only tells you how but also has amazing recipes to use with your sourdough culture once you've got it going. And once you have your culture, it can be kept alive for generations. It will get better with age and become part of your family tradition and heritage each time you divide and share it.

San Francisco is well known for its sourdough bread. At the bread bakery on Fisherman's Wharf they make the loaves small and cut the centres out to form bowls. You can order thick soups or chili in one of these bread bowls and use the top and the scooped-out innards for dipping and dredging.

I love this recipe because, if I make it using only white flour, it is close to, if not better than, San Francisco sourdough, and I don't have to travel there to get it! However, I generally include whole wheat flour because I like the added nutrition and the taste is equally heavenly, if slightly more rustic.

Wet ingredients

• 1½ cups Rotorua sourdough culture	375 ml
• 1 cup lukewarm water (or fresh whey from cheese making)	250 ml
• ½ tsp dry active yeast	2.5 ml

Dry ingredients

• 3 cups organic unbleached flour	375 ml
• ¾–1 cup fresh-ground whole wheat flour	175–250 ml
• cornmeal for sprinkling	
• 1 egg, beaten	

Directions

1. Pour sourdough starter and warm water into a large mixing bowl, sprinkle yeast on top and let it sit for 2 or 3 minutes.

2. Add the flours 1 cup at a time, starting with the white flour and then alternating. Stir vigorously while incorporating the flour.

3. When you cannot stir it any longer, turn the dough out onto a floured surface and continue mixing and kneading the rest of the flour into it until it has a nice doughy consistency. Note that the amount of flour may vary depending on the texture of your flours. Some hold more water than others, so be flexible with the amounts and vary accordingly.

4. When the dough is soft and smooth, turn it into a lightly oiled bowl and cover with plastic wrap. Let it rise for 3 or 4 hours or until nearly doubled in volume. I like to rise my bread dough in a warm oven. I let the oven temperature rise to its lowest reading then turn it off. I place a jelly roll pan on the bottom rack and fill it with water, then place the covered bread dough on the top rack, turn the oven light on, close the oven door and let it sit undisturbed for 3 hours or more. This system helps to keep the dough from drying out on top.

5. When the dough has risen to double its bulk, punch it down and turn it out onto a lightly floured work surface.

6. Sprinkle a baking sheet or pizza stone with cornmeal.

7. Gently pull and stretch the dough into a round loaf. Place the loaf on the sheet (or cut in two and place in pans), brush the loaf with beaten egg, slash with a knife if a free-form loaf (traditionally, San Francisco sourdough has a hash mark pattern on top), and place it back in the warm oven to rise until double in bulk, about 1–1½ hours.

8. Heat the oven to 425°F (218°C).

9. Place the loaf in the centre of the middle rack of the oven. Spritz the loaf with water and then spritz the oven walls quickly so as not to lose oven heat. This will give the crust that chewy texture that is the trademark of the classic San Francisco sourdough.

10. Bake for 40 to 45 minutes or until the loaf is a rich golden colour and it makes a hollow sound when you tap the top with your fingers.

11. Cool on rack.

I love this bread served with butter while it is still slightly warm. Yum-m-m!

was surprised at how well it performed, so he offered to buy it from me in exchange for permission to sell it to others. "You are not going to get rich off this," he said, laughing, but he offered me a sometime-in-the-future commission—"Once I've made some sales."

When I returned to Canada, I was really glad to have made that "deposit" with Ed Wood at Sourdoughs International because I had not been able to bring my Kiwi yeast back home with me, and the yeast that I caught in Bella Coola was, to put it mildly, lazy. I could not raise a decent loaf of bread with it to save my life, a fact I found quite upsetting in light of the fact that the Valley is so close to the Alaska Panhandle, as Alaskan sourdough pancakes have a certain rustic cache that true connoisseurs appreciate. After about a year of unsuccessful Bella Coola yeast wrangling and frustrated bread making, I gave in and contacted Ed Wood again. He kindly sent me a package of my Kiwi yeast starter. It was like having my own slow-food Ark of Taste or a private vault from which I could access my own heritage food!

The tough realities of food sovereignty

Back in New Zealand I had acquired a flock of chickens made up of an assortment of hand-me-downs and general cast-offs that were all very good at free-ranging for their own food and generally looking after themselves. All I provided was safe housing and water. We were building a house at the time, and Ian, one of the contractors, not only kept chickens but also showed them. I had never heard of such a thing but was curious enough to ask about the ins and outs of showing chickens. As well as giving us the grand tour of his chicken facility, he gave us a "chicken starter kit" of some of his less than show-perfect stock. He was getting out of that particular breed and was happy to let them go to a good home.

By that time he had been showing chickens for years and he related to us a charming, self-deprecating story of his first attempts. As a newcomer to this exciting world, he began with Leghorns, the only breed he knew. He bought a breeding pair, built them suitable housing and a run, and proceeded to take great care in feeding them, talking to them and paying them an inordinate amount of loving attention. Eventually he began to breed some of his own, and when it was time to go to his first show, he hand-selected two of what he thought were his most beautiful chickens, a cock and a hen that had been lovingly incubated and hand-raised. Both were plump and well plumed with gorgeous yellow legs.

At the show he stood proudly displaying his stock, but when the judges came to appraise them, he was shocked when some of them snickered and generally looked down their noses at his birds. He was dismayed when his chickens came in last. He had failed to check the conformation guidelines for Leghorns: legs were to be white! What Ian had considered a charming attribute was in fact a show-stopping conformational fault.

"And you know what?" he told us in horror. "Some breeders go so far as to bleach their chicken's legs to make them whiter before a show!"

Fast forward seven years to when the Howling Duck Ranch also acquired a bunch of hand-me-down, cast-off chickens. I wasn't worried about their lack of pedigree: I was quite happy to see them interbreeding and always fascinated to see how the chicks turned out. Consequently, we ended up with all sorts of shapes and sizes, and because I wasn't paying attention to breed conformation, it was inevitable that eventually one with yellow legs would appear.

Yellow Legs, as we appropriately called him, was a very striking bird. My husband—who had forgotten all about how Ian had been the laughing stock of the New Zealand chicken breeders' show—loved him. Night after night, David would return to the house after putting them to bed and wax lyrical about his beauty: "He's got these really beautiful yellow legs." I would then remind him of Ian's story, but he was undeterred.

Inevitably, Yellow Legs became one of the stars of our farm. Watching him walk, I would coo with each step he took, "Yellow ... legs ... yellow ... legs ... yellow ... legs." Sometimes I pretended to be the rooster himself: "Yellow ... legs ... yellow ... legs ... David likes my ... yellow ... legs." As it got closer to slaughter time, my voice changed intonation and I would chant to my husband as if Yellow Legs were trying to make a case for himself: "I'm Yellow Legs, Yellow Legs! Save me now, I'm Yellow Legs!"

Eventually friends were exposed to the drama and to Ian's background story, and Yellow Legs became a bit of a community legend. One day Carole and I were on a road trip to Williams Lake when an RCMP officer walked out in front of us. I found myself staring at the yellow stripe down his trousers, and beside me, without missing a beat, Carole suddenly blurted out, "Yellow legs, yellow legs, yellow legs," in time with his footfalls. I burst out laughing and hoped he didn't hear. How would I possibly explain?

Some time later that year, Carole and a host of others were at our house for dinner. I had placed a plateful of chicken on the table and people were helping themselves to it *al gusto*. I saw Carole pick up a drumstick, begin to devour it then suddenly burst out, "Oh my god!" The conversation came to an abrupt stop. Her hand, still holding the drumstick, was now poised at eye level over the centre of the table, demanding everyone's fullest attention. "Is this Yellow Legs?"

Taken aback, but not willing to lie, I admitted that somewhere on the plate among the pile of drumsticks were Yellow Legs' legs. Of course, I could not confirm that the one she was holding had indeed belonged to our show-stopping star. After a short pause of what could only be described as contemplative consideration, someone uttered a brief toast in honour of Yellow Legs. We all had a good laugh and continued eating. "Yellow legs, yellow legs, we all liked his yellow legs!"

Sadly, this conscious celebration of an animal's life was not the reaction that a farming colleague faced when she presented a sumptuous dinner of roast pork to her friends. She had raised and cooked it herself, but upon hearing that the pork had not been bought at the supermarket and had instead been one of the pigs they had "met" on a previous visit to the farm, her friends refused to eat and chose instead to take their meal at a local pub. And what did they order when they got there? Why, roast pork, of course.

The snubbed hostess, being much more polite than I, bit her tongue and did not reveal that she often supplied that pub with her own pork.

I had a similar, though less dramatic, experience while talking with a friend whom I had not seen in years about my homesteading work and my provisioning project.

He probed, "Are you growing your own veggies? How about wheat? Do you have fruit trees? What about protein?" Inevitably the conversation settled on the horrific revelation to a contemporary civilized person: "You mean you kill your own chickens!?"

"Yes, yes I do."

The tension mounted as the conversation took the obligatory tour through all-too-familiar terrain. "Oh, I could *never* kill an animal! Oh, those poor chickens (rabbits, cows, pigs, etc.)! How could you kill animals you know and then eat them?" And then there's my personal favourite: "You're not going to kill Bambi, are you?" All this from the mouth of a meat eater.

There are no moral lines in the sand to be drawn on this issue, only varying degrees of complicity and awareness. At one end of the spectrum are those who rejected the home-grown lunch in favour of a pig that was anonymously raised and slaughtered (and quite possibly factory-raised and processed under abysmal conditions) at the neighbourhood pub. At the other end are those who have chosen to walk the talk, the small land-holders who know first-hand just how intelligent, curious, funny—and yes, tasty—pigs, chickens, turkeys and cows can be.

In western cultures, animals such as serpents, cats, doves, lions, and (where I'm from) wolves, ravens, coyotes, eagles and so on were once honoured and looked upon as spiritual forces or god-like creatures. But agricultural peoples have never anthropomorphized the animals they worked with every day and then ate. Sure, the Hebrews told stories about sheep and goats, and the Greeks (think Aesop) told stories about hares and tortoises, and the First Nations told stories of raven, coyote and salmon, but only to illustrate important lessons and human concerns. The animals themselves were not sentimentalized into humanoids.

In Victorian England, however, under the influence of the Romantics' rediscovery of nature, animals in a new cuddly format were enlisted into a "cult of childhood." Since then, generations of children have grown up surrounded by humanized animals. Think of Kenneth Grahame's *The Wind in the Willows*, A.A. Milne's *Winnie the Pooh*, Beatrix Potter's *The Tale of Mrs. Tiggy-Winkle*, the legendary Brer Rabbit, Teddy Roosevelt's bear, the Forest Service's Smokey the Bear, E.B. White's *Charlotte's Web*, and the avatars from Looney Toons, Walt Disney and Pixar. We in the western world now have difficulty avoiding the anthropomorphized animal because it's everywhere, from cereal boxes to toilet paper.

On my farm I not only named a number of my animals but also anthropomorphized the heck out of them through my storytelling. I certainly didn't make a habit of naming every one of them, but it sometimes just happened, Yellow Legs being a good example. But the old adage that you cannot eat an animal that you have named is almost true, and I note that the ones I named were frequently those that were to be kept as breeding stock or egg layers and not destined for eating. However, I was able to eat animals such as Yellow Legs because I was aware of the hypocrisy and pernicious sentiment of any other option. None of this detracts from the wonderful fact that these animals gave me joy when they were alive. I watched them all, and by observation I learned about their unique personalities, their likes and dislikes. Who knew that a chicken would have a personality, that turkeys are curious and intelligent, that a goat can have an eating disorder, that a dog would like morning coffee (so long as it was instant), or that a duck would mope for days after its mate was taken by a fox? It's ironic that this close observation closed the loop and made it more difficult for me to consume these animals, yet consume I must because the alternative was to go back to purchasing from the factory system. At the same time my new, intimate knowledge of farm animals and their personalities made me even more horrified at how animals are treated in corporate agriculture's factory systems.

In the case of my farming colleague whose friends turned their noses up at the food she presented to them, ostensibly because they "knew" the pig, I have to ask, "How hypocritical can you be?" Animals in agribusiness suffer terribly in life and in death, but unlike the gorillas of Burundi, the grizzlies of the Great Bear Rain Forest, or the baby harp seals of the

Canadian Arctic, they usually don't get publicity, sympathy or donations. Those people who might self-righteously have an owner arrested for the way he or she treats a dog are able to ignore or simply not respond to the concentration camp–like conditions behind the walls of intensive livestock operations. What are the criteria that put an animal into the food category rather than the pet category? What is it that makes a food animal like a pig into an animal that those friends refused to eat?

Eating is a political act. When I kill and eat the chicken that was happily grazing outside my door in the sun yesterday, I am keeping my ecological footprint small. I am also not supporting the corporate agricultural system, its innate animal abuse and its host of other social atrocities. Today few of us have the opportunity to know the animal that nourishes our bodies. Few of us even consider the animals we eat to be in the same category as bears, gorillas or baby harp seals. But we should: they are all animals worthy of the same ethical consideration and humane protection. If anything, our food animals deserve more from us. In the food factory system they are not allowed the freedom of a natural environment, their bodies are doctored by humans in many ways, their natural life cycle of reproduction and rearing young is denied, interrupted or distorted. Their sole purpose in life is to be turned into food. Knowing these facts should be the grounds for any ethical decision-making.

I wish I had been there when my friend's colleagues had ordered their pork lunch at the pub. I would have explained how their food was made, and I would have told them, "Knowing agriculture and its practices is a responsibility. It is our money that is supporting it so we should spend it consciously. How we spend it and the food we choose to eat has a direct influence on how agriculture is practised and ultimately how hundreds of thousands of animals are treated."

Perhaps one of them would have said, "What are you trying to do? Put us off our lunch?"

I would have proudly answered, "Yes."

With a bit of luck, we would all have ended up back at the hostess's table where they had started.

City Girl Gets a Gun

I'M A CITY GAL BORN AND RAISED, and for most of my life have been utterly dependent upon the grocery store for my sustenance. So why on earth would I want to learn to hunt? Before living on the ranch and committing myself to self-provisioning, I'd never really thought about learning to hunt. In fact, I was once appalled by the idea of hunting. However, at the same time as I was leaving the world of vegetarianism behind me and recommitting to being a carnivore, I realized that we must respect the animals we cull for food, and that includes understanding and respecting the quality of life and necessary death of those animals. It also became clear to me that unless I could resign myself to eating only home-grown chicken or getting the nerve up to kill and eat one of my beloved goats, I was going to have to learn to hunt.

This fact left me with an overwhelming challenge: how would I learn to hunt? I was not raised around guns or with hunters. Until moving to the Valley, I'd never even known a hunter. Then I met Clarence. When I asked him to teach me he smiled broadly and said, "Hey, my dear, I'd love to." Not only was he thrilled to teach me but his family was also generous enough to supply me with the necessary support equipment and provisions. My first step, he explained, was to get a licence, so I signed up for the Firearms Acquisition Licensing course and the Conservation and Outdoor Recreation Examination (CORE), which, as it turns out, were just the first steps in a long line of necessary steps.

After completing my CORE, I waited patiently for my certificate to arrive in the mail, and when it finally showed up, I thought I was ready to go hunting. Not so. I had to go to the government agent in Bella Coola in order to get my hunter number, which would allow me to purchase my actual hunting licence. The government agent explained that she, too, didn't quite understand why there was a two-step system in order to get a licence, but she did laugh and say, "At least the number is free." For the actual licence I would have to pay, but I was pleased to discover that I could also purchase my hunting licence and species tag from her, although first I must fill out another whole set of papers. Finally I became the proud owner of a hunter number, a hunting licence and a mule deer species tag, all for the price of about $50. This did not include the money for the Firearms Acquisition Licensing course and Conservation and Outdoor Recreation Exam.

I also learned from the government agent that Canadian residents have to put their names into a lottery for what is called a limited entry hunting species tag (LEH tag). Non-residents simply fill out the requisite paperwork, sign on the dotted line and pay for the privilege of hunting whatever they want to hunt. Killing a grizzly bear, for instance, is worth about $1,100 plus GST, but having just filled out a mountain of paperwork for my licence, I doubted that the non-resident licence fee would even cover the cost of the paperwork involved in applying for it. This prompts the question, how much is the life of a Canadian bear or moose or wolf worth? Are we classifying these animals in the same category as such primary products as wood, oil or gas and selling them at bargain basement prices? Why do we not allow everyone to buy their way into a species hunt? The present system is cumbersome, inequitable and illogical.

It was too late for me to get an LEH tag that season, but I still hoped to get an actual hunting date nailed down with my coach, Clarence, a consummate bushman whose ease with the natural world shone through his every action and observation. He had also been the Valley's "cougar man" for more than forty years. Whenever a cougar was spotted where it shouldn't be—close to a home watching children on a swing set, or in a yard after having killed a dog—it was Clarence who our community turned to.

He already had his moose tag and was ready to hunt one moose between November 1 and 15. He gave me my first shooting lesson in his backyard using his 30-06.

"Aw, I'd just love to see you get your first moose!" he said excitedly as he handed me the rifle.

Apparently he thought we should start with moose. I, on the other hand, had been thinking grouse, but the look on his face when I suggested it said everything.

"Well then, Clarence, could we maybe start with a deer first?"

Once I shot off a few rounds, he went to check my accuracy. "Dead centre, six o'clock low," he said cryptically while walking back to me. As I watched him cross the muddy and uneven field effortlessly, I began to worry about how well I would keep up with him in the bush.

The following week Clarence was planning to go to "The Lake," by which the residents of Bella Coola mean Williams Lake (population 14,000), 458 kilometres to the east. It is the home of our nearest stoplight as well as all sorts of goodies that are otherwise unobtainable in Bella Coola—like Tim Hortons doughnuts. So for us, a trip to Williams Lake was a big deal. I asked Clarence if I could go with him to buy a gun suitable for deer and moose hunting and, if necessary (God forbid), for bear defence.

Then, because I knew next to nothing about guns, hunting or general bush safety, I called a friend, Gary Shelton, who is an avid hunter, ex-hunting guide, international expert on survival techniques and bear behaviour, bush safety instructor extraordinaire and renowned author. His books include *Bear Encounter Survival Guide* and two volumes of *Bear Attacks*. I asked him what kind of gun I should get to meet my needs.

"What you're going to need is something that will not only shoot a deer or moose but also be a bear defence weapon," he said. We talked about safety issues, my requirements as well as types and styles of guns, and he gave me a couple of options that he considered suitable for my requirements. One particularly helpful suggestion was that, whatever I got, I should have its stock cut down to match my diminutive size.

Being a natural teacher, Gary also talked about things to consider when hunting in the bush, and all of them had to do with safety. He told me how the parameters of hunting have shifted in the last twenty years and described some of the changes in the legislation with respect to the hunting and culling of animals, the result of which was an increase in the numbers of bears, particularly in our area. He explained that, according to Tony Hamilton, the province's carnivore specialist, the Bella Coola Valley's bear population had reached the point of saturation. Hamilton estimated there were sixty resident grizzlies within the Valley, a figure that probably rose to more than a hundred in the late summer and fall when the salmon runs drew bears from nearby areas. Of course, I wasn't surprised at this news. I had been seeing bears or evidence of bears on a daily basis.

"Because of the sheer increase in the bear population," Gary pointed out, "your chances of running into one have also increased significantly. Not only that, far more of them are no longer afraid of humans. This makes the situation more dangerous than it used to be when the bears feared humans. Historically, bears would run away when they came across a man in the bush. Now they don't leave the area just because you show up, and what is worse, some of them are becoming habituated to humans and now see them as a source of food, either directly by predating upon them or, if the bear has campsite or garbage dump experience, indirectly through their garbage."

Gary then praised the bushman skills and hunting prowess of my friend Clarence but added, "You and Clarence should have your bear defence strategy all worked out beforehand."

Pardon me, I thought, but did you say *beforehand*? Apparently a bear defence strategy was just part of a lunch list, like "don't forget your sandwiches and take some water with you. Oh, and remember to bring along your bear defence strategy. You won't want to be without that if you get hungry." I asked him what our bear defence strategy should look like and almost regretted the question immediately.

"One of you should be the lead, and this should be the more experienced person. The less experienced person should be prepared to follow the lead person's direction. The back-up person is exactly that—the back-up who's ready to follow the lead person's orders. During a bear encounter, the second person should move ninety degrees to one side of the lead person—about six or seven feet to the side—so if the need to shoot is determined, neither of you are in the other's line of sight. The lead person will make the call if there is a need to shoot, when to shoot, and if and when the back-up person should chamber a round."

In other words, I thought, this lead person will gallantly step aside, calmly watch the horror unfold, and after a quiet but complex calculation turn to his back-up and say, "Shoot." Meanwhile, the back-up will have moved into position, squared off with the bear and be poised to shoot, waiting only for the signal. Oh, and if necessary, this person should shoot well, for the love of god, *and* definitely accurately because the last thing you want on your hands is a wounded and therefore even angrier bear!

"It's important that your plan is discussed before going into the woods," Gary continued. "It's no use starting to discuss it once the bear encounter situation has begun. The lead person will make the decision whether or not there is a need for a defence based on the behaviour of the bear. This is very important because there will be bear encounter situations that never require anyone to shoot the animal. Of course, each situation will be

Sighting in my Remington .280 before the hunt. Photo David Dowling.

different, and just because you have a plan doesn't mean the event will unfold precisely how you imagine it. The above description is, of course, the ideal."

That is, I thought, if you can call any bear defence situation ideal!

"However," Gary went on, "there may be a situation where you can't move to the side. In that case, the back-up person will not chamber a round. Under no circumstances should a back-up person or anyone standing behind another person chamber a round—that's simply too dangerous."

Oh. My. God. These were not things I had considered when I committed myself to learning to hunt, nor were they things Clarence had ever talked to me about. I had presumed that if we came across a bear—or any dicey situation, for that matter—it would be Clarence's job to deal with it. My job would be to try not to pee myself, faint or become hysterical and run rough-shod through the forest, prompting a merry little chase in which the bear would, no doubt, participate lustily.

"So," I asked Gary, not sure I wanted to hear the answer, "will you recommend a gun that's sufficient for this?" After he listed the various merits of the guns he was recommending and why, as politely as possible I pressed him for a more precise answer. "Well (*for the love of God!*), which of the ones you have suggested is better for a bear defence situation?"

"Let me put it this way," he said matter-of-factly, "when a bear defence situation goes down, you're going to wish you both had bazookas!"

So besides needing to pick up a bazooka, another reason I wanted to join Clarence on his trip to Williams Lake was for the hunting prospects. Our nearly one-thousand-kilometre round trip through the best hunting territory in the province would provide us with ample chance to hunt on the way back home. When I relayed these thoughts to Clarence, he corrected me in no uncertain terms.

"What do you mean on the way back? My dear, we'll hunt both ways." His thumb motioned away from the centre of his chest toward the middle distance and then back again for emphasis, solidifying the plan right there in my driveway. "I'll lend you my 22-250 for the trip out. It's big enough to bring down a mule deer."

As it happened, we did not get away as early as intended so the hunting on the way out was limited to looking for animals from the comfort of the vehicle. We drove along slowly, more intent on spotting game or game tracks than actually getting to Williams Lake, and as we wended our way up "The Hill," our eyes were fixed on the snow on either side of the road.

"I don't like what I'm not seeing," Clarence muttered over and over, speaking more to the goddesses of the ungulates than to me. There was nary a deer nor moose track to be seen, though we spotted all sorts of predator tracks—wolf, coyote and fox. This is not to say we didn't see any animals at all. Before leaving the Valley, we met a big boar grizzly bear at the usual pee stop at the bottom of "The Hill"—the precise place where I had seen a mother sow and two cubs several weeks earlier. When I got out of the truck to pee, I watched the boar grazing just about fifty yards away across the road from me and I wondered if he might be the father of the cubs of my previous relief there. I stayed close to the truck and never took my eyes off the griz. Suffice it to say, you learn to pee fast around here.

As we drove on, we spotted a couple of foxes making their way into the forest. There were numerous snow geese and other waterfowl, even a few beavers. The most exciting moment, however, came as we were approaching Riske Creek village. As a big cat came up the incline on our left-hand side, I saw him first and called out, "Cougar, cougar, cougar!" and watched him leap from one side of the highway to the other, touching down only once. It was a beautiful sight and only the second cougar I'd seen in my life, the first being in my driveway early one summer morn.

I was anxious to see what the tracks looked like so we stopped the truck, got out and asked the earth to reveal the missing parts of the story. The prints from the cougar's take-off position were clearly marked, and he had touched down only once, almost perfectly on the centre-line of the road. Where he'd landed on the other side of the pavement his tracks were just as clear.

"Why, that cougar was moving!" Clarence exclaimed, then pointed at another set of tracks in the sand. "Look here! He was in hot pursuit of a deer."

There were lots and lots of deer tracks on either side of the cougar's prints, going both ways across the highway, but the ones right in front of the cougar's were very fresh. As Clarence made sense of the story, something took hold of him and he decided he wanted to track the cougar right then! The next thing I knew, he was talking about going back to get his son and their dogs, about how the dogs would be onto that cougar in a flash, about how cougars don't have the wind to run very far, about how it would likely tree very quickly in this country, about where he would place a shot if given the chance, about how he'd placed other shots at cougars past, about how exciting it would be for him to see me get my first cougar.

The more excitedly he talked, the more I needed to pee. It was beginning to sound like I was going to be hunting a cougar any minute and I wasn't prepared, emotionally or otherwise. I certainly wasn't comfortable with the picture of myself running behind Clarence in hot pursuit of this cougar, struggling to keep up and maintain composure. I didn't want to be walking deep into these rapidly darkening woods in the paw-prints of the cougar, knowing I may never again see Williams Lake, let alone my husband—or our farm.

Fortunately, in the middle of my panic-stricken reverie, Clarence finally worked his way around to sound reason. It was, after all, getting dark, he didn't have his dogs, his son was busy preparing for a moose hunt, and he himself was on his way to Williams Lake to go shopping with a greenhorn.

"I might have to come back with my son," he admitted.

Gee, ya think? But, while I had not been thrilled with the idea of spending the evening rummaging around the Chilcotin Plateau hoping to tree the cougar, it had been nonetheless interesting to have the earth give up the cougar's secrets even if only for a short distance. As we approached Williams Lake, we finally did see some deer—all of them does. We stopped counting at fifteen. They were beautiful, but does are not legal game. Nevertheless, my hunting partner reminded me, where there are does, there are also stags!

At the gun shop the next day I decided upon a Remington 700 series .280 rifle. (Later, back home, Gary approved my choice and listed off the various merits the gun store salesman had not revealed.) Now, I thought, I'm equipped to go hunting. We had planned to head back to Bella Coola that day, but over coffee and a Tim Hortons doughnut, Clarence announced

Fresh wolf tracks in the snow. The front feet are nearly as large as my hand.

that we would spend an extra night in Williams Lake and leave early in the morning to have a full day's hunting on the way back. No sense in leaving late in the day. No sense in travelling rushed. That would just cramp our hunting style. That would be no good, no good at all.

We got away early the following morning and enjoyed meandering our way home, stopping again and again in search of game. On foot we covered a lot of ground that Clarence was very familiar with and a bunch of ground he wasn't, but even though we were well and truly off the beaten path, we found no sign of deer or moose. Instead we spotted nearly everything else: foxes, coyotes, beavers, martins, muskrats, geese, squirrels, and more cougar prints in the snow. It was a great learning experience to find the different tracks, try to identify them and have my guesses confirmed or corrected by Clarence. While the whole experience was fascinating to me, Clarence didn't really get excited until we came upon fresh wolf tracks.

Suddenly, the *raison d'être* of the hunt shifted—we were now focussed on getting ourselves a wolf. Clarence immediately stopped talking and switched to sign language. "But I don't want to shoot a wolf," I whispered, looking into the face of utter bewilderment itself. Why not proved to be too difficult to explain in sign language, so at that moment I decided it would be easier to simply go along and hope we didn't catch up with the wolf. We followed one set of tracks alongside the road to where the wolf had peed on a sapling, which was demonstrated by three footprints around its base. Close by we found another set of prints coming toward us. There was clearly a reunion here. We tracked both pairs until Clarence observed the dwindling daylight. I was more than content to stop tracking and take photos, relieved it was not photos of an ex-wolf but instead evidence of its existence.

Clearly my first opportunity to hunt for a food animal would have to come at another time.

The only thing to fear ...

Later that month Clarence and I headed up the Valley on what was to be my first fully planned hunting trip, and that trip provided me with Clarence's hunting history: "That's where we shot a bear ... Over there we tracked a cougar ... My son shot his first buck in that field right over there ..." The monologue was interrupted only because Clarence decided to stop at Gary Shelton's place to discuss his malfunctioning gun. Gary's opinion was that while it could still be used safely, a gunsmith was required to restore its original mechanism.

As we left, Gary commented on our destination, "By the way, you know that Snowshoe Creek is where that hunter was attacked last spring by a grizzly sow?"

"Oh, I know," Clarence answered with unnerving enthusiasm.

As terror attempted to take its grip, I consoled myself with my father's advice when I was fifteen. We were standing in his kitchen when he told me, "You can do anything you want, Kristy. The only thing to fear is fear itself."

Thirty minutes later we pulled off the highway. There was one vehicle there already, but we decided it was a mushroom picker. When I hesitated to enter the thick bush, Clarence assured me, "Go ahead. I'm right here. I'll back you up." He discouraged me from shouldering my gun because I had to be ready to shoot. He meant "shoot a deer," but I was thinking, BEAR!

It was difficult climbing up the slope, which is one of the reasons that people don't often hunt within the Bella Coola Valley—on either side of the highway the only option is climbing. Clarence, ever the teacher, showed me the trees that had been rubbed by deer, bushes that had been nibbled and mushrooms that had been eaten. We came across a bone that Clarence determined was the forearm of a grizzly. Shortly afterwards, I heard something coming toward me through the bush—not heavy enough to be a bear but maybe something we could shoot. I turned back to Clarence, cupping my ear to indicate that I had heard something, and he nodded and motioned for me to get my gun ready. Just then a man appeared with a bag of pine mushrooms over his shoulder. After a short conversation in hushed tones about the quality of the harvest that year, we returned to our silence.

We came upon a ring of nine trees, four of which were cedar that had vertical scratches down their trunks. When Clarence went over to one and reached his hand up, I was shocked to see those scratch marks extending about four feet above his highest reach. Clarence's excitement and awe at our find was converted to panic in me that we were indeed in big bear territory, a long, long way from civilization or our truck.

I suppose every novice hunter has that moment of realization that there is no recourse other than his own skill with a gun to keep himself alive. Again I heard my father's voice: "The only thing to fear is fear itself." Yeah right, maybe when you're standing in your own kitchen! I started walking to refocus my attention from my sweating palms and panic attack, but it was fifteen minutes before my pulses stopped racing and I could think lovingly of my father—and Clarence—once again.

What helped me was that I began to imagine exactly what I would have to do in a confrontation. I would load my gun, cock it, aim, remove the safety, breathe and wait for Clarence's signal to shoot. Even as we encountered more and more signs of bear—tree scratches, rootings in the ground, and bear scat—I felt more and more at ease. That is, until I smelled cat!

It was like walking into a house full of cats that hadn't been visited for a month. When I signed to Clarence, he mouthed, "Watch yourself," and signed back that I should look up into the tree branches as we walked on. A tense time followed, with me glancing back from time to time at Clarence who was peering heavenward as we walked forward. The smell got stronger and stronger. Then I looked back again and Clarence was nowhere to be seen. My darting eyes finally focussed on his gun leaning against a tree. I chuckled at the thought that everyone has to pee sometime and turned away, knowing he would not have wanted me to know he'd been heeding the call of nature.

I walked on slowly and then I heard his voice whisper in my ear, "This reminds me of that old Indian trapper. He was hunting bear, you know, a couple of years back ... up north ... and the bear circled around behind him so he became the tracked. That grizzly got him."

"Oh my God, Clarence, don't tell me this now!"

"Cougar will track you, too," he went blithely on, "but with cougar ..." he turned and motioned behind us with his chin, "you have to look back ..." his eyebrows disappeared under his Elmer Fudd hat, " ... as well as up." He brought his rifle up in front of his chest then pointed it skyward to punctuate the lesson.

"Jesus, Clarence, can't the lessons wait until we're safely back in your truck?"

"No, no. No need to worry. Let that just be a lesson to us. We learn from others' misfortune, mm-hmm." He nodded, patted my arm reassuringly and went back to silence.

By the end of the day we had seen no cougar, no grizzly and no legal deer but lots of signs of all three critters, plenty of evidence that they were there. I felt satisfied that I had carried a gun through thick forest and was still alive and in one piece. I had faced down my panic, too, something I hadn't foreseen having to do without a bear encounter itself. At the truck Clarence shook my hand and said, "You know, in all my years of hunting, my wife never once came with me. She just wasn't interested. And there's no point in pushing someone not interested. Well done. You've got a lot going for you. I'm proud of you."

A time to kill

As it turned out, when I finally shot my first wild animal, I was not on a hunt. I caught a young red fox trying to dig his way into my turkey pen. This was the same little fellow that had been prowling around the place every night for several weeks, keeping me awake thanks to the vigilance of our new dog. I'd seen this fox on several of his midnight ramblings but hadn't bothered to try to shoot him. I just let the dog out to chase him off. But when he showed up around three in the afternoon, I decided enough was enough. David and I had just sat down for coffee when we noticed the turkeys' sudden agitation at something in the trees beyond their run. They were ringing their alarm bells, pressing themselves up against the near fence-line and generally making it known they were not happy about being captive. David ran toward the turkey pen, shouting that he'd spotted the fox.

I ran back to the house to get my smaller gun, which was a Ruger .22 semi-automatic. When I returned and closed in on the turkey pen, the little fox was not at all disturbed and was still trying to dig his way in. Well, this was not something you want in a wild animal. As I took aim through the fence, he felt my presence, stopped digging, sat down and looked at me, unblinking. Admittedly, he was a cute little thing, so I paused to consider what I was about to do. Should I shoot him? Could I really do this? Should I let him go on his way?

I let the safety catch off.

You have to shoot him. He will just be back and you might not be home when he comes. Just deal with him now and be done with it! You'll kill the fox and save your turkeys. They are your livelihood, your food security. Do you want to come home to a complete massacre? You know that's what foxes do. You've seen it. Yes, yes, he's very cute, but he's also a killer. You can't let him go and risk losing all your turkeys.

I took aim, targeting the centre of his chest.

Wait a minute. That shot might not be a good option. There's two layers of cross-wire fencing between you and him. The bullet could hit a wire, ricochet, miss him altogether—or worse, hit one of your turkeys. You'd better try to line up a better shot and just risk letting him escape this time.

As I repositioned myself, the fox went around the barn and behind the paddock fence-line. I ran around the other side of the paddock and then into it so I could take aim and not have the fence in my way. Meanwhile, he had taken off to the other side of the slough. Once across to what he thought was safety, he sat at the base of a tree and again turned and looked back at me.

God, he's adorable. And young, only a yearling. Must be the son of that gorgeous red fox that got Mr. Mallard last summer. In fact, that fox probably fed this little guy with Mr. Mallard! Such a sweet face. Jesus, Kristeva, don't go there!

I took a breath, aimed and fired. The bullet hit him in the chest. His face screwed up and he barrelled over backwards, recovered his footing and took off at a lope.

Oh no! Now you're going to have to track him across the slough! It couldn't get worse. There's all that devil's club to get through and it can take your eye out if you're not careful. This is not going to be easy. Crap, crap, crap! Why couldn't he have just collapsed in his tracks!

I rounded up my dog and my husband to help with the job. We found the blood trail and followed it but it was rough going. Following a blood trail sounds a lot easier than it is. Even with the dog trying to lead the way, we spent far too long crossing the slough and even longer trying to get through the dense brush. Eventually we came out on my neighbour's driveway and followed the blood trail along it, through the back of my neighbour's garden, out into the field and into the deep forest at the edge. While in the field, the dog got confused because the fox had obviously come to the neighbour's farm along this same path. Now the dog tracked him back and forth along the two paths until we spotted a drop of blood, then found another spot near where he had urinated. Even though the urine as still wet, we decided he must have done it on the way to the farm, marking his trail no doubt. When we finally picked up the blood trail again, it was along a slightly different path from the urine, so we backtracked and followed it to where the fox had crossed another slough and continued deeper into the forest.

Good Lord, this is all you need, to be tracking a fox at nightfall! Just your luck.

The light was rapidly disappearing and the forest was growing dim. I looked up at the ever-darkening sky and noticed clouds looming with humidity. Just what we needed, rain to wash away what precious little blood trail there was left. To make matters even worse, we spotted a fresh pile of bear scat. The last thing we wanted was a stand-off between Madame Grizzly and my pretty little pink .22, but the idea of leaving that little fox to bleed to death was terrible. However, with the light fading and a grizzly on the prowl, we had no choice but to turn back for home.

For the next few nights I struggled with my feelings of guilt at not being able to finish off that fox quickly. A few weeks later we had friends over for dinner and relayed the story. When my husband asked them if they thought the fox would die, our friend responded, "Let me ask you this—has he been back?"

Woman running fairly close to the wolves

In November Clarence and his family went moose hunting from their base camp at Louie Creek, above the Bella Coola Valley, as they had for over forty years. The cabin there had been built by a First Nations trapper many years earlier and Clarence had been given permission to use it. After the old trapper died, the cabin had been included within a hunting guide's territory, but the family still had access to it and they maintained it, making

additions and repairs. Over the years Clarence and his sons had also built trails from the cabin up into the mountains, so to say they knew the area intimately was an understatement. Through years of intensive use and collected experiences, they had named nearly every square inch of the mountain range— Jude's Meadow, Coffee Pot Trail, Trapper Ridge— and now each meadow was filled with cherished meaning, each ridge was a marker of successful hunting trips past.

My first moose hunt with Clarence at Louie Creek. The tree behind me is heavily marked by moose. Photo Clarence Hall.

In the midst of that hunting trip Clarence took the day off to take his great-grandson back to school, and he stopped in to see me on his way back to camp. He asked if I wanted to come up and see the country they were hunting in. Many of his family members would be there, and several of them had moose tags. It was a family thing, an inter-generational thing, a way of life for them, and I felt privileged to be included.

Unfortunately, Clarence and I returned from that hunt empty-handed. We spotted nineteen does but not a single buck. I didn't even put a round in the chamber of my gun as there was nothing legal that presented itself. We did see three grouse, but they were all on the side of the road where it's not legal to hunt them. But despite the lack of game, it was nice to get out and walk through the forest. The Little Rainbow Mountains were fringed with glory, and the smell of the fall air was delightful. We saw a sow grizzly with two cubs grazing on some grass and they were the most tame grizzly bears we'd ever seen. It was nice that we didn't feel threatened but at the same time alarming that they were accustomed to seeing humans.

Clarence the consummate bushman, wearing his trademark hat complete with cougar teeth marks from an attack when he was 71 years old. At 84 Clarence is still sprightly enough to challenge me to keep up with him.

What the trip lacked in face-to-face game hunting, it made up for in excitement and educational opportunities. I learned how to identify the tracks of all sorts of animals and spent some time tracking moose that managed to stay just out of our sights before they crossed the boundary of our legal hunting area. (The number of times they did this made me wonder if the Department of Conservation had supplied the moose with a free guide to our hunting plans.) But tracking is pretty easy in the kind of snow we had on that trip—snow that is not deep enough that the walking is difficult and is still fresh enough that it makes no sound as you walk and shows the tracks well.

The other members of Clarence's family took off on foot, snowshoes or ATVs, but Clarence's pace suited me just fine. We spent hours travelling the deactivated logging roads by vehicle, looking for fresh tracks. We covered mile after mile on the road west of the cabin and then on the east road but found not a single fresh moose track. We saw fresh wolf tracks and the tracks of foxes and martins. When I got excited over old moose tracks and wondered why we were not striking off on their trail, Clarence patiently explained that the moose that had made this track could be fifty kilometres or more away by now. While the other members of the family disappeared for six to nine hours at a time, often not reappearing until the early gathering dusk, we always returned to the cabin at a civilized hour for lunch or dinner.

Then finally we did come across some fresh moose tracks. "Oh, my aching back, look at those here, my dear," Clarence said, head hanging out the window while gently bringing the truck to a stop. "Here we go," he whispered, then reverted to his usual sign language. We got out of the truck, hung our rifles over our shoulders, and he signalled that I was to lead the way. I took note of the compass direction and saw that the moose was heading almost due north. I struck out in front of Clarence and followed the tracks through an old clear-cut. Moose like the openness of the clear-cuts, primarily because their favourite browse colonizes them so quickly.

The moose had woven its way through the young regrowth, looking for delicacies among the evergreen saplings. "Red willow," Clarence whispered and pointed to the chewed tips of the brush. About four hundred metres across the clear-cut, there were two more sets of moose tracks. These came from the east to meet up with our moose, and then they travelled on together, all heading north. This put a spring in Clarence's step. We were on the trail of three adult moose. Another few minutes into the tracking and a fourth set of tracks showed up, also coming from the east. "Aw, it's a baby moose," whispered Clarence. "It must be travelling with its mama." There was a surprising tenderness rather than disappointment in his voice.

We now knew that at least two of the moose we were tracking were not legal to hunt, but we carried on because the first two sets of tracks were definitely adult tracks. We clambered over the rough ground of an old clear-cut for about a kilometre and eventually entered into deeper forest on the other side. The tracking was not as easy at that point—the trees dropped snow and covered the tracks, and the sunlight didn't penetrate the forest easily. The tracks became obscure, and the density of the trees made the walking much more difficult. Finally Clarence announced it was time to turn back.

"Why?" I asked.

"Because we're almost back to the highway. Those moose will have crossed it by now."

In other words, they'd made it safely out of the legal area of Clarence's hunting tag. It amazed me that Clarence seemed to know exactly where we were anywhere in these Little Rainbow Mountains, no matter if we were in the truck, on the trail or deep in the bush. Each time he spoke to say, "We're going north now" or "Now we're heading southeast" or "northwest," I looked at my compass, and he was always dead on.

The next few days were spent in similar fashion. We would head out each morning looking for tracks. When we came across fresh ones, we would get out and track them for as long as it made sense—until they left the legal area, until it became too dark, and on one occasion until the weather abruptly turned sour, which happened so quickly I didn't see it coming. One minute it was warm and sunny; next thing I knew we were heading back on our tracks in a blizzard, donning more clothing and battening down the hatches of our hunting hats to keep warm.

Clarence was constantly teaching me as we went, and he often had me practising dry runs. I would pretend that a rock or tree up ahead was in fact a moose, load my rifle, take aim and pretend to fire, then unload and continue on the hunt. He quizzed me on every set of tracks we came across. On one occasion while we were tracking a moose, its tracks merged with another baby moose. Despite the fact that the first moose was obviously a mama and therefore not legal, we kept hoping to catch a glimpse of them. Clarence was happy to let me lead and guide me as we went, encouraging me to look at the browse they were eating, where they had bedded down for a rest, and then showing me the droppings of the baby.

"Look," he said, "it's a baby bull." He lifted a morsel between his fingers and held it up for me to look at.

"How can you tell?" I asked, trying not to show too much alarm over the fact that he had moose feces in his hands.

"One end is flat," he said and gently placed it back on the snow where he found it. "Don't worry, I won't hand you a cookie with that hand, okay?"

In the end he did *eat* a cookie with that hand. He also ate his favourite snack, Cheetos, and happily licked his fingers with each bite, then turned to me and laughed. "Well, the First Nations people used moose droppings to thicken their stews."

"So I guess it can't be that bad for you!" I replied.

I had noticed Clarence's lack of concern with "personal food hygiene" on numerous occasions. He was happy to pick an apple off the ground in my yard, take out his pocket knife and, without washing either the knife, which has a species-butchering résumé that is unbelievable, or the apple that was nestled on my grass where my chickens free-range, cut into it and start eating. While I was shocked each time he did it, I was also slightly suspicious that his lack of concern about sterile food conditions coupled with a regular bag of Cheetos might just be the answer to his longevity!

The hunting season for deer and moose finally ended on November 30, and I came home without my buck. Neither Clarence nor I had even fired our rifles that fall. In fact, on the whole trip (for me this meant seven days, and Clarence was gone for fourteen altogether) we didn't even see a legal deer or moose. This is not to say that the hunting party came back empty-handed. One of the others got a moose, and I had the opportunity to taste some of it. However, I didn't share the family's enthusiasm for the liver, an issue still lingering from my childhood. I also got a quick lesson in how to skin a moose and an overview of the merits of this particular moose with respect to its mounting appeal. Clarence's son Dave, an avid hunter and expert chainsaw operator, was also a professional taxidermist, and he kindly offered me the skin on the hind end of the moose for tanning but kept the cape because in his professional opinion this moose was particularly beautiful. Apparently its light colour was appealing, the markings on either side of the face were symmetrical—which hardly ever happens—and the dimensions of the skull and overall shape of the head were aesthetically pleasing.

Although my freezer was still gameless, I had learned much: how to identify the tracks of anything that walks through a British Columbia forest, how to identify moose and deer habitat and their feed, how to handle and fire my gun, and how to orient myself around the Little Rainbow Mountains. I now felt a lot more confident and prepared for the following year's hunting season.

Butchering 101

Clarence-style kosher butchering

WHEN WE BOUGHT the Howling Duck Ranch, most of what I knew about farming, animal husbandry, animal veterinary care and butchering had come from books. I had bought Carla Emery's book, *The Encyclopedia of Country Living*, which is a must-purchase for anyone wanting to learn about living "the good life." In it she describes various ways of killing a chicken. At the time the bloodless way seemed the most appealing because I just didn't think I could chop a chicken's head off. After studying the method carefully, the next onerous task was to choose which chicken to kill. I stood there deliberating, nearly heartsick over having to decide.

A neighbour had given us a bunch of free-range chickens, but we had also acquired a flock of about twenty rescue hens from a local intensive egg farm. These hens had lived a miserable existence and I was very proud of giving them a better life. But they were pitiful creatures. They couldn't stand for long, their feathers had been plucked out by other birds who were unimpressed with their cramped living quarters, and they all had under-bites because it is a common practice in battery farming to de-beak all chickens in order to keep the pecking down to a dull roar.

The first day I brought these hens home, they couldn't even walk. They'd been so used to their cramped conditions, they hadn't developed enough leg muscles to hold themselves up nor had they ever had the opportunity to stretch. Before I gave them the free-range existence we afforded our other hens, I decided to put them in transition houses. The previous year, we had built several "chicken tractors" to help convert our lawn to garden, and these structures now did double duty, providing a nice space for the battery hens to get used to this new-found freedom. As I put them down one by one into the chicken tractors, they stood for only a few seconds before sinking to the ground *in situ*. They sat in the dirt a long while before they seemed to realize that they could stretch out their wings and lean to one side then repeat the process with their legs, right down to the tips of their pointed toes. This activity was pure ecstasy for them, and a joy to watch.

It took several weeks but eventually those chickens gained strength and I moved them in with the others. There they learned from the free-rangers how to eke out much of their own living, scratching here and there in search of tasty grubs and greens. For the most part the chickens got along fine, but there was one bossy free-ranger who liked to bully everyone else, and she was very brutal with the new gals. So, as I stood there agonizing over who would be my first slaughter victim, she bullied her last hen and made herself the clear contender. I grabbed her up and got out the book. I'd have one more read through before attempting this.

The two of us sat together as I read through the options again, and she agreed that the bloodless option would be her first choice. With that settled, I took her in my left hand, holding her firmly under the chest, then grabbed her head with my right hand and swiftly jerked down with my right hand and up with my left, the idea being to break the neck so that the chicken dies instantly and bloodlessly. I yanked and she squawked. I tried again. She squawked again. Then again. And again. Her neck got longer and longer and my stress level went higher and higher. Finally, I could reach my arms no farther and her neck was stretched beyond imagination but she was still alive and I was nearing panic. I cried out for my husband to get a knife and he came and finished her off quickly. I cooked her up but neither of us could face her so I fed her to the dog. It was a miserable first experience and left me rattled enough not to attempt it again for a while.

After I had put several chickens through misery in my attempts to dispatch them "ethically" and "bloodlessly," it became my practice to simply cut their heads off and keep the suffering to a minimum. I managed to do it only a few times but then caved and left the actual killing and gutting to my husband while I helped with the plucking. Eventually we even stopped plucking and just took the skin off, feathers and all. While this made the work a little easier, the result was that we could never have a roast chicken because I found that, unless I was willing to drizzle cups of olive oil over the bird while it was cooking, the meat would dry out too much. Finally I decided that I would have to muster up the courage to do the job properly.

Thankfully, by this time I had become much better acquainted with Clarence and had begun discussing with him the various ways of killing a turkey. When he asked me how we had been doing it, I told him we cut the heads off.

"That's how we did it on the farm," he told me, "but I don't do it that way anymore."

A long time ago an old Jewish rabbi had taught him how to butcher turkeys the kosher way.

"You sever the jugular," he explained, gesturing to his neck with a slicing motion. "This way, they only flap a bit at the very end of their lives."

I had only read about this technique, but it sounded like a much better way than anything else I had encountered. It was also the way that Joel Salatin's books described the dispatching of chickens and turkeys. According to Salatin, it is the most humane and effective way because the animal quickly falls unconscious while its heart continues to work to pump all the blood from the body and veins. Thus the animal is clean for the rest of the process, and this is part of what makes it kosher. I had been thinking about attempting Salatin's process since reading about it, but I was wary of attempting to slaughter animals by following the directions in another book. However, here was an opportunity to learn first-hand a better way to do it under the guidance of someone well versed in the art.

In early October Clarence declared himself ready to butcher his turkeys in time for Thanksgiving. While I was theoretically prepared to learn, I was still having difficulty with the reality of it. I was still not quite there emotionally. But I, too, had turkeys ready, and I realized that I'd better get a grip on this or I would be once again hiring the task out to my husband.

My first day of working with Clarence was rough, and the first bird was the toughest to get through. After he caught it, I helped him fasten it by the legs into the hanging noose, and then he proceeded to slit its jugular. He was so matter-of-fact about it I hardly got the chance to get a photo or a description. What amazed me the most was that the turkey didn't even flinch as he cut through its jugular.

"Let's get another angle for the record, Clarence."

I have to admit I was taking refuge behind the camera, quite relieved not to be doing the actual cutting of the jugulars myself. I stood there watching, mouth agape. While he was cutting the other side of the neck open, I shared my astonishment about the relative ease of this killing method compared to chopping the head completely off.

"Oh, I know," he said without stopping to look up. "It's no way to kill a bird." He finished the second cut, stood up, gently cleaned off the end of his knife and put it back in his breast pocket. He turned to me and slowly reached his arms out to his sides and then, as if bouncing an imaginary basketball around in front of himself and looking around to see where it was headed, he continued, "When you chop their heads off, they bounce all over the place." His arms came to a rest at his sides, pausing there until the next thought requiring their participation was clearly formulated. "When you do that, they sometimes injure themselves, you know ..." He brought his right hand up to his chest, elbow sticking out askew, feigning injury. "They break a wing." He paused and stood erect once again. I watched as his mind flickered over his past, revisiting historic events where he'd seen this very thing happen. "No, it's no good at all. It'll hurt itself."

I was always impressed with this seeming dichotomy that he could balance in his mind, on the one hand the mindful care he provided for the life of a creature and its well-being and on the other his complete lack of squeamishness at killing it for food. As if reading my thoughts, he said, "Besides, it can wreck the meat." It was at that point the bird he had just "killed" came to life. It caught both of our attentions as it flapped strongly for about ten seconds. When it was done and had gone flaccid, Clarence stepped forward. "Well, that's it, my dear. That was his last gasp. That's how they do it ... just ... like ... that ... Uh-hmm." He then opened the eyelid of the bird and touched the eye. "That's how you can tell it's dead," he said, looking up at me, head of the bird in one hand, finger pointing at the now open eye. He explained that the cornea is very sensitive and if the bird was still conscious, it would have flinched or closed its eyelid when he touched it.

Satisfied that the bird was now truly dead, he dunked it in the scalding water, laid it out in his wheelbarrow and began peeling the feathers off. At this point I joined in the work. It smelled awful, like death in a wheelbarrow, I thought as I began to pull at the feathers. I actually had to forcibly keep my mind on the task, and it was a struggle to maintain composure.

This is it. This is where your food comes from, girl. If you want to eat turkey at Thanksgiving, then you should be able to help with getting it to your table. Suck it up, princess, and get on with the job.

I repeated this mantra in order to keep waves of nausea at bay and wondered how on earth I was ever going to be able to do it by myself. Feeling weak, I looked up at the granite cliffs around me with the vague hope of finding strength in the rock.

You can do this. You have to do this. Besides, if you don't do this, you will look pathetic.

Canning, butchering and processing meat is one of the essential tasks in preparation for winter.

Once the bird was de-feathered, Clarence lifted it onto the table and began to eviscerate it while I returned to safety behind my camera. The sounds, the sights and the smells had me swallowing hard and struggling to maintain composure. In contrast, Clarence was matter-of-fact in everything he did. But what truly amazed me was his attention to the job coupled with the occasional interaction with the other turkeys whose destiny was being revealed before their very eyes. "Hello, girls. How ya doing? You okay today?" he crooned to them as he stuck his hand inside their mate and pulled out the guts, carefully setting aside the heart, liver, gizzard and kidneys before dropping the remains unceremoniously in the garbage bucket below the table. By the time we were dressing out the third bird, I had mustered the courage to ask him to talk me through my first kill.

With Clarence watching over me, I gently took the turkey's head in my left hand and began the cut where Clarence pointed. I could feel myself pulling away physically with my upper body even though my hands were going through the motions. When the blood squirted from the wound, I let go for a moment before continuing quickly on the other side. I didn't want to lose momentum, let negative thoughts take over and not be able to finish the job. But that was the only turkey I cut that day.

I came back the following day determined to do more of

Two years earlier it was hard for me to imagine I would ever have the nerve to butcher my own goats.

the killing, having realized that I'd better get good at it while I had the chance because by the following week I would have to do my own birds if I was going to have them ready for Thanksgiving. Together we processed all of Clarence's fifteen turkeys. After we had five of them all lined up on the table looking like they'd just come from the store, I was feeling much better about it all. Now they just looked like food. And by the end of that day I felt much more prepared to attempt to slaughter on my own.

Two days later I began butchering on my own and was pleasantly surprised at how confident I felt about it. The first bird I chose was a duck, followed by two more. Then I moved on to a couple of turkeys. By the end of the day I'd butchered three ducks, three turkeys and a couple of chickens. When I had them all lined up, washed, cleaned and ready for the freezer, I took a moment to look at them. I have just made us food, I told myself. Beautiful, clean, healthy food. At some point I realized that I was enjoying the work. It was wholesome work. I was my own boss, working on my own farm. I was outdoors with my animals, providing food for my family and exhausted by the end of the day. I laughed to myself and thought, *You've come a long way, baby.*

Turkey plucking

After my lessons in Clarence-style kosher butchering, I dispatched twenty-seven roosters, eight turkeys and two ducks, plucking and eviscerating them as well. I began doing this all by hand, but that soon changed.

Several days into my planned massacre I had to attend a food security meeting at the hospital, this being the only venue in the Valley with video-conferencing capability. But on my way out of the farm, I noticed a dead bird caught up in the fishing net we used to protect our chickens and ducks. Aha, I thought, there's the little hawk that feasted on my ducklings. From a hatch of twelve that spring, only one had survived. The others had been pecked off, day by day. It was like living through scenes from Agatha Christie's *Ten Little Indians*—and then there was one. I didn't have time to cut the corpse out of the netting at that time but instead made a mental note to deal with it after I got home from the meeting.

Installed in the coldest room in the hospital, I listened diligently to the speakers in faraway Vancouver, though I admit that my mind occasionally drifted back to the little predator caught in the netting and all the other work I had to do back on the farm. Then I found myself thinking about how often I was having to sharpen my knife when butchering the turkeys, and it occurred to me that I might just be in the right place at the right time. After all, a hospital is a place where they cut people open. Why couldn't I use a scalpel? My mind began leafing through the possibilities of who might give me a contraband scalpel. I mentally checked off the doctors whom I knew well enough to ask and noted, sadly, that all were either out of town or recently retired. While I was lamenting the loss of such fruitful connections, one of the nurses walked by, as if on cue. As soon as the meeting ended, I sought him out and made my pitch.

"Sure, but you might want to consider buying an exacto knife instead," the nurse replied. He listed its virtues: cheaper, just as sharp, not made for a single use (who knew scalpels were made for one-time use?), more convenient and durable. "Besides, a scalpel is designed to make nice neat incisions that are repairable—not really what you're after."

As I left the nurses' station I had the good fortune to run into a neighbour, Karl, who I knew had at one time owned a chicken plucker. Convinced I was suffering the preliminary stages of arthritis but suppressing my desperation, I asked him nonchalantly if he still owned this contraption and whether I could borrow it.

"Well, it's actually a turkey plucker," he said, rubbing his chin then mercifully adding, "Sure, you can use it." With his hands in the air, he provided me with a quick virtual demonstration of how to use the machine, focussing on the final stages of turkey plucking—how to hold it by the feet and gently let it roll away from you, careful not to let it go but moving with it as it bounced up and down on the rubber prongs. As we made arrangements for me to pick it up the next day, I wondered what terrible ailment the other patients thought we were discussing as we stood there gesticulating in the corridor!

When I arrived home, Elmer, the man we had hired to build the poultry barn, was just leaving, having dropped by to finalize some minor details. We toured the new barn, and as he pointed out his workmanship, I ooh-ed and ah-ed at the appropriate pauses. Then as I escorted him off the farm and we stood at the gate discussing when he would return to complete the work, a movement caught my eye. The little creature in the net was staring at me as if to say, "I've got a bit of a situation here. Would you mind?"

"My gosh, it's alive," I blurted in mid-sentence and ran over to it. What I thought was a small hawk turned out to be a small owl.

The poor creature had been hanging there for hours. As I began to untangle it, Elmer hollered, "Watch yourself!" and launched himself through the gate. "Them little buggers can really bite." This he announced after I had already wrapped my bare hands around the feathery little body. Having previously been foolishly intimate—without protection—with a long and distinguished list of toothy wild animals during my life, I promptly let go and went to get my gloves.

All of fifteen centimtres tall, the owl gnashed its beak at me like a fero-cious little bear. I have always loved the feistiness of small creatures when they are in full swing, performing their best I-could-take-you-if-I-wanted repertoire, and this performance was quite hilarious, if not a bit unnerv-ing. Carefully I placed the owl in a box inside the garage where previous wounded—such as Gordon, the goat—had convalesced. Later that day we had a visit from Darrell, who had incubated our first batch of chicks and who was also responsible for the addition of Muscovy ducks to our pond. When I explained my planned release of the owl, he asked, "So you are going to liberate the animal that's been killing your stock?"

I nodded. "Not only that, I'm going to feed her."

There was a barely perceptible shaking of the head as he finished his coffee in silence. Darrell was raised on a farm and worked on ranches all his life, and this was clearly not in keeping with a rancher's idea of wildlife management.

Feeling compelled to plead my case, I added, "All the ducklings are gone now, and I think she has learned her lesson. She won't be back."

The next morning my husband set off to collect the turkey plucker from Karl and I went to check on the progress of the little owl. I was shocked to find her face-down in the straw, stone-cold dead. It was a sad little sight. It looked as if she had taken a couple of steps toward the meat I had put in the cage for her and had keeled over on the way to breakfast. I buried her near some of the other unfortunate animals of times past, where she could nourish the flowers in my garden. A few hours later when Elmer showed up for work, the first thing he did was ask about the little owl. When I told him she'd died, his face fell.

"Aw, I thought for sure she'd live," he said. "Did you put her in the freezer?" He explained that when something like this happened, people often saved the carcass, got a permit and asked a taxidermist to mount it.

It would never have occurred to me to do so. "Nope," I replied firmly. "She's in my flower garden next to the other fine creatures."

A few minutes later Karl and my husband arrived with the turkey plucker and man-handled the great machine onto the brick patio where I would be working. After they both left, I got myself organized, then slaughtered a chicken (for a test run) and scalded it for the plucker. I plugged the machine in and it whirred satisfyingly to life. Doing my best impersonation of my instructor, I gently laid the chicken over the turning rubber prongs. With a rapid-fire tuk-tuk-tuk-tuk-tuk (reminiscent of a playing card held by a clothes peg against the spokes of my bicycle wheel) the chicken sprang to life, leapt out of my hands, whisked itself through the plucker with nary a feather lost, and arced magnificently through the damp air before coming to an abrupt stop with an unceremonious thwap! on the wet grass beyond the machine.

In spite of this rude beginning, gradually I got the hang of it and decided that the plucker was a fantastic addition to my toolkit because it sped up the processing operation almost threefold! However, when I switched from chickens to turkeys, which are much heavier, the torque was several magnitudes greater, and once again I was caught off guard as the first turkey made its final attempt at flight. Determined to master the task, I hung on for dear life, bracing my gumboots against the machine in a desperate tug-of-war. But when I thrust my body backwards in one final attempt to control the process, the turkey, now battered and torn and still not exactly featherless, brought the whirling prongs to a momentary halt. As I retrieved the bird, lamenting the loss of my first investment in turkeys, my dog smiled smugly at the prospect of several gourmet meals. Fortunately, after a few more false starts, I developed a feel for it.

Clarence, who had grown up on a farm and raised birds all eighty-three years of his life, had never seen, let alone used, a poultry plucker. When I told him about the one I'd borrowed and how it was saving me so much time, he asked me to let him know the next time I was butchering so he could come over, lend a helping hand, and give it a whirl at the same time. Having learned so much from Clarence over the past couple of years, I was thrilled to be able to pass on some knowledge to him for a change, so before I lit the fire for the final butchering, I left a message on his answering machine.

I had brought the water up to scalding temperature and was just cutting my first turkey when Clarence appeared at my gate. "Don't you just have the perfect timing!" I called out when I saw him. I quickly finished the cuts on the turkey's neck, rinsed my hands and, wiping them dry on my pants, made my way over to greet him.

Clarence was almost a living caricature of himself: quilted red and white plaid jacket, buttoned-down shirt, blue jeans, Gore-Tex hunting boots and, to complete the picture, his green Elmer Fudd hunting hat—complete with permanent teeth marks from a cougar attack ten years earlier. This is his signature collection. You could take a photo of him and, by digitally changing the background scenery, make it true for any season: Clarence in the winter, Clarence in the spring, Clarence in the summer, Clarence in the fall. The only thing that would be altered to indicate the changing season would be what he was wielding in his hands: in spring a seed catalogue, in summer a shovel or pitchfork, in fall a rifle, and in winter a snow-shovel. Yet Clarence's simple tastes enchanted me—the more so because he was unaware of them. Underneath he was real, unassuming, and one of the most humble people I ever met, with not a pretentious bone in his body.

He never brought his truck into our yard, preferring to stop at the gate and walk in, talking to all the critters on his way to the house, meeting and greeting his way up the driveway. "Hello, goats! Hey there, duckies! How y' doing, doggy?" The animals always answered him: mm-baaaa, quack-quack-quack, gobble-gobble ... with one exception. Always absent was the dog's bark, which impressed Clarence to no end. He took this to show how intelligent the dog was, so on nearly every one of his visits he would happily report, "You know, my dear, she never barks at me. She knows me … you know … knows my voice. Mm-hmm."

The day of the turkey plucking Clarence had brought a big beef rib bone for the dog, and when I spotted him coming up the driveway, she was happily trotting beside him, head cocked to one side with the weight of the bone. She made her way back to her usual spot on the grass, flopped down and greedily started to work on it. The bone must have been about fifty centimetres long, and with this prize between her teeth and paws, her Christmas had come early.

As I drew closer to Clarence, I was not greeted by his usual "Hello, my dear," but instead with "Are your hands bloody?" Well, that's not a question I'd ever expected to hear aimed at me. I stuck out my freshly rinsed hands for him to inspect. Instead of waiting for my reply, he clutched my hands in his and, looking them over with care, triumphantly declared, "Yep, they're bloody!" He pointed to a spot of blood on my ring finger that I'd missed. "Okay, I'm satisfied," he said, dropping my hands and continuing his march toward the barn where I had my butchering station set up.

Then suddenly he veered off toward the hung turkey: "Oh, my dear, you haven't got him … her cut well enough on the right." Without a pause, he took out his knife and expertly finished the job that I had rushed in order to meet him a few minutes earlier. I was surprised by how good his eyesight was and impressed by how quickly he had judged the situation and worked deftly to rectify it. Clarence hated to see an animal suffer.

For the rest of the day, we worked steadily together, taking turns at catching the turkeys and scalding them. Then he asked that I show him how to use the plucker. Suitably impressed with my demonstration on the first bird and eager to try it, he did the next one. "Wow, this sure works, my dear!" he called out over the whir of the plucker. I looked over and saw his eyes widening in surprise as the feathers flew off. I was enjoying his pleasure in his newly learned skill when, in his excitement over the job the plucker was doing, he nearly lost the bird to the grip of the machine. "Wow, you see that?" he said, quickly recovering his grip on the fluttering bird. As he regained his composure, he laughed. "You ever drop one of these?" I shook my head. I let him do all the plucking that day.

"Did I tell you that I'm taking you for lunch today?" he asked suddenly. I turned to see him standing with one hand grasping the neck and the other the feet of a turkey, and the corpse, still steaming from the scalding water, sagging heavily between them. Mist rose up around him like a scene in a B-grade horror movie. Elmer Fudd butchers his first turkey.

"No," I replied. Having cut and plucked our way through the last of the turkeys, I asked him if he would mind if I added a couple of roosters.

"No better time than now, my dear," and he gestured to all the butchering paraphernalia about us. I'd been keeping the extra roosters—the Magnificent Seven, I called them—partly because they are really pretty but primarily because I like to let my hens (and thus my flock) "do their thing" when the desire suits them to go broody. Now, looking the roosters over, I began mentally weighing them because I wanted to cull the smallest and keep the heaviest for breeding stock in an effort to develop my flock into good, all-purpose egg layers and meat birds. The roosters that had watched their figures were destined for the knife. I spotted the two I thought were the smallest, caught them with my fishing net and brought them over to the hanging tree.

"Can you do this one, Clarence?" I asked, holding up one of my most beautiful roosters for him to see. "He's just too pretty. I can't do it." I was also concerned that my knife wouldn't do a quick enough job on the roosters. They had glorious manes, and after doing in a bunch of turkeys with no feathers on the neck, I knew my exacto blade was not sharp enough to get through all those feathers. I was relieved when Clarence obliged me.

Of course, once they were cut, I was fine and did the rest of the processing, minus the plucker, which Clarence was still pretty thrilled to be operating. Finally, as he was throwing the last of the feathers on the fire, Clarence asked, "You ready to go for lunch now?"

I rinsed the table-top and cutting board with soap and water, covered the blood with deep sawdust, stacked the buckets and other items away in their places, and carried the wrapped birds over to the garage. Clarence tipped out the scalding water and tidied up the fire and plucker mess.

That done, we headed into town for a hot lunch. It is amazing how good a hot meal feels after a day out working in the cold weather, and it was a lot closer to dinner time than lunch by the time we started for home. Reflecting upon the week, I realized that I'd come a long way from my sheltered upbringing and citified background. I had made the emotional trajectory necessary to kill and process meat for food from creatures I had hand-hatched, cared for and raised. I was now a lot closer to understanding Clarence's way than I had been only days before. I felt proud of having closed the loop on my sustenance. It all happened right outside my front door, made possible by my own hands and sweat equity.

To breed or not to breed

To breed or not to breed was the question, and if to breed, then how? I came home one day to find Fatty-Fat bleating away at me relentlessly. This was unusual because she is normally a very self-sustaining, quiet goat. On this late October day, however, she was insistent and seemed so needy that she convinced me to go into the goat pen to see if anything was wrong. I ended up staying and cuddling with her for a while. Within seconds Malcolm, who was not one to let such an opportunity go unattended, joined in the snuggle-fest.

At first I thought Fatty-Fat needed some scratching in places that horns just can't reach, but when Malcolm tried to mount her, it occurred to me that Fatty-Fat might be in heat, though I wasn't sure how to tell. I thought her vulva might be a bit more pink than normal, but then I couldn't say for certain since I'd not spent a lot of time considering that end of my goats.

In any case, I had to consider which of my goats to slaughter, and breeding would play a role in the decision. When I arrived home from my first hunting trip with Clarence, I felt as ready as I ever would be. As I walked past the goat pen with my rifle in hand (I had, to my credit, already butchered a variety of animals), a thought suddenly occurred to me: "They are just small deer. I can do this." It was then that I knew it was time.

I located a willing buck named Buddy, one of only two pygmy goat bucks in the whole Valley. Fortunately, although all the pygmy goats in the Valley had been brought there by the same man, Buddy was not related to my gals. I was worried about how he would get along with my two wethers, Gordon and Malcolm, but they all accepted each other nicely. In fact, he

Goat breeding was successful the first time around: Fatty-Fat and her kids, Fanny-Mae and Franky, take refuge from the summer heat inside a stump.

and Malcolm had once been kept on the same farm together so there was a historical familiarity between them that was noticeable. Buddy, the little rent-a-buck, was a hit with the ladies, too.

The books say a buck should run with the does for a month so he can attend to each of them as they come into their respective heats. But it seems he arrived just in time for Sundown's heat at the beginning of the month because the minute he entered the paddock he went straight to her and started flirting, and within minutes she had accepted him. In fact, she did more than just accept him—she got downright possessive. In no uncertain terms she let Shiraz and Fatty-Fat know that Buddy was to be hers first. I soon learned the goat equivalent for "Back off, bitch! He's mine!" It was the only time she acted like a bossy bitch and stood up to Shiraz, the top rank-ing doe who only let him breed her exactly once. But despite Sundown's amorous intent, in the end she was the only one of the three does that did not get pregnant, and later that year it was a mark against her. When deciding who to butcher first, Sundown's lack of fertility would prove to be the fatal strike against her.

Food insecurity and unpalatable realities

Although the concept of food sovereignty is high on the agenda of people throughout North America, in British Columbia recent changes to the Meat Inspection Regulations (MIR) have put more meat processors and producers out of business than they have created new processors. Because so many of the smaller custom operators have been forced to close up shop, the new regulations have reduced the capacity of small communities to produce their own meat. Thus, they are forced to be more dependent upon an already unsustainable and ecologically questionable food production and distribution system.

The new British Columbia Meat Inspection Regulations state that if the meat is intended only for your personal use, you have two slaughtering options:

1. You can take your animals to an abattoir, which can be either fixed or mobile. All British Columbia abattoirs that produce meat for human consumption must be licensed.

2. You can slaughter your own animals. It is legal to have friends or

neighbours help you with this task as long as nobody is paid or otherwise compensated. However, if you slaughter your own animals, you cannot sell any of the meat nor can you use it in any transaction that is commercial in nature, such as regular trading or bartering for other goods or services. Nor can you sell products such as sausages or meals made from this meat.

This legislation has effectively shut down "farm gate" sales. Yes, British Columbia farmers are still selling meat at their farm gates, but the place of sale is now meaningless. These farmers must now send their live animals to a provincially licensed slaughterhouse and then bring them back to their farms for sale. Therefore, this so-called right to sell from the farm gate does not in reality allow farm-gate sales. These are retail sales. The fact is that once the meat from that farm is slaughtered in a provincially legislated facility, anyone can buy it and resell it. The provincial government has effectively made retail outlets out of farmers' properties and taken away their right to sell their products directly to consumers. Not only does it mean a loss to farmers' incomes but it is also a loss to communities' food security and food sovereignty.

If you think you might get around the legislation by slaughtering for free, the Meat Processors of British Columbia have that one tied up with their own interpretation of the legislation: "Note: If the slaughtering of animals is part of the ordinary course of somebody's business, even if it is done for free, it would be considered operating an abattoir." Under this interpretation of the regulations, a farmer who wishes to sell live animals to his customers and offers to slaughter them for free will need to hold an abattoir licence. To date, this is not part of the law, but this interpretation by the Meat Processors organization is a warning to producers, and unfortunately has put many of them off entirely.

Because of British Columbia's geographically diverse topography and vastly dispersed populations, there are many rural or remote communities that have never had access to a local processor and have instead relied on doing their slaughtering themselves or with the help of the local butcher. With the new regulations these communities will have no way to legally process their meat, and thus they will no longer have the opportunity to be self-sufficient in their meat producing and processing capacity. For example, for farmers living in the Bella Coola Valley, the closest provincially inspected slaughter facility for red meat is over five hundred kilometres away (Beaver Valley) and the closest poultry slaughtering facility is around nine hundred kilometres away (Chilliwack or Salmon Arm). In economic terms, for the local farmer and his customers, these facilities might as well be on Mars. However, not to worry! The Meat Inspection Regulations have addressed this problem with the following:

> Producers in remote and isolated communities face special challenges because they may not have access to a licensed slaughter establishment. Some of these communities may need time to carry out feasibility studies before developing construction plans for new or updated facilities. In these limited circumstances, a Class C transitional licence applicant can apply for an exemption from the requirement to have a construction plan. This will allow the applicant to continue operating and selling direct to the consumer until feasibility studies are done and construction plans can be completed. As with all Class C licences, the meat produced must be labelled as uninspected and not for resale. Transitional licences are valid for six months, and renewal is subject to continued progress towards a fully approved and licensed operation. In exceptional circumstances, in remote and isolated areas, the Minister of Health has the authority under the Meat Inspection Regulation to exempt transitional Class C licence applicants from the necessity of getting an approved construction plan if in the Minister's opinion it is necessary to maintain slaughter capacity.

Well, thank goodness for small mercies! People in small rural or remote communities won't have to take any responsibility and make decisions for themselves because the minister will decide whether or not it is "necessary to maintain slaughter capacity." Five generations of farming families have been waiting for the minister to tell them if what they've been doing for a hundred and twenty years is worthwhile.

While our government produces tantalizing feasts of rhetoric about such things as rural economic development, food security and food sovereignty, their one-size-fits-all approach to food safety legislation is undercutting the contemporary interests of British Columbia's citizens. The overall result is food insecurity as communities lose their decentralized, locally controlled, economically diverse and thus more stable and sustainable food production and distribution systems. Already, as local producers throw in the towel, we are beginning to see these communities unravelling socially due to the breakdown of interdependency.

Overall, how do these legislative changes affect BC meat producers and processors? Some see the outcome as positive. I spoke to a beef producer near Quesnel who is quite happy with the changes because she can now supply people in Vancouver (670 kilometres away) with her pasture-fed beef. This is because she lives within an hour's drive of a licensed abattoir.

Other producers are not so lucky. Some in more populated areas who have had easy access to custom slaughtering in the past now find themselves without a processor willing to take their custom orders. Part of this is due to the fact that the regulations are geared to high-volume industrial packing plants that kill hundreds or thousands of animals per day. Not surprisingly, because the capital costs of the improvements required by the new regulations are so high, these plants cannot afford to take on small custom jobs. For the same economic reason, new processing operations are unlikely to open. When the costs of running a slaughterhouse are basically the same whether it is a small plant or a large one, it doesn't make economic sense to operate a small, custom plant. At the same time many of the smaller slaughterhouses, which traditionally did the majority of the custom and specialized work, are closing down or have already closed as they simply cannot afford to install the stainless steel equipment, high-end stun guns, saws and knives required to meet the new standards or such niceties as a separate office and bathroom facility for the meat inspector and an automatic, hands-free hand-washing system for the slaughtering staff. What exactly do a separate office and bathroom for the meat inspector have to do with meat safety?

What have we gained from the changes in the legislation? Local producers have been shut down. Real farm-gate sales have ended. Small specialized custom operators have been put out of business. Many small-scale, often specialized producers have nowhere to get their meat slaughtered unless they contravene environmental and animal rights standards by shipping their animals long distances to a licensed abattoir. How do these new regulations support food safety, eating locally, rural economic development, food security or food sovereignty? The answer is: they don't.

Readers who want to produce locally or support their regional producers in a way that is best for animals and communities should research local legislation and politics. They may well be surprised and shocked by what they find. In British Columbia the government launched an "Access to Produce" campaign for rural and remote communities and conducted community consultations both by task force meetings and by questionnaires. At one such meeting I attended someone from the audience said, "Look, we all want to have legislation like that in place. We just need it to be workable." Some people in the room agreed but I was unswayed. We didn't have a chance to debate the issue because the facilitator ended the meeting before we were given the opportunity to respond.

It is important to understand that the underlying foundation for all this legislation is the giving over of our rights to government and legislative bodies. And when we put a government in charge of our food, we accept that we are incapable of deciding for ourselves what is safe, healthy and nutritious. By acquiescing and accepting these "beyond ridiculous" laws, we are severely limiting our freedom of choice as consumers and obliterating the right of farmers to farm except on an industrial scale.

The most disquieting aspect of all this new legislation is that just because meat has been inspected by the government doesn't mean it is safe. The Maple Leaf Foods case is a poignant example. That company's government-inspected meats killed twenty-three people. Joel Salatin often says, "You can't legislate integrity," but I certainly can recognize it when I get to know my meat producer, look around his farm, see how his animals are cared for and see the relationship he has (or doesn't have) with his animals. I am not advocating the abolition of food legislation altogether. I believe that protections and policies need to be in place for large, centralized production and distribution systems, but I should have the right to farm and the right to sell my products from that farm, as should my neighbours, because there is a built-in safety system in play within a small food production and distribution system: my neighbours don't want to make me sick and vice versa. Moreover, in the unlikely event of a problem, we could track down its source quickly. There is a level of trust between community members who rely on each other for their food because their livelihoods depend on it.

Legislative policies need to support our communities and our farmers. With the contemporary focus on eating locally and developing community food systems, community food security and regional food sovereignty, we can't live with prohibitive policies and expect to make progress.

Bears I Have Known

They were here first

IN THE EARLY WINTER OF 2008, nine different properties in the settlement of Hagensborg had a collective loss of over seventy-five chickens, several turkeys and many ducks to marauding bears in the space of a week. By the grace of God, my own chicken sheds were still standing unharmed and my chickens were unravaged, but I had lost my last two female Muscovy ducks to a fox.

I ran into Clarence while out for lunch and he invited me to go with him to survey the damage a bear had wreaked at a friend's place two nights earlier. He wanted to read the signs and understand what happened, and he planned to reveal the story while I recorded and photo-documented the scene first-hand. We stopped at my place on the way up the Valley so I could change and grab my camera and my rifle. Clarence joked with my husband that he wanted me to be there to take care of him if a bear was still there. When I got back to his truck with my gear, he said, "You know we're not allowed to help the owner deal with her bear. If you shoot that bear, you'll be in trouble because you don't live there. Crazy, isn't it? And her all alone up there."

I threw the gun on the backseat anyway. "Well, we'll leave it in the truck," I said, echoing one of his regular pieces of advice. "I'd rather have it and not need it than need it and not have it." Clarence felt no need for his rifle; he just wanted to see what had taken place.

Once at the scene of the crime his sense of propriety and bushman safety took over and he had a sudden change of heart. "My dear, you best bring your gun, just in case," he said, stepping out of the truck and pointing to the backseat where my rifle lay. Then he laughed and gestured toward the chicken shed. "Wouldn't that just be the thing ... for us to get in trouble right there in the chicken shed? You just can't be too careful, can you?"

Agreeing, I loaded the gun. Heeding Gary Shelton's advice to let the more experienced person lead the parade in bear encounters, I closed the bolt with the chamber empty, set the safety and handed it over to Clarence. "I'll shoot with the camera. If the worst case goes down, at least I can get a nice photo of you!"

We moved cautiously forward through a foot of fresh snow, but not more than four feet from the driveway Clarence broke the silence.

"Hey my dear, looky here!" he said, pointing at a trail of footprints in the snow. "What we've got here is a grizzly bear. The owner doesn't know that. Just because a bear looks black doesn't mean it's a black bear. You see how those claw marks are turned down, distinctive in the snow?" He was also impressed with the size of those prints—it was certainly an adult bear.

As we approached the chicken shed, we surveyed her orchard. Clarence inspected every inch of the snow, providing me with a running commentary. "Oh man, look at those! Hey my dear, this is a big bear ... Oh my, look at her orchard ... Those bears have destroyed all her lovely trees ... and on top of all her chickens. Aw, look at those poor creatures all piled up in the snow ..."

When I started into the chicken house, Clarence warned, "Hold up! Watch yourself. That bear might still be in there. Look here where he left his teeth marks on the plywood ... Such power ... just ripped it all apart. No, no, this is no good at all ... Hey, look over here, my dear, there's his hair caught in the barbed wire. Whoo-ooo! Hair on five barbs! That's a wide bear! Oh man, he's broken that fence all apart ... Aw, wait a minute, that's a different track. I think we have two bears ... Yes, see here, the smaller print. This tells me it's probably a mama and I'd say a two-year-old cub. See where they tried getting back over the fence and turned around? Look, there's where they bedded down, right here at the edge of the forest ... See all those feathers? I bet they're bedded down right now within a hundred feet or so ... Wanna walk a ways into the bush?"

As attractive as that offer was, upon cooler consideration we concluded it would be better if we were *both* armed before rummaging through the dense forest at dusk in pursuit of the robbers, as Clarence called them. Back at the scene of the crime, I looked at the decimated trees, their limbs torn indiscriminately from trunks where the bears had tried to get the last of the fruit hanging there. Outside the shed, a pile of eleven lifeless little bodies were heaped this way and that against the wall with their legs, heads and wings askew, some with heads entirely missing, and most with their innards sucked out. A macabre sight. The force that had broken open the chickens' well-built home was impressive: the plywood sliding shutters that had covered the windows had been ripped to the ground along with their wooden frames, the heavy-gauge chicken wire over the windows had been crimped back as if from an explosion, and roosts and nesting boxes were tossed and shattered. The bears had taken away four of the chickens, leaving the pile of ordered chaos outside for their next meal.

I took photos as Clarence continued his commentary, "In all my forty-two years in this valley, I've never seen this. The bears should be hibernating at this time of year ... should have fattened up and gone to bed by now ... You know, there were no fish in the river for them this summer ... they need fish to build up the fat. The summer weather was no good—there weren't enough berries for them ... Gerald said he saw one in his yard the other day, do you know, scratching through the snow? He said it was looking for the frozen apples on the ground. Now what kinda food value could possibly be in an old frozen apple?" He paused before revealing his final analysis. "They're starving ... Suffering."

When I posted a story about the damage the bears had inflicted on this woman's property, I received this comment:

"What about the fact that you are placing tasty food morsels in the bears' territory? After all, they were there first."

"Tasty morsels" suggests that humans are responsible for attracting the bears. A few years back this idea led our Ministry of Environment and Conservation to promote a non-attractant policy and encouraged our town's elected officials to put an electric fence around the local dump. It kept the bears out for exactly two years by which time they had figured out that they could dig a hole and crawl under the fence. In the meantime, the barrier created new problems for the folks living in close proximity to the dump. Without access to their accustomed food source, the habituated bears went in search of a new one, entering people's yards and wreaking havoc. Among the dozens of livestock and pets killed and eaten were two horses. Property was damaged, gardens were raided and fruit trees were broken and in some cases destroyed.

But the seriousness of the problem cannot be ignored. The idea that we can prevent bears from entering our properties and our communities by adhering to the non-attractants philosophy and its resulting policies is a desperately hopeless fallacy that has been proven not to work in many places in North America. Even assuming it really is the community's collective responsibility to remove attractants, where does it end? What should you do about the freezer where you keep your own farm-raised meat or the dog food bag that you store in your home or your barbeque that is stored in the garage?

Where is the boundary line of "baiting" the bears? At your front door? In front of your fridge? Will the Ministry of Environment blame you if a bear smells the bacon frying on your stove and decides to come through your front door to get it? And I do mean *through* as few man-made structures can stop a marauding bear, even a small one. And if you're only allowed to shoot in self-defence, who will pay for the damage the bear causes to your chicken sheds? Who will pay for the loss of income and to replace the livestock? Certainly not the Ministry of the Environment. We already complain that local food is too expensive. If you, as a local farmer, have to pass on to your customers the cost of replacing a flock of chickens, repairing your sheds and the net loss to your income, the price of your eggs will increase dramatically. This is exactly what you face when you cannot protect your animals, fruit trees and vegetable patch—a local community food source that is also your livelihood.

This non-attractant idea also creates a legislative conflict of interest. On the one hand, the Ministry of Environment tells us to remove predator attractants, so the next logical step is to pass laws that forbid the keeping of chickens (or ducks, turkeys, pigs, goats, horses, dogs) or growing fruit trees or vegetable gardens because cherries, carrots and parsley are grizzly bear favourites. On the other hand, the Ministry of Health tells us to work toward community food security. In fact, at the 2008 Union of British Columbia Municipalities Annual General Meeting, this province's premier announced that a task force would be established to develop a strategy to help provide rural and remote communities with produce grown in British Columbia. These two directives are diametrically opposed.

Recently I pointed out this conflict to a friend in the Valley, and he recounted the advice given to several community members who had called the conservation officer about the most recent problem bear. "Chop down your fruit trees and get rid of the attractants," was the advice. How will this help us create a local food system and food security? The answer, which may come as a shock to our government, is not for humans to stop growing food or composting their food scraps at home, but the exact opposite. As he explains in his book, *Bear Attacks: Their Causes and Avoidance*, Professor Stephen Herrero found the answer in the Apennine Mountains of the Abruzzi region of Italy where he worked in 1971. In a town of nearly ten thousand people with about a hundred bears living in the vicinity, there was no bear problem, not even at the garbage dump. Being from Canada, Herrero was astounded and wanted to get to the bottom of it. "What are these people doing differently than we are back home?" he asked himself. The answer was that Italians don't throw away or waste food. No food scraps go to their dump sites—*ever*. They are either eaten or composted at home. As a consequence, Herrero found, there was no trace of bears near any of the dump sites nor did the bears go near the town. He concludes that food scraps left at dumps or at campsites will encourage marauding bears who may also break into nearby houses. The solution to the problem of bear attractants, therefore, is not to build fortress-type dumps where humans can continue to discard food scraps willy-nilly but to prohibit the dumping of scraps altogether. In short, we have to change our behaviour.

The second assertion of the commenter—that I am living in the bears' territory—reflects the misconstrued dichotomy of "their territory" versus "our territory" as if humans only belong in cities and those cities have always existed. The "our territory/their territory" attitude arises from a preservationist philosophy that drives policy and legislative decisions in British Columbia as well as North America in general. It presumes that bears have a territory that we humans have encroached upon, but the very concept of "territory" is a neat fiction that presumes a natural, agreed-upon boundary exists between the bears' territory and ours. But where is it? At the edge of cities? Around the surrounding rural areas? Should we all move out of the countryside and into cities, and if we do, who decides where the edge of the city lies?

As with so many issues, this debate is over boundaries, borders and margins, and yet there is no demarcated boundary to any natural creature's territory—only constantly changing niches or ill-defined ranges, regularly fought over with tooth and claw. The idea of identifiable borders is a human invention. Animals like bears do understand territory and mark theirs distinctively, but that territory is a living, changing thing, depending on each bear's condition, its niche in the population, and the state of the food supply. That food supply is intimately linked to the general bear population so that, if the food supply decreases or the bear population increases, the bear's fight for territory becomes more competitive.

The trouble in the Bella Coola Valley in late 2008 started with an increased bear population coupled with a late spring. In summer there was a poor wild berry crop and few fish entered the river, and the winter began very mildly so the hungry bears were late going into hibernation. All of this meant the bears' food sources were too scarce within their own food sheds, so the fight for territory between them became more vicious. Consequently, the weaker and younger bears that were denied access to prime habitat were pushed out of what we think of as their territory and into ours. The easiest pickings were our chicken houses, fruit trees, gardens and garbage, and when you combine that with a policy of eliminating attractants, it's not long before bears consider our territory theirs. And unlike the bears along the river, fishing for salmon and driving humans away in order to protect their food source, we humans didn't even put up a fight when they came and ate all our chickens, turkeys and ducks. Nor did we complain when they harvested all our carrots, parsley, plums and pears.

While some people may think we who live in rural areas are living in the bears' territory, under this system how should we establish and maintain *our* borders? Because a border, after all, only exists if both sides acknowledge and maintain it. In the past, in contrast to predators' shifting borders, humans have delineated their settlement boundaries precisely by mown lawns, driveways and fences, and they have defended that territory by shooting and trapping animal trespassers, thus training them not to intrude across the humans' relatively unshifting borders. As dogs can be trained, so can bears and cougars be trained, and that is why we humans have a residual idea that those predatory animals have a *natural* fear of humans. But in reality there is nothing innate about that fear at all. It is a learned behaviour and it was the direct result of the ancient human–wildlife conflict in which we have always been engaged.

That woman whose chicken house was damaged and whose flock was

When you live in a rural community your animals are always at risk of being killed or mauled by predators.

killed off told me that after forty-one years in the Valley she no longer enjoyed living there because of the dangers posed by bears and cougars. Normally under such circumstances she could have called the conservation officer and he might have brought a cage to trap the bear when it came back the next day to dine again. However, we were without a conservation officer and had been since June. Our only recourse was to try to convince the RCMP to help—if they had time and were so inclined.

Before the current legislative changes, my friend's husband had been in the habit of snaring invading bears or shooting them if they got too close, as many other people in the Valley did to protect their food source. Consequently, they rarely had a problem bear in their yards. They never wasted these animals, either. Her husband would skin them out and she would pressure-can the meat and give it to people who liked it or needed it. This was as close to living in harmony with nature as we could hope to get, and it came from the belief that humans, too, are a part of nature.

Today farmers and landowners are not allowed to patrol their borders to shoot or trap nuisance bears, wolves and cougars. They are not allowed to follow the sensible solution to a problem bear—converting that nuisance into a resource while protecting human welfare. And since we are no longer allowed to maintain the balance ourselves, the government may soon be forced to organize another of their "industrial harvests," as they did in Kelowna with nuisance rabbits or in the Yukon with nuisance geese. Just imagine the hue and cry if that were to happen with bears—but that is where we are headed.

I am not advocating eradication of predators, as has been done in many other countries. Indeed, one of the main reasons I came back to Canada from New Zealand was because of our vast wild spaces and the variety of wildlife that live within them. However, if we want humans and wild animals to co-exist in perpetuity we need to establish and maintain, through enforcement and policing, that boundary between our and their territories. In order to achieve this, we will have to make serious social changes—both nationally and internationally—the most crucial of which is to curb our human practice of limitless territorial expansion. Once we have decided where our human territory ends and that of the animals begins, we will have to be diligent about reinforcing that border and training the predators to be wary of our presence. Perhaps this sounds harsh, but as in raising a child, it is only fair to set clear boundaries. Consider it tough love.

Electric fencing deters black bears and sometimes grizzlies if they have not already had access to the fruit or beehives or chickens that you are trying to fence off. But this is not a foolproof tool. You often can't electric-fence a grizzly out once it's had access as it will just push on through. And God forbid you should get a bear on the inside of your fence! It won't leave.

In British Columbia we are allowed (theoretically at least) to kill animals that threaten our livestock. I say theoretically because, thanks to our overly proscriptive gun storage laws, it is extremely difficult to get a weapon ready when you really need it in an emergency situation. For example, say a bear (or perhaps two) is wreaking havoc in your chicken shed. You hear the commotion and run out to see what is happening. You assess the situation and decide you need to shoot the bear. You run back to your house to get your gun, rummage around to find the key, unlock the gun from the case. Then you get the key that unlocks the trigger and run to where you have to store your ammo separately from the gun. You unlock that case and load the gun. You race back to the scene of the crime, and if you are not too out of breath and the nightmare is still unfolding, you may legally use your gun. If things go your way, you may be able to save a chicken or two. Complying with this law has meant the loss of lives (some of them children's) to the claws of bears and cougars. One child was killed by a black bear because a neighbour could not find the key to unlock his correctly stored gun. Gary Shelton recalls, "I asked them about the neighbour who had run to the fence [when he heard Lisa's screams of terror], then ran back to his house. Dave explained that he had run to get a gun, but the rifle had a trigger lock on it, and he couldn't find the key. ... He suffered terribly and had to get counselling, not just because of losing Ian, but also because he hadn't been able to do anything to help save Ian." (*Bear Attacks*, Shelton, 1998, page 70)

In the sad case of my farming friend, if her husband had been still alive, he could have stood on the porch and shot the bear. Or he might

This cougar killed my neighbour's three guard dogs over the course of a few nights.

have tracked it the next morning and set a snare, as was the practice here until recent legislative changes made it illegal. This might have saved some of her chickens who suffered at the claws of the bear and might have prevented the bear's suffering through slow starvation. However, she could not legally ask for a neighbour's help to deal with the bear because the law says you can only protect your own livestock, not your neighbour's. In the old days our community would have been able to deal directly with this situation by phoning any number of qualified, experienced and willing hunter-neighbours. They could have effectively and safely destroyed the bear at once, either using their own guns or the Ministry of Environment's bear trap, which was sitting idle just across the road from my house.

Instead, our community had to wait to plead the case to the Ministry. During the delay of several days, several more people's flocks were massacred and sheds destroyed. In one instance, the bears ripped straight through the half-inch plywood walls of a poultry shed to get at the chickens. By the time the community had mustered two local hunters willing to work within the legal hunting regulations for our region, which allow the hunting of grizzly bears on a limited entry hunting tag and bow-hunting for black bear for a limited season, the conservation officer from Williams Lake was just beginning his six-hour drive to get here.

At the same time that we were being victimized by marauding bears, a cougar began terrorizing the neighbourhood. The cougar's games started with the killing and eating of several pet cats and attacks on two dogs, killing one. It was also feeding on deer in the wild. Thankfully cougar hunting season was open so a couple of hunters took up the challenge and started tracking the cat. After a long chase that led the hunters through neighbouring barns, yards and even someone's shop, they finally shot it just beyond the airport, not far from my house.

Knowing that there was a cougar on the prowl, I worried about my goats and dog. On the one hand, it was good to leave my dog outdoors because she was our early warning system and possibly just enough of a deterrent to make an inexperienced cougar change his mind. However, the dog was no match for a determined cougar, so if I let her stay outside, she might have been killed—even during the day. In fact, dogs here are often referred to as "cougar bait" because so many are taken each year from yards and even when walking with their owners.

When I had encountered the cougar in my yard, the conservation officer had commented that we were in a rural environment and I had to expect such wildlife conflicts. He told me the Ministry of Environment's policy reads, "Calls that involve nuisance bears ... coyote sightings in urban areas, cougar sightings in rural areas ... are usually low-risk." He said that conservation officers are only required to respond when a cougar "poses a direct threat to human safety," and according to the Ministry's policy, my cougar didn't pose a risk to human welfare because it was in a rural area and only looking at my goats. I pointed out that the cougar was in my driveway four feet from my house, that it had been watching me while I worked in the garden, and that the street bordering my property was remote but well-used by the locals, including mothers with small babies and young children on bikes or waiting for the school bus. None of these facts helped sway the officer to rate this cougar incident medium or high-risk.

The Ministry's policy goes on to assert that human–wildlife conflict is "usually preventable," and can be "largely resolved" through increased public education and a "collective effort to stop attracting" wildlife to our communities. According to the conservation officer, I had been attracting the cougar.

While discussing our community's cougar problems with another conservation officer I was told that, in accordance with the Ministry's "Safety Guide to Cougar Attacks" literature, which has not been updated since February 1996, we shouldn't fear cougars but respect them. When I reported this advice to a hunter friend who had helped track and shoot a cougar that had been terrorizing our neighbourhood, he laughed. Most people in the Valley would laugh at such ridiculous advice because they know what a cougar can do to you and how limited our resources are. The doctors and nurses here know what cougar injuries look like, and they know that it only takes four and a half minutes for someone to bleed out if a jugular vein—a cougar's preferred incision point—is cut by a claw or fang. They understand just how lucky are the few who have escaped with their lives after a cougar attack. They are acutely aware of the severe limits to our remote hospital's operating capacity, that our community relies solely on a volunteer ambulance service and that we do not have a fully trained paramedic team for first-aid treatment.

People in our community put these facts into the equation when considering wildlife–human conflict. They also know that the change in the Ministry of Environment's policies, outlawing the hunting and trapping of cougars and bears as a preventative protection measure, is at least partially responsible for the change in predator behaviour toward habituation and the increase in predator populations. These policies drive real action—or inaction—and foster skewed thinking.

That officer who told me we shouldn't fear cougars backed up this assertion by telling me that in Washington State, conservation officers put tracking devices on cougars and then go into classrooms to show children where those cougars are on computer screens. He explained enthusiastically that the children are learning that, while cougars are all around them, they are still safe. "See kids? These nice cougars obviously don't want to harm us!" Is it really a good idea to teach our children not to be wary of creatures that are by nature predators, especially given that cougars are more likely to attack humans of smaller stature?

Ironically, the Ministry's literature advises us to defend ourselves strenuously if attacked by a cougar. Other more current cougar literature goes further and warns us not to play dead because, unlike in the majority of bear attacks, which are not predatory in nature (with a few exceptions), an attacking cougar intends to kill and eat you.

The Project in Full Swing

The Rod and Gun Club dinner and dance

EVERY FEBRUARY the local Rod and Gun Club hosted a dinner and dance to raise money for the club and to raise awareness of hunting and animal conservation. Many might find it curious, if not ironic, that the hunters in this valley are some of those most aware of conservation and environmental issues and the most active in environmental conservation and preservation of animals. However, they are by far the most knowledgeable bunch of folks from whom I have had the pleasure of learning about the complexities of the natural world around us and the balance of nature.

In preparation for the big event, the members of the club prepared the meat they had hunted the previous fall as well as the farm-raised animals that they butchered for food, and the local amateur and professional taxidermists prepared animals for the display. I had helped Clarence butcher the turkey he donated, and I also helped his son, Dave, skin and butcher out the cougar that he brought to the event. The dinner had also provided me with the opportunity to bring my duck-breeding venture to a close; I butchered the last of the Muscovy ducks and took them to the dinner along with a loaf of my homemade bread.

Given the small community, the array of foods at the dinner was surprising, but it was also a testament to the industry of the people in the Valley. I could have tried every kind of meat on offer but managed to limit myself to what I could fit on my plate and as many varieties as I could still remember by the time I got from the smorgasbord back to the dinner table. On offer were deer, moose, caribou, elk, wild boar, duck, turkey, beaver, llama, black bear, grizzly bear, smoked sausages and hams and of course Dave's cougar, which he presented freshly roasted. I tried everything except the caribou and beaver. I had eaten caribou before, and by the time I got to the beaver it just wouldn't fit anywhere on the plate, though it did look delectable, having been made up into a beautifully presented stir-fry. I was surprised to see that the dinner even catered to vegetarians with salads of various kinds and several versions of tofu, vegetable stir-fries and bean dishes. The meal was scrumptious and most of us ate far too much, although I did manage to save room for dessert.

What struck me most about the dinner, besides the fact that it was such a unique example of local culture and so particular to the Valley, was that although I was expecting a greater difference in texture and taste between the carnivorous animals and the ruminants, they differed very little from each other. My favourite was the elk, with the cougar and the grizzly bear roasts tied for second place, and of all the options I sampled, the llama had the most distinctive taste, but so similar in taste and texture were most meats that I'm certain I could feed my mother a grizzly bear roast and tell her it was beef!

Crouching farmer, soaring feed costs

Spring arrived late in 2009 and as a result I found myself rapidly running out of hay for my goats. Worried that my supply wouldn't last until the new season's crop was ready, I began phoning around to see if anyone had extra to sell. The answer was a resounding no from everyone.

When you live in a remote place and your neighbours have no hay for sale, there is nowhere else you can go to buy more. Or if there is, it is five hundred kilometres away and you cannot justify the cost. The later than normal growth of the new crop had everyone concerned, and they were either hanging on to their own hay because they were as worried as I was, or they didn't have any extra to sell. I was down to my last two bales, and I realized that I would have to figure out how to supplement the goats' feed with something else. It occurred to me that I could let them have free range on the property, but that was a desperate measure. I just couldn't stomach the potential loss in terms of fruit tree and vine damage. Finally I decided I would just have to take the browse to them.

Armed with a hand weed trimmer I began hacking at the wilder areas of the property, and knowing that goats like thimbleberry bushes, I started with them. Within days I had run out of fodder on the farm and was soon making my way up and down the highway cutting the brush and carrying it back to the goats.

"Isn't there something wrong with this picture?" one passerby commented. Indeed there was. It would have been much easier if I could tether the goats and move them up and down the highway, letting them do the work of getting their own browse. In fact, at one point it had occurred to me that I should rent my goats out to the Interior Roads, the office that

The goats were a constant source of entertainment, but keeping enough feed to over-winter them proved to be a challenge.

maintains the roads for the Ministry of Highways. I would call them "Interior Goats." After all, they would probably do a much better job of keeping the sides of the roads cleared, not to mention that they would love the job and perform as if they were being paid to do it. Alas, this would never be. I couldn't really see the government going for this plan, and I couldn't possibly tether them out there even if I wanted to because they would become instant cougar bait. Instead, brush-cutting became part of my morning chores—a half-hour or so of labour donated to the Minister of Highways on behalf of my goats. It was my volunteer duty to the province and the goats loved me for it.

As I crouched down in the brush and chopped fodder each morning, they would line up along their paddock fence, watching diligently as I worked. There was a chorus of preferences baa'd in my general direction, the likes of which I imagined went something like this: "Mo-o-o-ore h-o-o-o-rse ta-a-a-il, less dock, please. I w-a-a-a-a-nt bra-a-aa-mbles! How ab-o-u-t some lilies and a s-i-i-i-de of c-o-o-mphrey ..." I wondered why I hadn't thought to do this before. It was, after all, free supplemental feed.

I tried turning this thinking to the other areas of the farm. What other feed could I supplement easily? The chickens and ducks already free-ranged so they more or less fed themselves, and when there were occasions that I couldn't let them free-range, I used chickweed to supply them with fresh greens. No, the highway belonged to the goats.

Eventually the new crop of hay was cut and baled, and we gathered it from the fields and stacked it into our shed. There were 132 bales in total.

Sweetness and light

As part of my goal of self-provisioning I wanted to extract myself from dependency on store-bought sugar. One way of doing this would be to get bees, and this had been on my wish list for several years. I had fantasized that it would be easy, thanks to the research I had done on that possibility while living in New Zealand, where there are more kinds of honey on the shelves of every grocery store than I ever thought could exist. As I had been lucky enough to live next to Tony the Greek, who kept his own hives, I had been able to do without sugar for a couple of years because each summer he gave me several pounds of his harvest. When I ran out of Tony's honey, I could drive about a mile further down the road and buy more from Robin, the honeyman. I used honey for everything—it sweetened coffee and jams, I baked with it, I even used it as a skin softener.

"Bees are the easiest animals you'll ever keep on your farm," New Zealanders had told me time after time. It was true that until very recently beekeepers there were able to raise organic honey almost effortlessly. The country did not have varroa mites and had very few bee diseases in general, so apiarists could raise bees in natural conditions. Sadly, this is no longer the case as the varroa mite moved into New Zealand sometime just before 2000.

Now that I was seriously trying to provision organically for my family, I figured that keeping my own bees would be the answer to getting off my dependency on the grocery store for sugar. While I was in New Zealand I had never been ready to accommodate bees by early spring, which is when you need to get organized and order them, but now I figured I finally had the time and space to set up my own apiary, and I began the task of finding the equipment and sourcing bees. But quite in contrast to the advice I received in New Zealand where beekeeping is easy, the general consensus in Bella Coola was "Don't bother!" Two agriculture extension specialists I consulted said, "You're living in a very marginal area for bees. There simply isn't enough natural forage for them."

When I spoke with two of the local fellows who have kept bees, they both confirmed what the professionals had said. Indeed, these Valley beekeepers had been struggling for several years, one of them losing all of his hives and the other all but one. Both had been successful in harvesting honey each year, but they'd had to work hard at it and devote a lot of time to keeping their hives alive, and they explained some of the realities of the time commitment and the difficulties involved in raising bees in this climate. I learned that bees like warmer weather than the Valley can provide. They don't appreciate the lack of sunshine, the wet weather or the damp, and they need acres and acres of good fodder, such as fireweed and clovers, in order to keep healthy and well fed.

As Bella Coola is in a rain forest and there is relatively little cleared farmland, there simply is not enough fodder to support them. I also learned that bees are not the easiest farm animal to keep anywhere in British Columbia, even in the warmer, drier parts of the province because there are more diseases here. As one of the local men told me, "You have to be prepared to devote a lot of time to raising bees here," and this was not what I had in mind.

Ultimately, I decided that I just didn't have the spare time it would take to devote to bee husbandry on top of all my other tasks. So I put my beekeeping aspirations on hold and started to look for another source of sugar. Eventually I came across a source of sweetness that is not only more traditional in this part of the world than beekeeping, but is also easier to manage. Birch and Douglas maple trees grow wild in my front yard! I began to wonder how easy it would be to simply tap them, extract their subtly flavoured sap and render it down into a sweet, tasty syrup.

We were experiencing a bit of a warm spring and suddenly I realized that, if I wanted to give tree tapping a try, I'd better get moving. Luckily it turned much colder again so the trees remained in their hibernation state. I found a local man who had experimented over the years with both maple and birch syrup making, and he was kind enough

I tapped my three maples and seven of the birches to make syrup. I boiled the sap over an open campfire. Truly, self-provisioning doesn't get any better than this.

to tell me about his experiments and provide advice and even loaned me ten spiles—the official term for the little metal "thingies" used to tap the trees—and ten ice cream buckets in which to catch the sap.

Not wanting to inadvertently poison myself, I showed him what I thought were my Douglas maples. I needed verification because locally they are called vine maples, and not being a woodsman, I really wasn't sure if I was on the right track. He verified that indeed these were Douglas maples and assured me that in terms of flavour they are repudiated to be one of the best maples for syrup. In fact, they are such good producers that he had stopped tapping the birch trees altogether and was now focussing entirely on maples. "I've found a few Norway maples and I'm going to experiment with that type this year," he said quietly as he left me with buckets and spiles in hand.

Now it happened that over the past few years a grizzly mama and her cubs had been bedding down each summer just behind my pergola, which was in the vicinity of the birches and maples I wanted to tap. I had once watched in horror as she stole a whole garbage pail full of duck feed right out from under the ducks' beaks, and on another occasion I was startled while hanging my laundry when her cubs raced through my front yard, having been scared off by the neighbour's dog. I had also seen them come into the yard and harvest many of my apples, breaking valuable tree branches as they went.

Because of these visitors and other bears that had been coming through the property each summer, one of the tasks I had been working on over the winter was clearing the dense undergrowth from the second-growth forest on the front half of the property, a two-acre tangle of alder, birch, maple, fir, hemlock, spruce, and a host of dense, scrubby bushes. The worst of these is devil's club, a beautiful but deadly plant with two-inch thorns that grab hold of passersby and cling to them with the tenacity of barbed wire. But while this undergrowth is impossible to get through if you are a human, the bears managed just fine, tunnelling their way through it to create a network of trails. With practice, I learned to identify their paths, and I found it interesting to see that each one went past several different native berry species.

With spring almost upon us, I found myself out there again hacking and hewing my way through this barely identifiable network to open it up for human accessibility. I found it hard going without machines but reminded myself it was better exercise than paying to go to the gym and running on a treadmill. While I was hard at work, Clarence came by and tenderly reminded me that I should be looking up every now and then in case a cougar was watching from on high. He then took me on a little walk-about in order to point out a nearby spruce tree. "Why, it was just there I shot a cougar a couple of years ago."

I told him I always brought my dog with me and sometimes even the goats. It was a sad reality of living in the Valley that one of my animals might save my life by sacrificing its life. Clarence nodded as I added that goats are efficient browsers and made short order of clearing much of the brush for me, although I couldn't possibly have let them out there alone to do the work as it would be like sentencing them to certain death. I reasoned that when we were out there together, we all stood a better chance because there is safety in numbers.

Clarence stood amazed at what we were doing, never having witnessed this kind of activity in the Valley. "And what are you doing all this here clearing for, my dear?" he asked at last.

"I need better access to these trees," I explained. "I'm going to tap those three maples and seven of the birches to make syrup."

He smiled and told me he'd never known anyone to tap birches before but that he'd tapped plenty of maples back home on the family farm in Pennsylvania while growing up. Most people think of maple sugar production as quintessentially Canadian and located either in Quebec or Ontario. It's not an activity one associates with the prairies or here on the West Coast, but it is possible.

Whenever I worked at clearing the brush on this part of our property, I had always built a huge bonfire to burn the brush, and at the end of a hard day's clearing I would sit by the last of the glowing embers and enjoy a sip of whiskey. That year, instead of enjoying the fire at the end of the day, I planned to use the brush to boil down my sap and transform it into syrup, the difference being that I would start the fire at the beginning of the day and keep it going for two whole days to render one large pot of sap. While it wouldn't be exactly cost-effective, we would taste the *terroir* of our own birch and maple syrup. And yes, the word terroir does extend beyond wine to other earthy products like syrup: syrups have local flavours, too.

Through Internet research, I discovered that if you mix the saps from maples and birches, they will form a uniquely flavoured syrup. Maple provides a better conversion of sap to syrup than birch (forty to one versus eighty or a hundred to one) so blending the two would make the rendering process less time-consuming than straight birch sap—or so my theory went. By my calculations our syrup ended up as a mix of about 20 percent maple and 80 percent birch.

As we had been away for a few days after I tapped the trees, we weren't sure how much of the fluid in the buckets was in fact just rain water—but we remained hopeful as we lit the fire to begin the rendering process. David and I then shared two days outside under grey skies with temperatures hovering just above freezing, but we were able to celebrate our spring break pleasantly warmed by the fire and dreaming of future spring days when the air would smell of turned earth and chlorophyll rather than smoke and birch sugar. As I looked across at my little yellow buckets hanging from their spiles in the tree trunks, I wondered why we are not all harvesting from our woodlots in this serene, labour-free way. Much of our radio news these days is filled with catastrophists predicting global economic ruin and advocating getting out of cities. It made me glad to be in a place where there was still so much self-sufficiency and that we had enough space to practice it.

After the sap had boiled down, I brought the pot indoors to complete the task on the stove. I had read that you can easily burn syrup in the last stages. Mind you, you can also easily boil it all away thinking it is still just water, because it looks that way for most of the process—no lovely amber colour, no viscosity. Sure enough, miraculously, at about one-inch depth the liquid suddenly thickened, darkened and looked like real maple syrup. I had about a quarter of a cup of pure gold in a jam jar.

I took my first tentative, frugal sip. Delicious! I had read that boiling over an open fire imparts a smoky campfire taste, and that proved to be true. It enhanced the caramel flavour while underneath there was an earthy mineral flavour. I contrasted this with the clearer, crisper taste of some birch syrup we had bought in Quesnel, a town up on the plateau.

My attitude toward time had shifted. As a self-provisioner, I was now geared to food availability rather than the clock and the standard calendar. In the old days I had regarded my year of activity as beginning on May 24, the traditional date for beginning safe frost-free outdoor gardening. With the discovery of fiddleheads I had expanded my provisioning calendar, and now thanks to the birch-maple syrup discovery it had been expanded even further.

My world was now measured by food, not only in time, but in space also, because wherever I walked or drove I remembered what food I had gathered there or what I might gather in the future. This must be how animals map their worlds, too.

While clearing the front of our property, I had realized by examining the bear trails that they travel east and west but deer travel north and south because their food sources lie in those directions. Bears follow the streams to the salmon rivers via the berry bushes, and deer travel to the meadows via my vegetable garden. Like the Aborigines of Australia with their song lines, I was making my own tracks across our property and across the Valley, and like the deer and bears, my map was taking shape along paths of sustenance. The more self-sufficient I became, the more I learned about how much effort it takes to feed one person. While my goal of food sovereignty was not always about cost effectiveness, the syrup-making exercise had renewed my appreciation for how cheap the food in this country really is. A jug of Quebec maple syrup at our supermarket was about $12. But I realized that this was far too cheap for the resources used, even considering the efficiency of mass production. I now also looked at our land and its resources differently. What only a month earlier had been a tangled mass of vine maples that I had considered sawing down because, according to several sources, it was no good for anything had become a precious resource. I already had a second batch of sap on the stove and intended to make several more batches over the next few weeks.

As in many aspects of our lives, the necessary decisions one makes when focussing on food security are full of compromises. When raising food for ourselves, climate and geography are important environmental factors, which to one degree or another dictate the terms of what is possible. "Location, location, location" is not just good advice for real estate speculators. I had to let go of my fantasies of growing great tomatoes and shell-out beans and raising bees because in spite of all my efforts, they would not do well given the geography of the Valley. But, while maple and birch syrup take a huge amount of energy to produce, they turned out to be a much more environmentally suitable solution to my sweetener needs than honey. The trees are native to the area and only Mother Nature tends to them, cultivating the sweetness we reap each year.

The Jenny Craig Cornish Crosses

With spring rapidly approaching, it was time to start thinking about our dietary needs for the upcoming year. I had been told that Cornish Cross chickens were easier to raise than the straight-run Cornish broilers that you buy in the supermarket, with lower chances of heart attacks and water-belly, so I decided to try them. I had two reasons: I wanted a heavier meat bird for my table, and I wanted to breed larger size and greater growth rate into my range birds. I'd been breeding a heavy heritage mix of bird over the past few years in an attempt to get the best of all worlds: a good egg layer, good meat bird, efficient range bird, and a hardy bird for the cold. But in the end, the heritage breeds can only grow so big and they don't have the real meatiness of the breast that we've become accustomed to in the hybrid birds of the commercial flocks.

I ordered fifty day-old Cornish Cross chicks and was told they would arrive in Bella Coola on the mail truck that Friday afternoon. However, around eleven on Friday morning I received a phone call from the Williams Lake post office letting me know the chicks would be arriving there at five that afternoon, and could I please pick them up before they closed for the weekend? The Williams Lake post office is a nearly five-hundred-kilometre one-way trip from Bella Coola!

Needless to say, I spent the better part of the afternoon in a panic, trying to locate someone in Williams Lake who would care for the chicks over the weekend and to arrange for a courier company to pick them up on Monday and bring them to Bella Coola. Thankfully, the feed store owner came through for me, picking the chicks up on Friday night, and Gerald of Chilcotin Freights agreed to bring them on his truck on Monday. Even so, as the chicks would be less than a week old by Monday, the feed store owner was worried about them making another long trip without food and water. As luck would have it, someone from Bella Coola dropped into the feed store on Saturday and the feed store owner pounced. "Would you mind taking these chicks with that order of yours?"

Being a neighbourly sort, the man kindly obliged and my wee-uns arrived safely that night in the gentle care of a man I'd only met once at a party. He did a fine job as they all arrived alive and well.

These little creatures had a much higher rate of poopy-bum than the other chicks I'd raised. I don't know if that is typical for the breed or because they were highly stressed by their perilous journey. There is also

I was warned that the rapid growth of these Rhode Island Red and Cornish Cross chicks could be a problem, so I supplemented their diet with fresh greens to slow their growth rate and help prevent poopy-bum.

the possibility that the people at the feed store fed them medicated starter while under their care, even though I'd already had them vaccinated for coccidiosis, which is caused by a common protozoan parasite present in almost all chicken yards and which can lay dormant for years until chickens are reintroduced. Heavy infections of coccidia cause serious disease and may kill many chickens, and while chickens of all ages can come down with coccidiosis, four- to sixteen-week-old chickens are most commonly affected. Therefore, having them vaccinated at the hatchery as day-olds provides the best protection and long-lasting immunity. It also does not affect organic status whereas medicated feed can. At any rate, I had to do daily patrols and cleanings for several days with about forty percent of the chicks, but as a result they all grew well.

Mostly my chickens took care of themselves, as well as doing their mating and hatching on their own. My only hand in the process was to cull the Jenny Craigs (the skinny light-bodied chooks) and ensure good breeding stock, and up to this point we were all quite happy with the program.

When I first got the Cornish Crosses I was worried about their rapid growth. The literature warns this can be a problem and advises restricting their food intake in order to keep them from going "off their legs." I was not exactly sure how to restrict these little guys' food. They were the messiest birds I'd kept when it came to feeding from the hopper. There was more food on the ground around the hopper than I'd seen with any other bird. But I was worried that I would starve them if I restricted the amount I gave them, so I tried another route to resolving this problem. As with all my baby chicks, I began taking them fresh greens as a daily supplement. Not only does this help with poopy-bum prevention but it also slows their growth rate a bit. But I was worried that these little guys might not like the greens, and at first it did look like they wouldn't eat them. Of course, only a few of the braver ones had to take an interest before the whole flock was jockeying for positions around the plate. Now I just had to hope that the ol' Weight Watchers rule—"Fill up on vegetables"—was a universal principle!

After I moved them out onto the free-range pasture, their alarming growth seemed to slow to a more natural rate of development, but by nine weeks, they were still too skinny to butcher, and I had to postpone butchering day to see if they would reach two kilograms. At least they looked happy and healthy, with no sign of the dreaded list of possibilities: heart attacks, water bellies, laying down to eat, coming off the legs and so on.

Taking Stock

In the summer we started a roadside stall to see what we could sell of my excess produce, but we learned it takes a huge effort to stock a stall and keep things fresh, and if we were lucky, at the end of the day the average return was $5. As the summer wore on, I felt more and more like an average global peasant.

Although we were now completely self-sufficient in eggs, chicken and turkey, I had not yet managed to be completely self-sufficient in all aspects of chicken and turkey raising. Despite my best efforts to incubate my own chicken eggs, I was still relying on buying day-old turkeys and some day-old chickens. However, I now had a much better idea of how much chicken and turkey meat we ate in a year, and I was learning how to raise the birds on a more profitable scale. Ducks, however, had proved to be unreliable layers of eggs and were not very good mothers, and I am not all that fond of their meat. I sometimes wondered if this had something to do with my feelings toward them—they were very cute and I enjoyed watching and listening to their antics.

Having bred the goats, I would now have to learn to butcher and eat the kids, which was not something I was looking forward to. I still wanted to milk the goats and make cheese, but the realities of our farm's location and its host of predators made this an impractical idea, and the regulations for selling the milk prohibited that possibility. I came to understand why Joel Salatin had written a book called *Everything I Want to Do is Illegal*.

Despite all that I had learned, I was having doubts about the whole enterprise. A friend from New Zealand asked why I was staying here when there were much easier places to farm, and I was beginning to wonder that myself. It is just not enough to have a cute farm and funny animals. I needed a wage like everybody else. The funny animals were taking time and effort, and while I could justify having them as pets when I had a nice salary, I was having a more difficult time justifying them now that I didn't.

Surprisingly, when I said that to people (who had nice salaried jobs), they were shocked. "Oh, you can't get rid of your goats, they're so cute!" was the most common response. Yes, they were cute. So were the ducks. But cute wasn't paying the taxes, replacing the roof or replacing the truck as it rusted away. When did our society come to expect farms to be cute, and farmers to lose money on their farms? When did we stop caring that, like any other service industry, if a farm is not supported and can't make a profit, it won't last?

This principle is well understood for all sorts of businesses and services, and yet farms seem to be thought of as something that shouldn't make money. It is as if we've all come to accept it as logical that farmers should work outside their farms to pay for their farms. What other business would this apply to? Would you run a restaurant that way and work somewhere else to pay to keep the restaurant open?

My life, I realized, had become an artistic expression of my politics, and my garden was my palette.

Searching for that one percent

"What you're looking for is 1 percent of a moose," Dave, Clarence's son, said softly as we followed some fresh tracks in the snow. "You're not going to see 99 percent of him." Then slowly bringing his hand up through the air between us, he motioned delicately as if caressing part of the woman he loved and whispered, "You'll see a leg ..." That example clearly outlined, he shifted his body posture completely to prepare for the next example. Standing tall, he arched his neck and head the way a horse does just before it is going to strike out at you and brought his index finger down the length of his nose. "You'll just see the tip of his nose." His face loomed over me while his body squared off in an aggressive stance. Maintaining that pose, he brought his other hand up to the side of his head, placed his thumb in his ear and extended his arm to its limit. He whispered, "Or an antler," and for a brief moment he was a moose. Then, turning, he pointed at a patch of willow brush and his finger traced a half moon through the air. "Or, you might just see his butt."

There was a pause in the lesson. I could see he was lost in memories of hunting trips past, when the visions he'd just described had unfolded before him. It's this kind of thing that makes Dave a good teacher: not only is he a very experienced hunter but he also has an accurate recall of minute details and uses them to punctuate his lessons. Suddenly back in the moment, he looked directly at me and said, "What you're not going to see is a whole moose."

It turned out that he couldn't have been more wrong, but the point he was making would stay with me as would his next lesson. It was the morning of the big day and he was revisiting things he'd said several times before. "I can't stress this enough, Kristeva," he said. Then he contextualized the lesson by footnoting the pedigree of this knowledge: "My dad always stressed this to me and so I'm going to stress it to you."

Like his father, Dave never just says something with his mouth. Instead, his whole body has a role to play, and the more important he deems the information, the more body parts are engaged.

He leaned toward me. "The hunt is not over until you're back in camp," he said, and his hands became quad bikes moving along imaginary trails and parking in front of the cabin. "And your gun is hung up." His hands glided daintily through the air as if hanging women's lingerie rather than a gun-strap. "I don't know how many times I've seen it ... you know, guys on their way back to camp ..." His hands squeezed down hard on an imaginary throttle. "Buzzing home as fast as they can like the hunt is over ... you know, just because they've turned back toward home." A look of disgust washed across his face. "You can't move slow enough when you're hunting," he insisted. He went on to describe several occasions when he'd seen moose or deer or whatever he was hunting while he was on his way back to camp when he'd thought the day was over.

"One time I was here," he said, pointing to the meat pole hanging in front of the cabin, "butchering out a moose when I heard a shot go off right there!" He pointed. "I tell you, honey," he paused and laughed, recalling the incident, "that shot was so close it scared the living daylights out of me ... but I knew it had to be Dad." In fact, his dad had seen a big buck deer standing on the other side of the cabin just metres from where Dave was butchering. Dave's smile disappeared and the stern look returned to his face. "He made his point that day."

My pre-hunt lessons over, we struck out for the day—and it was a glorious one to boot, a nice change from several days of the worst conditions Dave had ever seen in his forty-two years of hunting in the area. Yes, I had braved those days, too—though more for the experience of driving the quad than looking for moose. Although it was not all that cold, the heavy rain and sleet had made the going tough. "The animals will hole up in this weather," Dave had yelled over the incessant pounding of the rain, "but we can break trail!" And break trail we did. For two solid days we climbed hills and plunged through meadows and even very nearly got stuck in a bog that should have been iced over by that time of year. But that was the first time I'd ever seen a mole. Dave was ahead of me as we came to the bog, and I watched with horror as his bike broke through the ice before beginning to sink. He increased his throttle until his tires spun and the bike lurched

Learning to hunt successfully was the last step in achieving my goal to provide food for my family.

forward out of danger, but as the tires spun, they spat a wee mole out of its shelter and onto the ice. I watched, fascinated, as it scurried across the path in front of me and disappeared a few metres away into another of its snow-covered tunnels.

Today was a different story. While we made our way from the cabin at our usual top speed, me in the lead, I was mindful of all that he had taught me. "I see you're practising," he said, manoeuvring his quad beside mine. Wherever we stopped for one of his smoke breaks, it was a signal that class was in session, and his stories enlivened each new lesson. But this time, instead of waiting to hear what he had to tell me, I took the opportunity to get an answer to a question about a tiny detail in one of his earlier stories.

"Last year you told me that when you shoot a moose you always wait for twenty minutes before going after him—why?"

"Oh, okay. You need to know this." He finished rolling his cigarette, lit it, and took one long drag before continuing. "If you take off after a moose once you've shot it, you'll be running for miles." He took another drag on his cigarette and the smoke billowed up around his face. "But if you wait, he'll just go over there and lie down and not get up again."

We headed out on the trail again. I took the lead and puttered quietly along the meadow, looking from side to side for that 1 percent of a moose. My eyes scanned the foreground and then the recesses of the forest but encountered nothing. We were now getting close to camp again and I could feel my disappointment rising.

Trying to lift my spirits, I reminded myself of Dave's lesson that morning: "The hunt is not over until it is over." I kept repeating this to myself as we crept our way homeward. One might say that the mantra paid off because, as I was just turning a corner to inch out into an open meadow, suddenly there it was—a whole moose. *Jesus God, there he is!* I got off the quad quickly and quietly, keeping myself small beside the bike and hoping the moose wouldn't notice any change. He'd obviously not been spooked by the sound of the approaching bike.

I reached into my pocket and got out two cartridges and loaded them into my gun. I winced as they clicked into place, worried that the moose would react to the unnatural noise. But it was the sound of my bolt action that got his attention. His head came up from the willow brush he had been ruminating over, but he was too late. Now on one knee with the moose's chest in my sights, I pulled the trigger.

The moose flinched, but I wasn't sure if it was from the sound of the gun or if I'd actually hit him. "Again!" Dave directed from behind me, bringing me back to the task at hand. I reloaded, aimed at the now moving target and fired. This time he stumbled and it was obvious he'd been shot. He disappeared into the bush and it was all I could do not to take off running after him. "You did it!" Dave cheered as he grabbed me up into a bear hug. "Isn't this exciting?" Indeed it was.

Not one to miss an opportunity to prove a point, while we waited out the requisite twenty minutes before tracking him down, Dave held forth. "Well, this didn't quite go as I said it would, but I was right about one thing." He reached into his pocket for his tobacco pouch. "I told you that you wouldn't see a whole moose." Before proceeding with the explanation, he opened up a Zig-Zag rolling paper and stuffed it full of tobacco. "And you didn't," he continued, pausing to bring the rolling paper to his lips to lick and seal it. He stuck the freshly made cigarette into the corner of his mouth. "You only saw 99 percent of that moose." He took a deep drag on his smoke, savouring both the moment and the smoky flavour. Then, eyes twinkling, he stuck one leg out and pointed at his boot. "His toes were buried in the snow."

Now that I am a hunter, I feel a little bit less like a domestic animal and a lot more like a natural human being, a real member of our species. I feel like the predator that God (or the universe or whoever) intended us to be, like the Aboriginal women of the Australian outback who take their food from the world around them, who track their food down and kill it with their own hands, women that I'd want with me under desperate circumstances. I am now one of *those* women.

Your Money and Your Mouth

In 2008 I started a blog on which I posted an article called "What can I do to take back some control over my diet when I'm living in the middle of a city?" I had many responses, and while on the one hand I understood the enthusiasm of those who responded, I was disheartened by the number who felt that we, the ordinary people, are to blame for the problems that are inherent in the system. I am philosophically opposed to what I now call "The Al Gore Effect": that is, I don't believe that we, the people, are to blame. Moreover, I don't believe that we are going to be able to fix all the problems by riding our bikes to work once a week or only buying green or organic or local. In fact, I don't believe there are any personal behavioural changes that can wholly affect the game itself because the problems we are facing are systemic and the rules are wrong.

The people we elect to government may think that they can manipulate the rules of that system and that, if they choose, they can right the wrongs in it, but they can't. The system is controlled by the financial markets, and those markets are driven by fear and greed. That is why food prices around the world have surged to levels they haven't reached in twenty years. According to the latest United Nations Food and Agriculture Organization's food price index, "in just six months the price of soybeans is up 46 percent, the price of sugar is up 34 percent and there are fears that if nothing changes on that front we could see widespread food riots around the world" (CBC, February 8, 2011). This is the result of the financialization of food that has led to a completely new kind of speculation in food markets.

"Some of the largest banks and financial institutions of the world are going long on commodities and bringing on a tremendous 'buy' pressure," says Fred Kaufman, a contributing editor for *Harper's Magazine* and author of *A Short History of the American Stomach*. So in addition to the supply and demand equation (population growth and economic development that drive prices up and the natural disasters that drive supply down), what the world is facing today is "a group of specialized financiers who are making a bundle of money on hunger" (CBC, February 8, 2011). But, Kaufman adds, "Everybody has to understand ... that there is more than enough food to feed the world. In fact, we have double the food [we need] to feed the world. The problem [is that there] are new kinds of demands and new kinds of speculation." What is needed, he says, are policies that support the small farmers around the world because it is these small farmers who are feeding more than half the world. "Globalistic policies which drive prices down don't necessarily help the small farmers and don't necessarily help the people who need help the most."

There are things that government can do to support those small farmers, says Evan Fraser, who holds the Canada Research Chair on Global Human Security at the University of Guelph. He specializes in food security issues and is the co-author of *Empires of Food: Feast, Famine, and the Rise and Fall of Civilizations*. Governments need "a new approach and for science to invest in small-scale agriculture and get away from the large-scale agriculture that we've tended to invest in. We need a new approach to trade that recognizes the importance of diversity and food sovereignty. We need to store food at a local and a regional level as a buffer against a crisis." But at the same time, he points out that "consumers need to develop a consciousness about food so that we are aware of these issues and are aware that when we buy a Big Mac or a tofu burger we're voting for a kind of system, and we need to vote for a system that is kinder and gentler on the planet" (CBC, February 8, 2011).

Recently I attended a community meeting put on by the provincial government as part of their think-tank sessions for rural and remote communities. One of the participants said she was struggling with her decisions on what to buy in the grocery store if she followed the rule of buy local first, buy Canadian second, buy Washington State third, and so on. She explained that she was puzzled that buying from Canadian sources came before buying from Washington State because of the gas/oil kilometres involved, Ontario being a lot farther away than Washington or Idaho. She also struggled with the choice of organic imports versus the non-organic from somewhere closer. Should she buy the organic potatoes from Washington State or the regional non-organic potatoes? She wanted to simplify the process and buy local, ethically raised, sustainable products. However, because these often didn't exist, she was forced to make other complex choices, and in many cases these choices were beyond her personal philosophical guidelines.

Listening to her ethical dilemma helped me realize a fundamental truth: it is not enough that we get informed and make ethical choices because if the items we want to choose are not available, then we cannot be effective even if we want to be. The power to make the needed changes lies in the hands of our governments and their policy makers. The best we can do is find out about the agricultural policies of our governments and advocate for ethical changes. We must look closely at our food distribution and production system and the legislation that supports its get-big-or-get-out infrastructure. Ultimately, government legislation supports factory farming with its industrial pollution, animal abuses and environmental degradation. At the same time, these factory farmers are provided with access to loans, subsidies and crop insurance and are backed up by research and development programs (think Monsanto and Roundup Ready crops) and the latest marketing and distribution techniques.

On the other hand, growers who are committed to ethical, holistic, biodynamic, spray-free, organic and otherwise unconventional farming have no meaningful support from government and their ability to survive, let alone thrive, is always on the line. On top of such expected farming variables as bad weather, pests, diseases and the fluctuations of the market, they must deal with higher production costs than their conventional farming counterparts. For example, a steer finished at a "concentrated animal feeding operation" is fit for slaughter in just twelve months, while a pasture-raised animal can take thirty months. As a result, the price of the food that is produced by these "unconventional farmers" is higher than what you will pay for factory foods.

Friends and colleagues complain they can't afford these prices, yet these excuses often come from the mouths of people who take a holiday to a remote location at least once a year, eat out regularly, buy their children every new toy, iPod or cell phone that comes onto the market, wear the latest in athletic, eye- and footwear, and buy expensive name-brand clothing. While they think nothing of spending five dollars for a fancy coffee at Starbucks, they demur at the idea of paying the same for a dozen healthy eggs or an extra dollar for food that is an investment in their own health—not to mention the additional benefits of supporting a farmer who cares for his or her animals humanely, protects the environment and watershed, and thereby keeps the economy local and the community supported.

According to the Love Food Hate Waste organization (lovefood-hatewaste.com) based in the United Kingdom, people in the developed world throw out one-third of their food annually, which brings me to ask, is good quality food really too expensive or are we just so accustomed to cheap food that we have become lazy and wasteful? Quite apart from the careless waste of food by those who have enough when there are others in the world who don't have enough, this wasteful practice sheds light on why it is difficult to convince people that good quality food is worth more money. If we "haves" can afford to throw out that much food then surely, if we got organized and didn't waste so much, we could afford to pay more up front for better food. Unfortunately, the only marker of value generally recognized by the people of the developed world is consumption, not quality, which in the case of food means taste, nutritional value, ethics of origin, environmental impact and so on.

Since moving from the city and investing time and money into supplying my own food, I have come to understand that how we spend our money is a choice. I know how strong the pull is to buy superfluous items; I feel it every time I enter a city and the splash and ripple of the window dressings catch my eye and excite my imagination. I know first-hand how easy it is to get caught up by the continuous bombardment of advertisements and to suddenly find myself "needing" things I have absolutely no use for.

The urban system of value and priority is shaped by our consumer society to prioritize accessories and cauterize any sense of where each meal comes from. Many people truly believe in health and justice and may assiduously buy from their local fair trade store and write generous cheques to the NGO that is saving the giant panda in China, but still they mindlessly shop at the supermarket, buying factory-farmed beef, chicken and turkey, or choose the cheaper "free-range" eggs from some anonymous corporate farm rather than buy from a local farmer whose animals have something like a normal life.

As Michael Pollan, author of *In Defense of Food,* and Barbara King-solver, author of *Animal, Vegetable, Miracle*, have so eloquently explained, when eating mindlessly from the supermarket supplies, we are in effect eating oil, thanks to the huge distances that most food has to travel to be available in local supermarkets. Re-localizing our food is the most important thing we can do to save the planet, and it is something that each of us can support by choosing to eat differently and demanding from our governments legislation that supports our ability to do so.

Today, if you live in a city in a temperate climate, you can find a wide variety of foods that are grown in your area all year round or at least for a large percentage of the year. You can, therefore, choose to spend your dollars ethically. Your local farmers' market should be your first stop, and you won't have any trouble finding one; in BC alone there are almost a hundred of them, usually open on Fridays or Saturdays. According to a report issued by Farmers Markets Canada, an umbrella organization dedicated to furthering the viability, growth and prosperity of Canadian farmers' markets and helping farmers connect with consumers, there were 28 million shopper visits to farmers' markets across the country in 2008. The biggest problem for farmers who sell at these markets is the lack of government support for advertising and marketing.

Smith and McKinnon, the authors of *The 100-Mile Diet,* lived in downtown Vancouver and had access to a panoply of good food at their local farmers' market as well as to farmers on the outskirts of the city who could supply nearly everything they wanted. Like them, you can also locate community farmers and become really connected to the origins of your purchased food. Go beyond the single purchase transaction and open a dialogue with these farmers around agricultural issues. Start by asking about the challenges, problems and legislated prohibitions the farmer faces. Learn what is and is not allowed to be sold directly from the farm without first having to take a circuitous route off the farm—for example, to a slaughterhouse and back again. If you invest in the issues surrounding food production and distribution, you can become an effective, informed lobbyist, either in the next elections or in your daily life.

The most important interactive step an urban dweller can take is to buy from a local farmer, preferably as part of a group that is committed to providing a secure market to that farmer. If you can get out of the grocery store and into the farmers' market, you may be able to find such a farmer, just as you found a dentist, a doctor, a personal trainer, a piano teacher for your daughter, a soccer coach for your son. If you line up some like-minded friends to patronize these farmers, you may even be able to influence what they grow because farmers need secure markets for their products. For example, if a farmer knows that twenty families would buy honey from him each year, it may be worth his while to start keeping bees, especially if one of his other crops would benefit from the bees' pollinating activities.

Another idea is to stage a farmer appreciation night. Food is culture and culture is food. It unites us and is the centre of much socialization. Invite your farmer to a dinner you've made using his or her produce and introduce him or her to your friends. The farmers I know all love to talk about their products: they work hard to grow the food you buy and yet don't often get the opportunity to talk about it. Farming is a calling, not just a career. Farmers reveal this through the passion in their voices when they talk about their products, or when they take a second job to keep their farms going, or when they sleep outside with their chickens to catch the fox that's been killing them.

We need to honour our farmers. Farming should be the most noble profession we have, yet when was the last time a high school counselor or university career counselor suggested someone choose farming as a career? I wish mine had. We revere our doctors, but why are we not looking at our farmers as part of our public health system, too? After all, healthy food is considered a central part of preventative medicine. My greatest heartbreak in the past four years was talking to a group of fifth-generation farmers in Saskatchewan now older than their fathers were when they passed their family farms on to them, who found themselves working harder than their fathers ever had. Yet not one of those farmers was able to make a living off his farm, let alone a dignified living. They and their spouses had taken part-time jobs to support themselves. We have made farming like a drug habit, something the farmer does surreptitiously and almost with embarrassment, so small are the economic returns and so low is the social prestige in which we hold it. So perhaps you could honour your farmer's skills by learning a few of them from him, and instead of taking another trip to Hawaii, you might want to offer to farm-sit so that your farmer might have a holiday in Hawaii, perhaps for the first time.

Thinking even more locally, the smallest steps to food security that you can make may involve growing your own food: herbs in pots, a tomato in the corner of the deck, strawberries in a hanging basket. Try to grow what you like to eat. When I suggested this to a friend who likes potatoes, she asked me, "Why should I bother growing potatoes when they're so cheap at the store?" My answer was that they are easy to grow, help break up the soil for future crops, and won't have the chemical sprays that are dumped on those cheap commercial potatoes. Don't grow difficult vegetables that you eat relatively rarely, like eggplants or peppers, unless you live somewhere hot and you have the know-how, the space and the time—especially if this is your first attempt. You don't want to be turned off the whole venture by making it complicated. Share some of the work with your friends and neighbours. Perhaps you could construct a greenhouse where you and your neighbour can grow some favourites like tomatoes and peppers without having to bear the cost of the whole structure alone.

One of the happiest aspects of gardening is the community it attracts. Where I live, I deliberately seek out the old-timers and learn from them. You can sign up for a community garden plot and meet the neighbouring gardeners. If you make the effort, you will find like-minded folks and, if you are lucky, a Tony the Greek or a Clarence of your own with whom you can trade succulent recipes and learn valuable skills. A garden fertilizes an amazing web of interconnectivity (pardon the pun!).

Someone recently contacted me from the city asking if I knew where she could get a small flock of Barred Rock chickens. I suggested she try her local feed dealer or to get together with some neighbours to make up a big enough order to get them from a hatchery. But the following day I had a better idea: I suggested she go to a factory farm and buy some of their "spent" hens. The typical factory hen is discarded after one year of service, and because factory farms maximize their profits at the expense of the animals' lives, these hens are typically sent to the food mill or, worse, ground up into blood and bone meal for garden centres to sell. But these hens still have a lot of life and good laying potential left in them, and I joked to my caller that she could start a movement in concert with Vancouver's Farm Folk/City Folk, who are working to get "a chicken in every backyard." I had already met with some of the Farm Folk/City Folk people and talked about their support for heritage breeds—another worthy cause—but perhaps it makes more sense to give a factory farm hen a nice life in return for her service in our factory egg production system.

Check your city's bylaws. Many cities are now allowing small backyard flocks of chickens. You keep backyard poultry very easily and without much work if you put them in a mobile coop—a chicken tractor in permaculture terms—which will help to avoid any off-putting smells and provide some of the best nitrogen-rich fertilizer on the planet. For a tiny amount of grain and access to your lawn, chickens will provide you with the healthiest, tastiest eggs you'll ever have the pleasure of eating. There truly is nothing like taking an egg, still warm from the nest, and making it into an omelette just minutes after it's laid—now that's fresh! You can raise rabbits in the same way, providing some of your own meat for the price of a few alfalfa cubes, your fresh vegetable peelings and access to your lawn. Really, how attached are you to mowing your lawn?

There are many other ways you can make food production your business rather than somebody else's. For example, you can learn to use your kitchen gadgets for other purposes such as grinding your wheat in your coffee grinder, just minutes before you turn that wheat into a delicious loaf of fresh bread. You can also learn some food preservation techniques so that you can buy cheap in season and eat out of season. It's not compli-cated: making yoghurt is one of the easiest ways of preserving a food and it takes just minutes. Fermenting vegetables is also easy. A friend made sauerkraut in her apartment, leaving it in a Ziploc bag in her pantry beside the light while it fermented. Dehydrating is even easier and can pro-vide a ready-made meal: a jar of meat, a jar of tomato sauce, and a handful of dehydrated peas, carrots, onions and zucchini, and within an hour you have a delicious, healthy dinner with virtually no preparation. And it's a dinner you know is not going to make you sick! In addition to increasing your food security, preserves look beautiful on your counter—trophies of your industry, promises of future enjoyment. Even without costly kitchen appliances, you can still get creative. For example, while living in New Zea-land, too mortgage-strapped to buy a dehydrator, I laid out our tomatoes on a cookie tray and put them on the back window ledge of our sedan. Each day my husband parked his car at the school, and the sun did its work. Soon our car became known in the staff room as the "sun-dried tomato car." (One piece of advice: if you dry fruit and veggies this way, crack a window open slightly, lest you end up with sun-broiled tomatoes!)

With the purchase of one or two very simple pieces of equipment, your kitchen table can easily become a family focus of food production, and you can invite your kids to be part of the food-making equation. One of my local friends told me what great pleasure he gets from spending time around the family table processing food. His children are involved in all aspects of their food production, from helping in the garden to caring for the newly acquired chickens to the final processing and storing for winter. He waxed lyrical about how he felt during cherry season when the family was processing their bounty. "I looked around the table and each of us had a task: one was in charge of washing, one was drying, they were taking turns with the cherry pitting machine, and we were laying them out in trays, making them ready for the dehydrator. I felt like Santa Claus in his workshop with his elves before Christmas!"

If you want to go on an excursion, don't just mountain bike or jog or play but become a hiker-gatherer. Gather while you go so that your activity is educational and productive. You can return with a bag of mushrooms or blueberries or black currants. Plan seasonal excursions: the fiddlehead hiking season, followed by the alpine blueberry camping trip, the fall mushroom hunt backpack trip, and so on. Of course, not every location will have the same gathering options or potential, but every location will have something to offer. Take up the challenge of re-educating yourself and make a part of your life revolve around the gathering and eating of local foods. Put the "culture" back in your area's agriculture.

What all this amounts to is rethinking your choices and re-evaluating them under the rubric of differentiating your wants from your needs. Identify some things you can live without, such as the pineapple in January if you live where pineapples don't grow. Redirect some of your superfluous spending into something worthwhile. For example, a friend of mine quit drinking beer and now donates that money to a needy family—and this friend is living in a city on a half-time salary. Whatever you do, try to keep your money in your community and spend it according to your newly reassessed value system. Every dollar you spend is a commitment, a testament to what you believe in, and you can put your money where your mouth is, literally.

Epilogue

Farming: The social nexus

A FARM IS LIKE A WEAVING LOOM, embracing the threads that become the social fabric of a community. Every time I expanded my farming endeavours, I met a variety of people from the community who, had I not been doing this work, I would not have had reason to meet. There were myriad gardeners and farmers with whom I shared my trade secrets, but more importantly, they shared their vast wealth of knowledge with me. For that I will be eternally grateful, and I am thrilled to call them friends. There is also an extensive list of people that I hired to help build and develop parts of the farm, people who have skills and knowledge (and machines) that I did not have. The list includes loggers, builders, electricians, farmers, back-hoe operators, cement truck drivers and providers, gravel operators and (occasionally) the conservation officers.

I had lived in the community for five years before I met Cliff, even though he lived and farmed just two hundred metres away as the crow flies. A friend recommended him as a source of good hay, and soon he and his tractor became regular visitors delivering rotted hay, which I used to mulch the garden. For him it was a bad reminder of a poor haying time last year but it was worth its weight in gold to me.

Ed, who often helped Cliff to deliver the rotting hay, was another new acquaintance. It was Ed I hired to rotovate the new 2,000-square-foot garden in the front yard after hiring Mitch to chop down a couple of old, rotting willow trees and clear the area of brush. Ed was also a wealth of knowledge. Had I not spent some time chatting with him after he completed the rotovating, I would never have known how to sow my wheat! I also would not have had a source of local beef because the farmer I usually bought meat from had all his cows spoken for that year.

Colleen, my neighbour, a long-time friend and the one-time landlord of our property, was another regular visitor to my garden. She would come over for coffee in the morning and survey my work, her little dog Winston at her side. She told me some of the history of the land we now called ours, pointing out which fruit trees she had planted and which had been planted by the previous owner. She knew the varieties of some of the old apple trees and, when we went together to the nursery, helped me choose new varieties. She generously shared starter flowers from her garden and showed me how to transplant the tender plants safely. Colleen was an avid gardener and collector of plants, both domesticated and wild, and whenever she went camping, she would come back with her truck loaded down with new possibilities, which she'd often shared with me. I credited her with the establishment of most of my flower gardens.

Finally there was Clarence, from whom I gained more knowledge and gardening secrets than any other gardener I ever met. Keen to share both his knowledge and his plants, he was integral to getting parts of my garden populated, providing potatoes, beautiful purple dahlias, blackberries, three six-metre-long rows of strawberry plants, three young cherry trees that had self-seeded voluntarily into his garden from his older trees and that transplanted successfully into mine, and some of the gorgeous trademark red tulips from his vegetable patch. So Clarence's garden continued to be a living inheritance to our community.

Of course, there was also the growing list of people who bought my eggs or wanted my veggies. Just as importantly, there was a list of people who simply came by to visit, check out the farm, or bring their children and grandchildren to meet the animals. In her book *Animal, Vegetable, Miracle*, Barbara Kingsolver shares the history of the farmhouse she lived in, and how, through stories from the family whose parents had built the home, she had come to know and experience place. "[The] surviving Webbs ... now in their seventies ... unfailingly invite us to their family reunions. Along with the pleasure of friendship and help with anything from binding a quilt to canning, we've been granted a full century's worth of stories attached to this farm." I too have experienced this way of knowing the place that I called home through the stories of the land, because there were many folks in the Valley who not only were born there but are the fourth or fifth generation on the land, and their stories were often punctuated with remnants of local historic experience.

When we hired some local builders to build our poultry barn, I learned yet another dimension of the area's history. One of the builders was born and raised in the Valley and, needless to say, had raised a lot of buildings there over his fifty-odd years. Listening to him, I conjured a picture in my mind of a skyline of barns, homes, and shops scattered throughout the Valley, indelibly marking the land, a painting of his life's history through his work.

When Cliff delivered his hay, he told us how as a child he had played on our farm as it had belonged to his uncle. "Their house was over there, they had a cabin there, and their barn was right there. Then so-and-so bought the place and they built a slate walkway and fireplace." He told me more about the place than I learned in the previous three years of living there. Not long after that, another neighbour revealed he had also once owned the place and run cattle on it. After a bit more discussion we discovered he was the original breeder and owner of my horse, Nick, and he told me that Nick had a sister. It seemed that nearly every person who came through our front gate brought along another piece of material, fleshing out the patchwork of our land's history and even its recent existence.

One day a vehicle I didn't recognize stopped at the end of our driveway. I was in the yard working and so I went to greet him. He was probably in his seventies and now lived on the Sunshine Coast. He told me he had once lived on our farm, too, and asked if he could come in and have a look around. We spent some time with him and listened to his stories. He was one of the original owners of the land, and I'd never dreamed I'd meet that person. His stories were the final threads that quilted the patchwork of our history together. We were now officially bound, completed, marked into place, protectors and sovereigns of a land rich with history, community and possibility.

Additional Recipes

Canning Martha Stewart–Style

Canning Pears Martha Stewart–Style has a ring to it, rather like *Crouching Tiger, Hidden Dragon*, but less threatening. I picture Martha in her kitchen, crouched low beside her compost bucket, knife in hand, slowly creeping up on her pears, ready to pounce. My process is a little less dramatic but successful nonetheless.

In October I made two kinds of chutney. One was a plum chutney that I recommend for pork and chicken, and the other was apricot, which I serve with samosas.

Apricot Late-Night-Guilt Chutney

Ingredients

• 3 cups dried apricots	750 ml
• 3 cups boiling water	750 ml
• 2 medium onions, finely chopped	
• 2 tart apples, peeled, cored and chopped	
• 1 cup white sugar	250 ml
• 1 cup demerara sugar	250 ml
• 4 cloves garlic, minced	
• 1½ cups apple cider vinegar	375 ml
• ½ cup raisins	125 ml
• 2 tbsp fresh ginger root, finely chopped	30 ml
• 2 tsp mustard seeds	10 ml
• 1½ tsp ground cinnamon	7.5 ml
• 1 tsp ground allspice	5 ml
• 1 tsp cracked black pepper	5 ml
• ½ tsp cayenne pepper (more or less to taste)	2.5 ml
• ¼ tsp salt	1.25 ml

Directions

1. Combine all ingredients in a large stainless steel saucepan and bring to a boil, stirring to prevent scorching. Boil gently for about 45 minutes or until mixture is thick.

2. Fill the canner with hot water. Place 7 clean half-pint (275 ml) jars in the canner over high heat, boil for 10 minutes and remove from canner.

3. At the same time, place snap lids in boiling water and boil for 5 minutes to soften the sealing compound.

4. Ladle chutney into the hot jars, leaving a ½" (1.3 cm) head space. If necessary, remove air bubbles by sliding a rubber spatula between glass and food. Wipe jar rims to remove any stickiness and twist on screw bands until just fingertip tight. Place jars in the canner.

5. Cover the canner and bring the water to a boil. Process for 10 minutes. Remove jars from water bath and cool for 24 hours. Check jars for seal. (Sealed lids curve downward in the middle.)

6. Remove screw bands and store separately. Wipe jars, label and store in a cool, dark place.

Lavender jelly

Lavender, while not a wild-crafted plant, acts like a wild plant in that it is perennial and needs next to no tending. Thanks to my discovery of a recipe for lavender jelly, I anticipate its season as much as I do fiddleheads'. This recipe is courtesy of Linda Stradley of What's Cooking America (whatscookingamerica.net).

Lavender jelly is so pretty it is fit for a queen, and apparently the first Queen Elizabeth made sure her chef always had it on hand. The story goes that she tasted it while on a trip to Provence where lavender fields abound. When I made it, I was alarmed at first by the colour of the lavender water because it turns an ugly purplish-grey. But when I added the sugar and cooked the mixture, it turned a delightful light pink.

Ingredients
- 3½ cups water   875 ml
- ½ cup dried lavender flowers   125 ml
- juice of 1 lemon (¼ cup)   60 ml
- 1 (1¾-ounce/49 g) box powdered pectin or 1 pouch (3 ounces/90 ml) liquid pectin
- 4 cups sugar   1 kg

Directions
1. In a large saucepan over high heat bring water to a boil. Remove the pan from the heat, stir in the dried lavender flowers and let them steep for 20 minutes.

2. Strain the mixture into a deep kettle or pot and discard the lavender flowers.

3. Stir in the lemon juice and pectin and continue stirring until the pectin is dissolved.

4. Bring the mixture to a boil over high heat and add sugar. When the mixture returns to a hard rolling boil, allow it to boil for 2–4 minutes, stirring occasionally.

5. Transfer the jelly into hot sterilized jars, filling them to within ¼" (6 mm) of the top. Wipe any spilled jelly off the rims of the jars, seat the lids and tighten the rings around them.

Makes 5 half-pints (275 ml).

Notes and Sources

Seed resources

- Seed Saving Sanctuary: www.seedsanctuary.com/articles/seedsaving.cfm
- International Seed Saving Institute: www.seedsave.org
- Seeds of Diversity: www.seeds.ca/en.php
- Dan Jason: www.saltspringseeds.com
- The Natural Gardening Company: www.naturalgardening.com/shop/index.php3
- Hometown seeds: Jared West and Scott Peterson,
www.hometownseeds.com
- Stellar Seeds: Patrick Steiner, www.stellarseeds.com
- West Coast Seeds: www.westcoastseeds.com

References

CBC, (February 8, 2011). "Global Food, part two": www.cbc.ca/video/news/audioplayer.html?clipid=1785321271 (Date accessed: Febuary 9, 2011).

Statistics Canada, (2004). Canadian exports and imports: www.statcan.gc.ca/pub/15-515-x/2004001/4064688-eng.htm, 2004-07-30. (Date accessed: February 16, 2011)

Staff Writer, (April 2, 2007). Grizzly attacks plague central coast. The *Vancouver Sun*: www.canada.com/vancouversun/news/story

Joel Salatin, (2007). *Everything I Want to Do is Illegal: War Stories from the Local Food Front*. Polyface Publishers.

Gary Shelton, (1998). *Bear Attacks: The Deadly Truth*. Shelton Productions: Bella Coola.

Acknowledgements

Joel Salatin, an inspiration to all small, ethical, subversive farmers, kindly read the manuscript, and was a virtual mentor.

Jon Steinman of the radio program *Deconstructing Dinner* found time in his busy schedule to review my book and provide a recommendation that struck the heart of the matter.

Rebecca Wellman, one of my best and most supportive friends, encouraged me to blog and inspires me every day through her photography.

Clarence, my chosen grandfather, head of a remarkable family, shares his life and inspires me every day.

David (aka Big Bull), who is generous beyond words and whose wife has the kindest heart, inducted me into the wolf pack.

David, who supported me in every way imaginable, listened to my ideas tirelessly, and has made me shed tears of joy, exhaustion, frustration and, through it all, develop my writing ability.

Thanks to Pammy, for helping me edit all night long; to Brenda, for helping me find my way forward; to Russ, for his generosity and willingness to open his farm to me and my group of seven.

And thanks to my virtual friends in the blogosphere: *Musings from a Stonehead*, who helped put me on the blogosphere map and inspired some of my writing; *Little Farm Dairy, Throwback at Trapper Creek, Art of Proprietation* and *A Homesteading Neophyte*, who came to my rescue when I had goat emergencies; Mitch, Fred, Tony, Mike, Robin, Carole, *Subsistence Pattern, Suburban Bushwacker*, Kevin Kossowan, *The Kitchen Playground, Powell River Food Security Project, City Mouse, Small Pines* and *Bring Me Sunshine*, who regularly made me feel I had something of interest to say; *Not Dabbling in Normal*, who invited me to join them as an author in their cooperative project; and those who made me feel that I was part of a family by simply being there to rely on, who left challenging comments that spurred me on, made me virtual birthday cakes that made me hanker for a real life visit, and have touched my soul by what they're doing and by making it accessible to the world (you know who you are).

Thanks to my publisher, Vici Johnstone, and my editor, Betty Keller, for having faith in this project and for the blood, sweat and tears they put into it.